GOD & SCIENCE

Divine Causation and the Laws of Nature

RICHARD L. THOMPSON

GHP
GOVARDHAN HILL PUBLISHING
Alachua, Florida

Readers interested in the subject matter of this book
are invited to correspond with the author at:

Richard L. Thompson
P. O. Box 1920
Alachua, FL 32616-1920

First edition. First printing: 2004

Published by Govardhan Hill Publishing.
Printed in the United States of America.

Cataloging-in-Publication Data

Thompson, Richard L.
God and science: divine causation and the laws of nature / by Richard L. Thompson
p. cm.
Includes bibliographical references.
ISBN: 0-9635309-9-2

Library of Congress Control Number: 2004110362

CONTENTS

Dedicated to

His Divine Grace
A. C. Bhaktivedanta Swami Prabhupāda

oṁ ajñāna-timirāndhasya
jñānāñjana-śalākayā
cakṣur unmīlitaṁ yena
tasmai śrī-gurave namaḥ

FOREWORD

Richard L. Thompson, a scholar of Vedic texts, is well read in contemporary science as well as the history of western science. He correctly places himself in the intellectual-spiritual genealogy of the Perennial Philosophy. He finds ways in which information encoded in Vedic texts illuminate findings—and puzzles—of contemporary science. He demonstrates again and again the remarkable wisdom about the world yet to be mined from the ancient civilizations of India, China, Babylonia, even Greece and Rome, and from the oral cultures of many indigenous peoples.

The presumption of much modern science is that consciousness arises in the process of evolution as an emergent property. Vedic sources agree with other ancient civilizations that it makes far more sense to see the embodied world as deriving from spiritual worlds rather than as the foundation of the spiritual dimension. He argues convincingly for the primacy of spirit, even given all that science tells us about the material world. The stories of the New Physics may be closer to our traditional myths than we imagine.

Thompson's ability to explain clearly very difficult concepts of traditional and contemporary physics and cosmology is extraordinary. In a sense, his work is within the same overall movement that, in the highly Christian west, includes the debates about Creationism. His erudition, the elegance of his prose, and his deep understanding of traditional and contemporary science give a different kind of credibility to the knowledge and wisdom of our intellectual and spiritual ancestors, east and west, which they encoded into their legends, myths, and rituals. One begins to suspect that we have forgotten at least as much as we've discovered.

—Sheldon R. Isenberg, Ph.D., associate professor and chair of the Department of Religion, University of Florida, co-founder and associate director of the Center for Spirituality and Health

INTRODUCTION

What is the relationship between science and religion? Some see it as one of inevitable conflict, others see it as harmonious, and still others see differences that they hope to reconcile. For many years, I have been one of the latter. I have felt that science has fundamentally challenged the very roots of religion, but that this challenge can be answered in a way that agrees with basic scientific and religious principles. Framing such answers was the purpose of the essays in this book (which were written between 1986 and 2000). However, on reviewing these essays, I have come to realize another potential relationship between religion and science. Both religion and science can cross fertilize one another with inspiring new ideas that may ultimately culminate in a synthesis that goes beyond our present understanding of either science or religion.

The particular religion that I am following in this book is Gauḍīya Vaiṣṇavism, a subdivision of the Hindu faith of India. Vaiṣṇavism is a strongly monotheistic tradition devoted to the worship of the Supreme Being as Viṣṇu or Kṛṣṇa. Gauḍīya Vaiṣṇavism, in particular, was founded in the 16th century in Bengal by the famous saint Caitanya Mahāprabhu. Gauḍīya refers to Gauḍa-deśa, a name for Bengal, but Gauḍīya Vaiṣṇavism is widespread in India and has taken root throughout the world.

Although its nomenclature may seem strange to people of Western background, there is a fundamental similarity between the basic teachings of Gauḍīya Vaiṣṇavism and the Judeo-Christian tradition. Both traditions hold that the material universe is created and maintained by a supreme personal God. As a result, both give rise to similar issues regarding the relation between religion and science. Thus many of the essays in this book are also relevant to Christianity.

While on the topic of nomenclature, I should note that followers of Vaiṣṇavism regard their tradition as Vedic. The term "Vedic" refers to followers of the ancient scriptures called the *Vedas*. Modern scholars generally limit these scriptures to the four *Vedas—Ṛg, Yajur, Sāma,* and *Atharva*—which they date to the centuries following 1500 B.C. However, Vaiṣṇavas, and Hindus in general, tend to use the word Vedic in a broader context. They include as Vedic a series of texts, including the *Rāmāyaṇa,* the *Mahābhārata,* and the *Bhāgavata Purāṇa* or *Śrīmad-Bhāgavatam.* They may also use the term Vedic to refer to more recent texts that follow the basic Vedic tradition. In this book, I use the term Vedic in this broad sense.

The essays are arranged more or less chronologically under subject. The first essay deals with the fundamental question of how matter can be controlled by a transcendent God while, at the same time, obeying the laws of physics. A possible answer is based on the many-worlds theory of quantum mechanics, which allows for the possibility that a transcendental being, operating beyond time, could choose branches of the universal wave function in such a way as to bring about desired courses of action in the material universe. Looking back on this work, it is interesting that theological ideas dealing with the trans-temporal nature of God mesh nicely with trans-temporal approaches to quantum physics.

The question of how God relates to the laws of physics has been the cause of a great deal of soul searching among scientists. What it comes down to is that something has to give. The known laws of physics do not contain any terms which express divine will. Therefore, if divine will does influence matter, either it wills that everything should precisely obey physical laws or it must in some sense violate these laws. Essays two and three look at this dilemma from the standpoint of science, Christianity, and Vaiṣṇavism.

The first three essays have examined how science must be modified if it is to allow for the survival of basic tenets of religion. The fourth essay looks at ways in which religion may retreat in order to allow for well-established findings of science and modern scholarship. In Vaiṣṇavism, as in other religious traditions, there is a great deal of "mythological" material which seems to directly contradict modern thinking. How are we to deal with such material, while at the same time preserving what is valuable in the tradition?

One approach is to, in effect, "kick God upstairs." By arguing that God is totally transcendental to matter, and by interpreting all of God's material actions as symbolic, all conflict with science can be resolved. This approach is compatible with some strictly monistic approaches to metaphysics, but it does not agree with theistic schools of thought that attribute to God an active role in nature.

A less drastic approach is to give indirect interpretations to scriptural topics which are in strong conflict with modern thinking. Historical chronology is an important example. In Indian tradition, the history of human life is said to extend over vast periods called *yuga* cycles, each of which lasts for 4,320,000 years. This was rejected by early British Indologists, who adhered to Biblical chronology with its creation date of around 4000 B.C. In response to this, the 19th-century Vaiṣṇava teacher, Bhaktivinoda Ṭhākura, gave an interpretation of Indian chronology that compressed it into the Biblical framework. He likewise stated, in some writings, that the heavens and hells described in Vaiṣṇava scriptures were imaginary.

Inevitably, this interpretive approach gives rise to the question of how far we should go. Are some topics open to interpretation while others are sacrosanct? How do we decide?

One approach is to view all of the mythological material in the scriptures as referring to another dimension of reality. According to this idea, all of the entities mentioned in the texts really exist, but in another world. Our only link with this higher-dimensional world (at least while we are living) is through visions, in which information from the higher world is projected as through a window into this world. I discuss the pros and cons of this idea and go on to consider how it can be extended by allowing more things to pass through the window. Here again, we encounter the question of how far we should go.

The question of the plurality of religions also arises in this context. The mythological systems of different religions tend to be mutually exclusive, at least at a first glance. If we are to interpret mythology as being true in some sense, then what mythology do we choose, and how do we reconcile conflicting claims? In this regard, the *Bhāgavatam* states that intelligent species throughout the universe follow different Vedic systems that are adapted to their particular natures. This is a truly universal definition of "Vedic," which includes all religious systems on this planet and beyond.

The fifth essay in this section deals with the topic of miracles, starting with the famous "miracle of the milk," in which milk offered to Gaṇeśa seemed to mysteriously disappear. Miracles are apparent violations of natural law which may point to the operation of higher laws that allow divine influence to percolate into the material world. As such, miracles have generally been unacceptable to scientists, and they also pose a problem for religious authorities. However, they are popular among people in general since they tend to confirm religious faith.

Finally, the sixth essay discusses a number of areas where there are possible conflicts or synergistic interactions between science and religion. These include God and the laws of physics, Einstein's theory of relativity, quantum physics, the brain and consciousness, near death experiences, extraordinary events (miracles), the fossil record, and Darwin's theory of evolution. I conclude that there is tremendous scope for the development of new findings and ideas through the interaction of science and religion. But we should avoid blocking such developments by scientific or religious dogmatism.

Under the heading of the fossil record, I compare the scientific chronology of the geological ages with Indian chronology. Here we see a remarkable agreement between the two chronological systems. This shows that there may be more than one way of interpreting Indian chronology in an attempt to bring it into agreement with modern science. It again raises the question of how the process of scriptural interpretation is to be understood.

In the second section of the book, I include two essays dealing with theories of physics. The first deals with David Bohm's theory of the implicate order, in which information encrypted into matter "unfolds" and becomes manifest. Bohm intended this as a theory of monism, in which everything is enfolded in oneness within the Absolute. By making a comparison with the technology of phase conjugate mirrors, I show how Bohm's ideas can be used to allow for the windows from higher realms that I mentioned above.

Bohm follows Eastern tradition in pointing out that the Absolute is beyond human reason. This is a serious impediment to progress in rational understanding. But I point out that if a sentient higher intelligence is on the other side of the window, there is the possibility—also well known in Eastern tradition—of learning through direct communication with the Absolute.

In the second essay of this section, I discuss how in the theory of relativity, time for one observer may pass more slowly than it does for another. A similar idea turns up in the *Bhāgavatam,* where it is explained that time passes more slowly on the higher planet of Brahmaloka than it does on the earth. This leads to the idea that both time and space may be radically transformed for an observer who passes out of the material universe and enters into transcendental timelessness.

The third section of the book deals with consciousness and the mind-body problem. Here the first essay begins by examining the idea of artificial life through computer simulation. By drawing on ideas from the *Bhāgavatam* and the *Bhagavad-gītā,* I develop the idea of virtual reality as a model for the relation between mind and brain. Interestingly, this was written at the time when Jaron Lanier was experimenting with his early virtual realities. (The virtual reality model is developed further in my book, *Maya: The World as Virtual Reality.*)

The second essay examines the process of vision and the much ridiculed notion that vision depends on a "little man in the brain." The little man idea makes no sense as long as he is required to be a physical subsystem of the brain. However, it does make sense to postulate the existence of a non-physical conscious entity which is the ultimate perceiver of sense data.

In the third essay I make a historical digression and examine old Sanskrit texts from India which describe various kinds of automata. These include practical machines that could have actually been built, as well as fictional robots with human capacities. Ironically, the scholar V. Raghavan laments in his discussion of these machines that in India they were not developed technically but were simply used to illustrate the relation between the soul and the body.

The next essay turns to long distance hypnosis. Experiments in Russia by professor Leonid Vasiliev indicate that one mind can somehow influence another, even though there is no known means of physical communication between them. This corresponds to one of the *siddhis* or natural yogic powers discussed in the *Bhāgavatam.*

Finally, the fifth essay in this section discusses quantum mechanics and consciousness. Although it is popular to suppose that quantum mechanics brings consciousness into physics, the "experimental observers" in the theory are actually physical devices. It is difficult to bring non-physical conscious observers into the quantum picture, because too much consciousness, or consciousness in the wrong places, would interfere with quantum phenomena. The relationship between quantum mechanics and consciousness still needs careful consideration.

The fourth section of the book deals with the theory of evolution. This has long been one of the main areas of conflict between scientists and traditional Christians. The latter (including scientists with Christian convictions) have generally been dissatisfied with the Darwinian emphasis on chance and physical causation as the sole basis for the evolution of species. They have proposed alternatives to Darwinism, ranging from guided evolution and the theory of design to literal Biblical creationism.

Since Vaiṣṇavism is a theistic tradition, it tends to generate similar responses to the Darwinian theory of evolution. One of the most basic responses is to critique different areas of evolutionary theory, pointing out drawbacks. Thus in the first essay I discuss the theory that living organisms arose from disorganized molecules on the early earth. Although this theory is essential for a purely physical account of the origin of species, it is still lacking in supporting evidence and an adequate theoretical model.

It is easy to point out flaws in the Darwinian theory of evolution, but what is the alternative? In the second essay I point out that the Vaiṣṇava texts assume descent with modification, and in that sense they agree with the theory of evolution. However, the process of descent begins not with primitive organisms, but with higher beings whose bodies are made of subtle forms of energy not known to modern science. For descent with modification to pass from such beings to physically embodied organisms as we know them, there must be some process whereby subtle energy transforms into gross physical energy. Or perhaps this is simply a process in which information on a subtle level is transmitted through a suitable "window" into the physical realm. This is an area where extensive research is needed.

In the last essay in this section, I turn to the "rational seeds" (*rationes seminales*) discussed by Saint Augustine in the early days of Christianity. Augustine proposed that subtle seeds were planted in nature at the time of creation, and later they produced living organisms through a process of natural unfolding. Some scientists have seen this as a forerunner of the idea of evolution. (See "Does God Go Against the Laws of Nature?" in Section I.) However, Augustine's idea is closer to the Vedic idea of subtle *bījas*, or generative seed forms.

The final section of the book deals with cosmology and ancient history. One persistent theme of the Vedic literature is that thousands of years ago (say, about five thousand) there flourished a highly advanced Vedic civilization that was worldwide in scope. Taken literally, this seems to fly in the face of archeology and modern historical scholarship. Nonetheless, there are tantalizing hints that some kind of culture exhibiting Vedic themes did leave traces around the world. At the very least, there seems to have been an extensive cultural diffusion of ideas that show up in old Indian texts.

Much of the evidence for this has to do with astronomy and cosmology. In the first two essays in this section, I show that common astronomical themes can be found in old stories from cultures around the world. The specific shared details of many of these stories suggests that they are products of cultural diffusion, rather than independent invention.

In the third essay I examine a detailed cosmology presented in the Fifth Canto of the *Śrīmad-Bhāgavatam.* This brings us back to the question of how scriptural texts are to be interpreted. Taken literally, the cosmology of the Fifth Canto seems to be an imaginary, poetic exhibition that has little in common with the findings of modern astronomy. However, a closer examination of the text reveals an overlay of several distinct layers of interpretation. These are: (1) a description of the earth globe in polar or stereographic projection, (2) a realistic map of the solar system out to Saturn, (3) a topographical map of a region of south-central Asia, and (4) a map of the celestial realm of the demigods. These interpretations indicate a surprising level of scientific sophistication. The existence of distinct, valid interpretations of the same text suggests that a simple literal approach to old Sanskrit texts may be inadequate to reveal their real meaning.

The fourth essay examines the second of these interpretations in greater depth. There I argue that the ring-shaped features of the "earth disk" (Bhū-maṇḍala) in the Fifth Canto correspond accurately with the geocentric orbits of the planets as given by modern astronomy. (I note in passing that heliocentric orbits can be cast into geocentric form, simply by changing the point of reference to the earth.) This topic is discussed in greater detail in my book *Mysteries of the Sacred Universe*, which includes a statistical analysis of the correlation between planetary orbits and features of Bhū-maṇḍala.

This orbit correlation requires us to know the length of the *yojana*, the unit of distance used in the Fifth Canto to define the structure of Bhū-maṇḍala. If the orbit correlation is real, then a *yojana* of a precisely determined length should have been in use historically. In the last essay in this section, I show that there is in fact historical evidence from Egypt for such a *yojana* length. This suggests that in ancient times there must have existed advanced astronomical knowledge that was shared by India and Egypt. Such knowledge would have to antedate the relatively crude astronomy of the known Greek and Near-Eastern texts.

In summary, by bringing together modern scientific ideas and Vedic literature, many interesting ideas arise. It is widely believed that there is a fundamental conflict between science and religion, and that this can be reconciled only by either drastically editing religion to agree with science or drastically doing violence to science in order to bring it into line with religion. However, these essays suggest a different approach. Science and religion can cross-fertilize one another and give rise to possible fruitful ideas that might not have been thought of from the standpoint of science or religion, taken separately.

In the publication of this work, I was assisted by Jayādvaita Swami, who edited most of the articles, Yamarāja Dāsa, who designed both the book and its cover, and Christopher Beetle, who helped in the production in different ways. I want to express my gratitude to them.

RELIGION AND THE LAWS OF NATURE

1

God and the Laws of Physics*

Introduction

The rise of classical mechanics marked the culmination of a major shift in Western thinking from Aristotle's idea of the world as an organism to the conception of the world as a clocklike mechanism operating according to mechanistic laws.The distinguishing feature of classical mechanics is determinism—the idea that the history of events for all time is rigidly determined by the precise material conditions existing at one time.

Determinism has many profound philosophical implications. For example, if nature is indeed strictly governed by deterministic laws, then sentient beings must be pure machines, and the possibility of a nonmaterial mind that interacts with matter is ruled out. Thus a recent book on the relation between minds and machines begins with the premise that, "the price of mind/body interaction is violation of the laws of physics—a price that few philosophers (or scientists) are willing to pay."[1]

> Determinism also rules out the idea that God is in direct conscious control of day to day events. Historically, this led to the development of deism, the philosophy that God created the physical laws and initial conditions, and then ceased to play an active role in the universe. According to this philosophy, since God's only role in the universe is to create it in the beginning and then strictly enforce the deterministic laws of physics, no real exchange can take place between God and human beings through prayer or meditation. Thus if God seems to respond to our prayers it can only be because the initial conditions of the universe determine the later occurrence of both the prayer and the

---

*Originally a lecture given by Dr. Richard L. Thompson at the World Congress for the Synthesis of Science and Religion in Bombay, India during January 10–13, 1986. Reprinted from *Synthesis of Science and Religion: Critical Essays and Dialogues.*

> response. The natural conclusion of this philosophy is that we should pay attention only to the laws of nature; whether or not God exists in the background is of little practical significance.

In the twentieth century, classical physics has been supplanted by quantum mechanics, with the result that physics ceased to be strictly deterministic. This development led to a number of attempts by prominent physicists to reintroduce the idea of conscious volition into our physical world view.[2–5] However, the advent of quantum mechanics did more than simply add an element of indeterminism. In its standard formulation, quantum mechanics requires us to renounce the idea of forming a coherent theoretical picture of objective reality. This tends to discourage attempts to harmonize physics with any worldview that presents God, the material world, and the conscious living beings as real entities standing in some kind of mutual relationship. Thus, attempts to relate quantum mechanics to metaphysical ideas have often centered on the drawing of parallels[6] and the use of physical theories to provide metaphors illustrating transcendental philosophies.[7]

In this chapter I will discuss a reformulation of quantum mechanics and classical mechanics which presents both as nondeterministic theories of an objectively real material energy. Such a formulation can be of interest in the domain of physics since it suggests new ways of carrying out calculations, and it may even suggest new avenues of experimental investigation. But here my main purpose is to explore the relation between modern physical theories and broader metaphysical and theological ideas. My thesis is that both classical and quantum physics are compatible with the idea that a transcendental superconscious being directs the course of events within a flexible framework of nondeterministic laws. I should stress that this exercise in philosophical speculation can at best suggest tentative possibilities. However, it is only by considering possibilities that we can decide which way to go in the search for truth.

Classical Physics

The first observation to make is that the idea of strict determinism in classical physics was never necessary, even in the eighteenth and nineteenth centuries. To see why this is so, consider Figure 1. Here we see a latticework of metal rods, arranged in the form of a helix. We can use this arrangement as a metaphor for the idea of determinism in classical physics. The rods are arranged in triangles in such a way that the entire structure is rigid. Thus the shape of the structure as a whole is determined by the lengths of the individual rods, and the position in space of any part of the structure is determined by the orientation of a few of the rods. (These could be the rods at one end of the coil for example.) The rods play the role of the relations of cause and effect that are expressed in terms of differential equations in classical physics. Given the initial state of affairs in a physical system (i.e. the

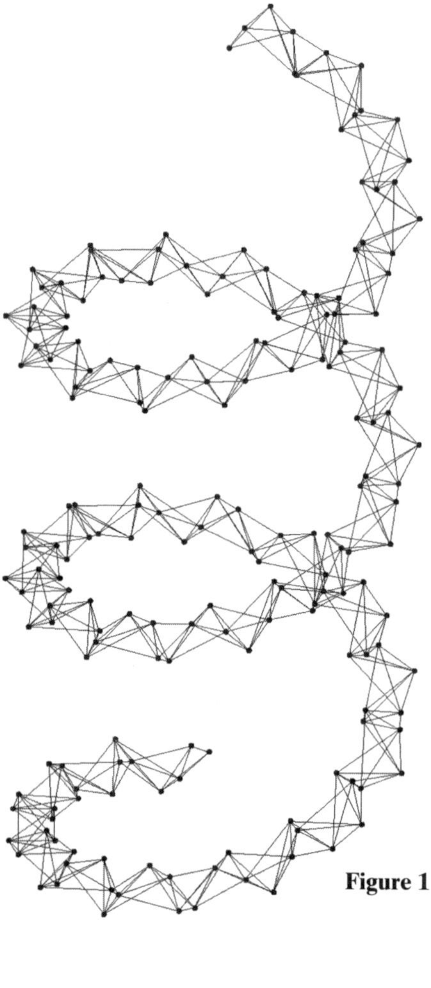

Figure 1

orientation of some of the rods), these causal relations exactly determine the course of events in the system. This is true if the lengths of the rods are precisely specified.

But suppose that we don't know the lengths precisely, and suppose that in nature their lengths are not rigidly pinned down to exact values. (For example, the rods might be slightly springy.) Figure 2 shows what happens if some of the rods are shortened by one percent of their lengths. The helix has changed markedly, adding an extra turn, and increasing in length by some 66 percent. Thus, if we cannot measure the lengths of the rods with more than one percent accuracy, we cannot even roughly calculate the shape of the structure.

Given slightly imperfect knowledge of the rods, the structure may take on a wide variety of overall shapes. Only the local curvature of the helix is more or less insensitive to small changes in the lengths of the rods. This observation can be generalized to classical physical

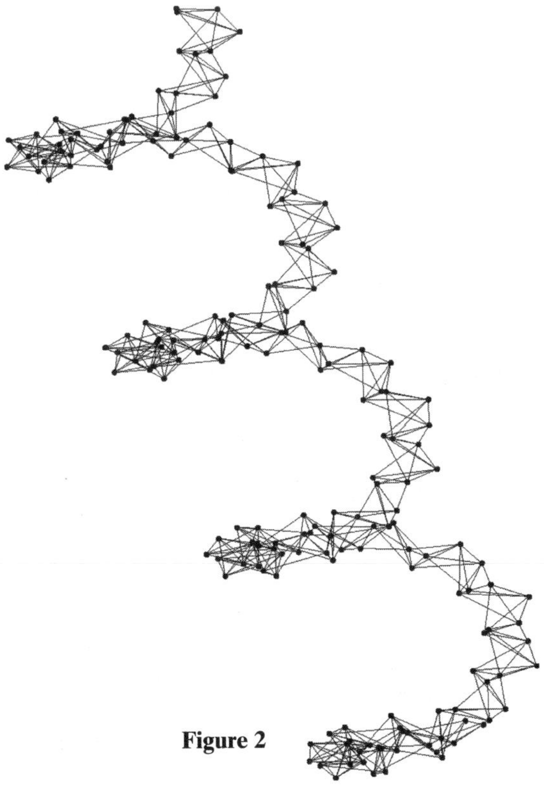

Figure 2

systems in general. The history of such a system is exactly determined from the initial conditions if the equations of motion are exactly satisfied. But if we only require the equations to be satisfied within the limits of experimental error, then the history is generally free to take on a wide variety of different courses. It is only the local linking together of events over short times that is narrowly prescribed by the natural laws. We can regard the complete history of events as a kind of flexible, spring-like continuum that tends to curve in a certain way in accordance with the physical laws of cause and effect, but can be freely bent into many different shapes.

To illustrate how flexible this continuum can be, it is useful to consider a simple example from classical physics. Figure 3 shows a two dimensional potential well, which is called the Henon-Heiles potential.[8] The contours represent lines of equal potential and the lowest point is in the center. This potential well corresponds to a force field directed toward the center of the triangle. We can imagine a

Figure 3

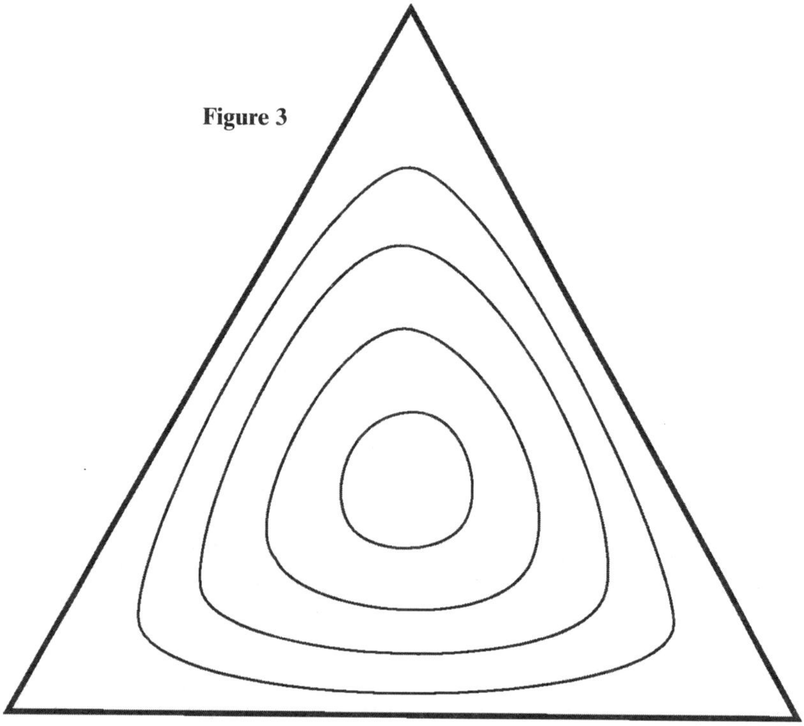

particle with a mass of, say, one gram, moving in this field in accordance with Newton's laws like a marble rolling in a bowl. The classically determined path of the particle cannot be predicted for very far into the future since tiny changes in the direction of the particle will result in large changes in its motion in a very short time.

The diagram in Figure 4 represents a closed orbit for the particle. According to the classical equations of motion, the particle should cycle indefinitely around this closed path if it starts out with the right values of initial position and momentum. However, if the initial position or momentum differ from these values by as little as 10^{-12} (in cgs units) then the particle can quickly deviate from this orbit, and within 140 seconds it can be following a completely different path.

In this example, the position and momentum values at each time correspond to the rigid rods in the example of the helical lattice. We cannot actually measure position and momentum with an accuracy of greater than 10^{-12}, and thus we are not required on the basis of em-

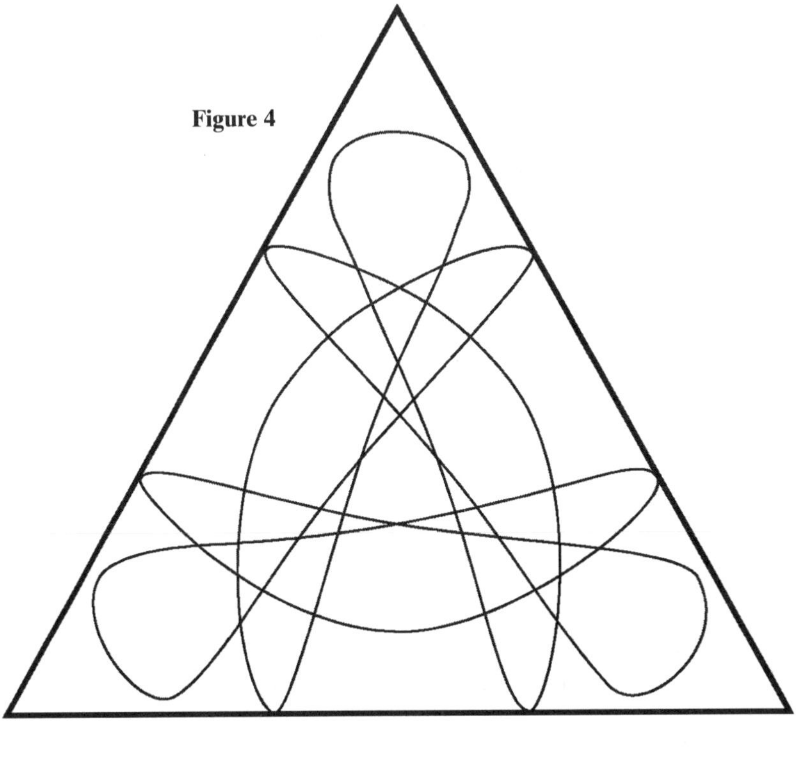

Figure 4

pirical evidence to accept that in nature these quantities are more precisely defined than this. It is possible to view the classical equations of motion as approximate relationships which allow for an immeasurably small degree of flexibility in position and momentum. However, if we do this, then it follows that the overall trajectory of the particle is not even approximately determined by the equations of motion. Its curvature over short times is nearly determined by these equations but its shape over longer times can be freely chosen.

In recent years scientists have noticed that classical equations of motion generally have solutions which are extremely sensitive to the conditions at each given time, and which are therefore unpredictable over fairly short periods of time. They have called this unpredictability "deterministic chaos" and there is now a large literature on the subject. What is surprising is that this was not discovered before (although it was noticed by some physicists, such as James Clerk Maxwell.[9]) One reason for this is that classical equations that can be easily solved and analyzed have solutions that do behave in a predictable way, and it was natural for people to think the same must be true for the equations that they couldn't solve.

Another reason for the bias in favor of determinism is that the equations governing machines must necessarily generate predictable behavior, and the image of the universe as a machine has had a powerful infuence on Western thinking. In this connection the historian Stanley Jaki has observed that the idea of the universe as a clocklike machine became prominent in Europe many years before the rise of classical physics.[10] He argues that this idea was an outgrowth of medieval Christian theology, which regarded God as being extremely remote from the material world. In fact, Jaki proposes that mechanistic science arose in Europe as an indirect outgrowth of this theological outlook.

If a classical trajectory is extremely sensitive to small variations in position and momentum, then it is possible for the trajectory to follow a wide variety of complex courses. Figure 5 shows a simple example of this. Here a series of steel pins are arranged as in an old-fashioned pinball machine, and one movable ball bounces from one pin to another. We assume that there are ideal elastic collisions and no friction, and we assume that the array of pins extends to infinity in all directions. As the ball moves, each bounce exactly follows the laws for elastic collision (i.e. the angle of incidence equals the angle of reflection.) However, it can be shown mathematically that by properly choosing the initial angle of motion for the ball, we can select practically any path that we might like for the ball's overall motion. For example, the angle can be specified so that the path spells out Shakespeare's plays in some particular handwriting. This shows that, in principle, it is possible in a classical system for highly complex patterns to arise that are independent of the classical laws and yet consistent with them.

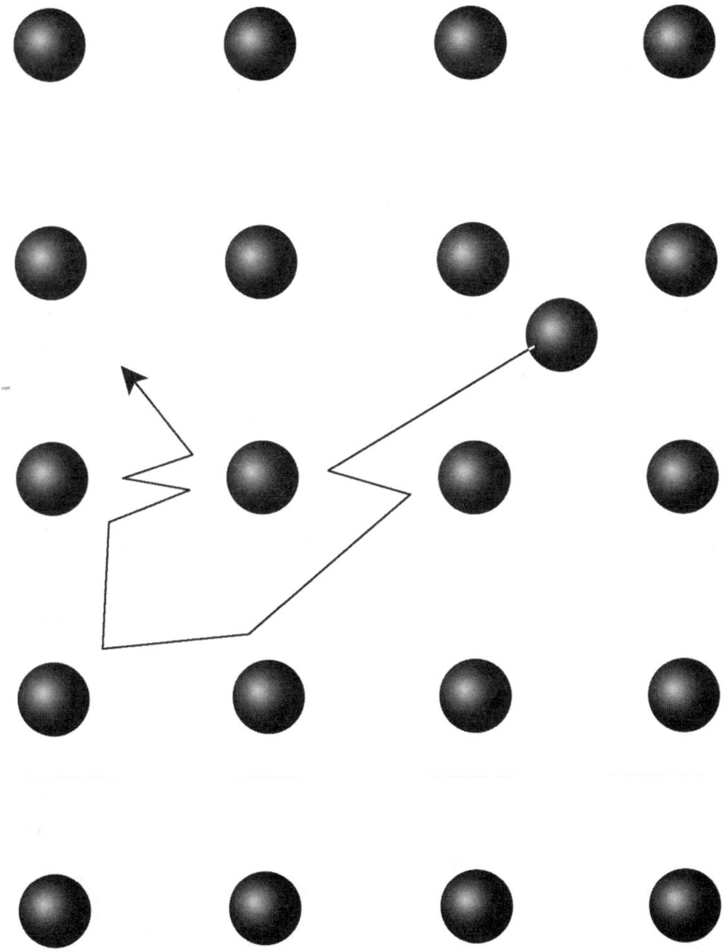

Figure 5

The examples I have given thus far are for very simple, idealized systems. However, similar conclusions also apply to complex systems involving many degrees of freedom. I will not discuss the analysis of complex systems here, since this would require much time, and would involve many mathematical technicalities. Figure 6 sums up the general picture of classical physics that emerges from this analysis. Here the vertical axis stands for what is called configuration space. Each point in this highly multidimensional space represents the complete state of affairs in a complex system at one point in time. If we can be so audacious as to try to apply physics to the world as a whole, then such a point encodes a complete numerical description of the configuration of matter in the entire world (or universe) at one time.

The curved line in Figure 6 represents a particular history of events that unfolds within the complex system. The point where the curve touches the vertical axis represents the initial state of affairs in the system. In the deterministic interpretation of classical physics, the rest of the curve is rigidly determined, given the laws of motion and this initial point. However, it is also possible to formulate classical physics in a nondeterministic way in which the laws of motion determine the local shape of the curve around any particular time, but the overall shape of the curve can be chosen with great freedom.

I should briefly note that in standard treatments of physics, the second law of thermodynamics is introduced by making restrictions on the choice of the initial state of the system. This allows for the irreversible increase of entropy with increasing time. In the nondeterministic approach to classical physics, the second law of thermodynamics can be introduced in the same way. I should also note that this nondeterministic approach can be formulated mathematically by modifying Hamilton's principle, which requires that the action should be stationary with respect to variations in the path. This is discussed in detail in a technical paper.[11]

The nondeterministic picture of classical physics is compatible with the idea of God as an omniscient and omnipotent transcendental being who directly controls the course of events, but who also requires these events to follow certain fixed laws. It is also compatible with the idea that the conscious self is nonphysical, and can interact with the brain without violating the laws of physics. Later on,

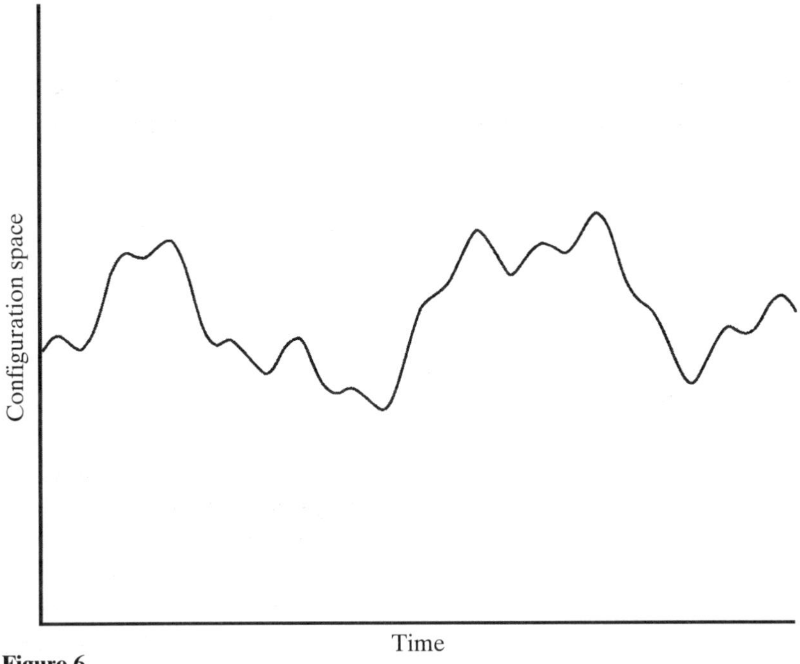

Figure 6

I will discuss in greater detail how God and the conscious self may be related, and how they can interact with the material world. First, however, we should briefly discuss the revolutionary development in physics known as quantum mechanics.

Quantum Mechanics

One possible objection to the nondeterministic formulation of classical mechanics is that, after all, it depends on certain limitations in our ability to measure such quantities as position and momentum, and in the future these limitations may be overcome. However, the historical development of physics has led to a quite different conclusion. With the advent of quantum mechanics and the Heisenberg uncertainty principle, position and momentum came to be regarded as possessing a certain degree of absolute uncertainty.

The quantum theory describes nature by means of a mathematical entity called the wave function which attributes many different classical configurations to a system at any given time. To convey some idea of what this means, consider Figure 7, which presents an artist's rendition of the quantum mechanical wave function. Here the vertical axis represents the space of all possible configurations, as before. But now, instead of a trajectory that passes through one configuration at a time, we have a blurry, wave-like construction that always spreads out over many configurations. On an atomic level this spreading out is absolutely essential for the theory. For example, the spreading out of the electron orbiting the nucleus of a hydrogen atom plays an important role in the calculation of the atom's energy levels.

However, the wave function can also spread out on a macroscopic level. The standard illustration of this is the Schrödinger cat paradox. Imagine a cat in an apparatus that either kills the animal or lets it live, depending on whether or not a radioactive atom decays within a certain time interval. If we try to use quantum mechanics to describe this arrangement, we find that the wave function divides into (at least) two branches, as shown in Figure 7. One branch represents a dead cat and the other represents a live cat. Furthermore, if we introduce a human observer into the picture, then we find that the wave function comes to simultaneously represent the observer seeing a live cat *and* the observer seeing a dead cat.

This creates a problem if we consider that the wave function is supposed to give the most complete description of nature that is possible. I will briefly describe some of the approaches people have taken to cope with this problem. However, this subject is both vast and highly controversial, and I will have to leave out many important points.

The standard response to the problem is to conclude that quantum mechanics does not provide a description of objective reality, and that we should indeed renounce the idea of trying to make such a description. According to this approach, the quantum theory simply provides a system for predicting correlations in our observations, and the wave function represents the state of human knowledge rather than the state of nature. It is hard to find fault with this approach empirically. Yet it leads to bewildering conclusions if we try to make it the basis of a consistent world view.

If the wave function simply represents knowledge, then whose knowledge does it represent? If we say that it represents the knowledge of a community of physicists, then we must posit a macroscopic world containing physicists and measuring instruments. But what is

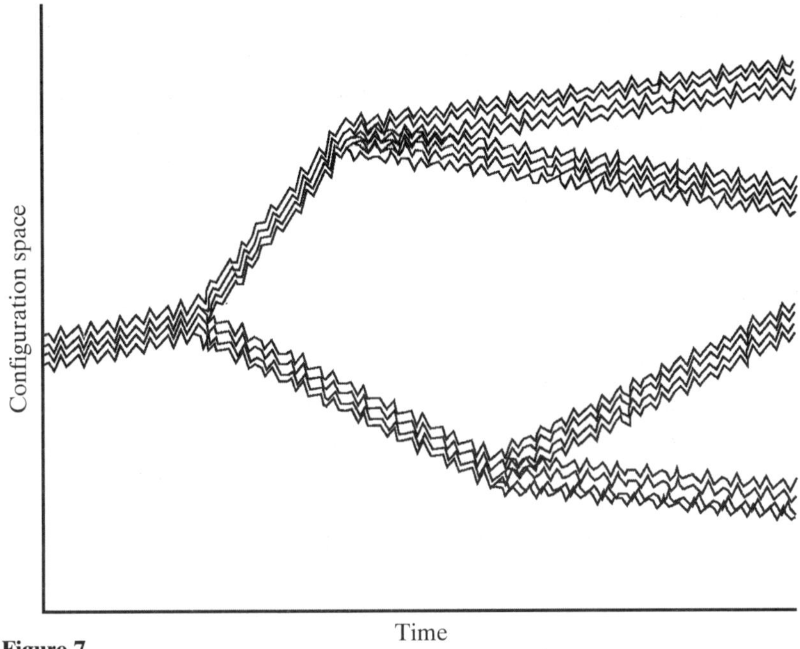

Figure 7

that world made of? If we try to represent it by physical theory, it is natural to suppose that it is made of atoms which must be described quantum mechanically. This tempts us to try to construct a quantum mechanical description of the macroscopic world, and von Neumann showed how one can go about this mathematically.[12]

Yet if the wave function represents an observer's knowledge and not objective reality, then at least one observer must be left out of the quantum mechanical analysis, and be regarded as *the* observer whose knowledge is being represented. Thus, we arrive at different pictures of reality, depending on which observer we single out. An observer is either part of a wave function and not objectively real, or he is the one whose knowledge is represented by that wave function. It seems difficult to build a consistent world picture on this basis, even from the viewpoint of an idealistic philosophy.

One standard feature of quantum mechanics is the postulate of collapse of the wave function. According to this idea, when the wave function splits into two or more branches representing measurably different states of affairs, all of the branches except one are erased,

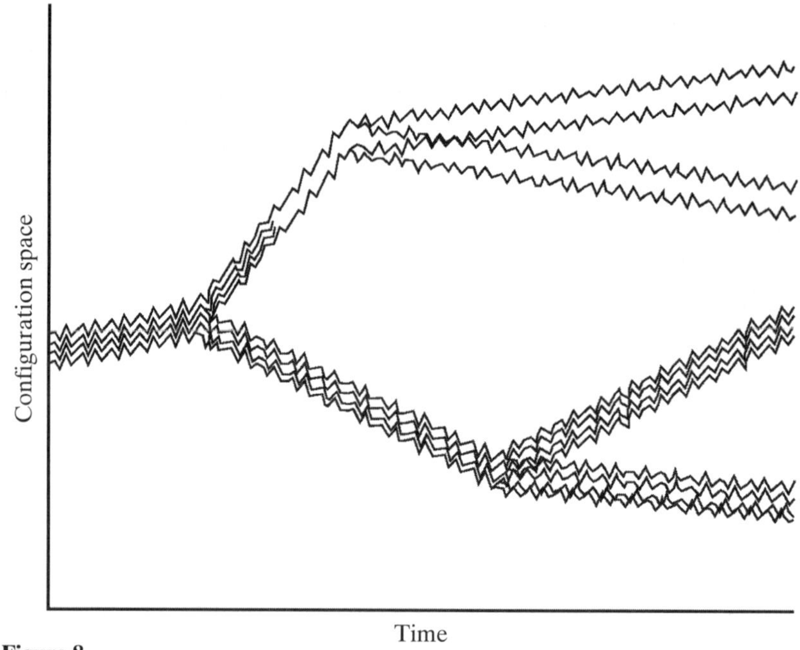

Figure 8

yielding a new wave function that represents one of the measurement results. This is depicted in Figure 8. Often the idea of wave function collapse is accompanied by the idea that the wave function *does* describe what is actually there in nature. Collapse is postulated to keep the wave function consistent with our ordinary experience (and thus assure that a cat is either dead or alive). However, quantum theory provides no physical reason for the collapse to occur at any given time, and it has the appearance of an awkward, *ad hoc* addition to the theory. We note that Wigner has proposed that the consciousness of the observer causes the collapse of the wave function, and that the quantum theory may have to be substantially modified to properly take consciousness into account.[13]

These difficulties have induced some physicists to search for alternative formulations of quantum mechanics. One such formulation is the "many worlds" theory of Everett, Wheeler, and Graham. Here a wave function is assumed for the universe as a whole, and the entire wave function is taken as a direct, one-to-one representation of objective reality. The many macroscopically distinct branches of this wave function are interpreted as distinct, mutually inaccessible universes. As each branch subdivides into further macroscopically distinct branches, the universes bifurcate further into new, divergent copies. This theory does offer an account of objective reality, and it was once advocated by the physicist John Wheeler as the only workable scheme for a quantum theory of the universe as a whole.[14] However, it suffers from the drawback that it is impossible in principle for us to observe the other universes which would constitute most of this reality.

Another approach is to add "hidden variables" to the quantum theory and thereby transform it into an objective, deterministic (or stochastic) model of nature. A prominent example is the quantum potential theory of David Bohm.[15] Unfortunately, I do not have time to discuss this topic in detail.

Quantum Mechanics and Objective Reality

At this point I would like to indicate briefly how it is possible to formulate quantum mechanics in such a way that it preserves its nondeterministic character, and also presents an objective description of nature. The starting point for this is the idea that classical physics describes the history of events as a path through configuration space. The physicist Richard Feynman noted that one could think of quantum mechanics as a scheme in which events are described not by one path, but by the sum total of all possible paths through configuration space.[16,17] He showed how paths could be said to "interfere" with one another and cancel one another out, so that only the paths allowed by quantum mechanics remain. (This is done using what is known as a Feynman path integral.) His formulation in terms of paths generates the same pattern of branching possibilities as the wave function formulation, and in fact it is simply another way of mathematically expressing the wave function.

One way of modifying quantum mechanics to obtain an objective model of reality is to strike a compromise between the classical scheme of one path, and Feynman's scheme of all possible paths. One can represent the history of events in nature by a bundle of closely similar paths. Using Feynman's methods, one can evaluate this bundle to see to what extent the paths in the bundle interfere with one

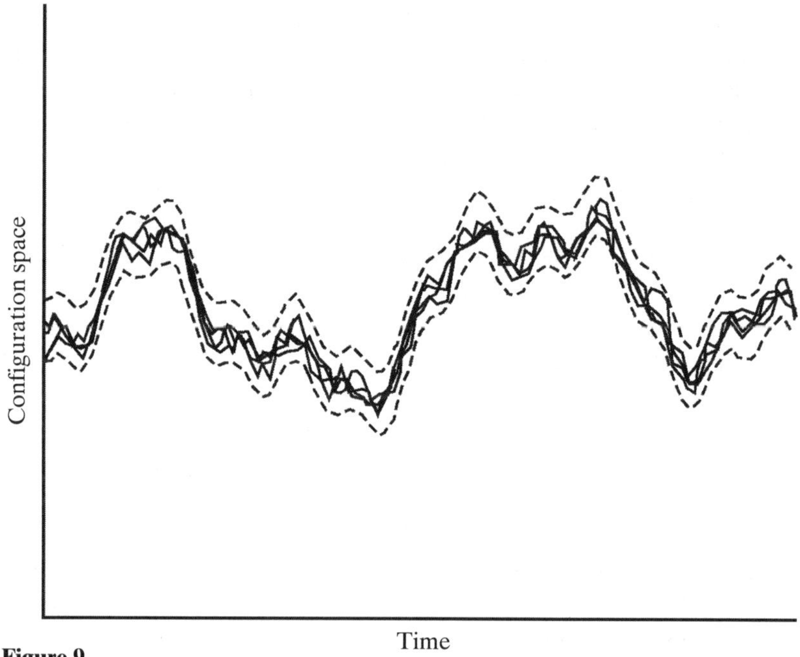

Figure 9

another. If these paths are "harmonious", or non-interfering, the bundle is quantum mechanically acceptable as a possible history of events in nature, and if they are inharmonious and tend to cancel out, then it is not acceptable. We can posit one trans-temporal act of selection that chooses a harmonious bundle of paths representing *the* complete history of events in nature.

Figure 9 depicts such a bundle of paths. The bundle is constructed in such a way that it displays no detectable ambiguity in the values of measurable variables (such as the state of health of cats.) However, it also allows for the inherent uncertainty required by quantum mechanics on the atomic level. The technical details of this formulation of quantum mechanics are presented in an unpublished paper.[18] Formally, it adds nothing new to quantum mechanics, but it shows how this theory can be seen to provide a nondeterministic account of objective reality.

It also shows how quantum mechanics and classical mechanics can be given a similar form. The selection of the bundle of paths in this version of quantum mechanics is comparable to the selection of the single flexible path in the nondeterministic formulation of classical mechanics. The local shape of the bundle is sharply constrained by the physical laws, but the bundle's overall shape can be freely chosen. The difference between quantum mechanics and classical mechanics lies in the fact that the quantum mechanical bundle of paths is free to flex in more ways than the classical path. Thus we can say that quantum mechanics is more undeterministic than classical mechanics.

Transcendental Dimensions

At this point let us return to the topic of the relationship between God, the conscious self, and the material world. I do not want to tie this discussion too closely to the particular formulations of physical theory presented here, since physical theories are always subject to change, and it is unlikely that we will ever be able to give a complete theory of matter in all of its diverse aspects. Rather, I would like to simply abstract from these formulations the idea of the history of material events in space and time as a kind of flexible continuum that can both satisfy nondeterministic laws of physics and be molded with great freedom in accordance with other considerations. Such a formulation of natural laws has been consistent with the developments in physics from Newton's time down to the present.

I will discuss a particular model of the relation between consciousness and matter which is based on Vedic literatures such as the *Bhagavad-gītā*[19] and the *Brahma-saṁhitā*[20]. It is useful to consider such a specific concrete model since by doing so we have a solid basis for raising questions and engaging in further discussion. Hopefully the points that I make will be relevant from the points of view of many different schools of thought.

The Vedic literature presents the concept that there are two fundamental types of conscious entities, the beings of limited individualized consciousness such as ourselves, and a supreme, superconscious being who simultaneously perceives and directs all phenomena. The innumerable limited beings are referred to in Sanskrit by the term *jivātmā*, and the supreme being is known by many different names. Here the name Paramātmā is the most appropriate since it refers to the role of the supreme being as the overseer of the material energy.

The material energy is described as an emanation of the supreme which is manipulated in such a way as to create a world of illusion, or *māyā*. In the diagram of the bundle of paths in Figure 9, the bundle corresponds to this material energy, which is manifested as a realm of space and time. Both the Paramātmā and the *jivātmās* have no place in the diagram since they are both transcendental. Indeed, the material energy is also of a transcendental or spiritual nature since it is an emanation of the supreme, and in this sense matter does not exist as a independent substance. However, we can portray matter as having an independent existence, since its behavior is adjusted by the Paramātmā to create this impression.

The Paramātmā creates the illusion that the material energy acts independently by imposing certain regular laws on its behavior. These laws allow for many mechanical processes to take place in nature without any apparent need for higher intelligent guidance. According to the Vedic literatures, these laws include not only the familiar laws of physics, but also psychological laws governing the functioning of material minds.

The entire system is intended to provide a field of activity for limited conscious selves or *jivātmās* who are connected with machine-like bodies and minds fashioned from the material energy. The connection between the transcendental conscious self and the material body is maintained by the Paramātmā, and this is done due to the inner desire of the self to experience material enjoyment. If the laws imposed on the material energy were strictly deterministic, then we would have a model in which the *jīvātmās* are essentially epiphenomena, going helplessly along for the ride as the material elements interact. However, according to the Vedic literature, the laws are actually nondeterministic, and thus the conscious self is able to manifest free will.

The conscious entity associated with a particular body is not directly able to govern the actions of that body, and thus it is stated in the *Bhagavad-gītā* that the individual soul is not the performer of actions within the material world. However the Paramātmā provides an interactive link between the individual self and the material energy. The Paramātmā is aware of the desires of the individual conscious selves, and he directs the course of material events accordingly. Thus, the material elements move in accordance with the desires of individuals, but the connecting link between inner desire and material action is extremely subtle.

It is not possible, of course for all desires to be fully granted. The free will of the individual is constrained by the laws of nature, which exhibit a considerable degree of determinism, even though they are not entirely deterministic. Also, different conscious selves have conflicting desires, and the Paramātmā must strike a balance among them. Thus a rich man will wish to protect his valuables while a thief desires to steal them. Finally, the will of individuals is constrained by the laws of karma, which modify the course of the individual's fortunes in accordance with his past deeds.

In the *Bhagavad-gītā* it is described that the superconsciousness or Paramātmā completely transcends material time and space. However, this does not mean that he exists in a timeless void. Rather, the events at all moments and locations in space-time are directly perceived and directed by the supreme being. In addition, there exist other space-time continua and completely nonmaterial realms of experience which all lie within the field of consciousness of the supreme. The shaping of the material space-time history by the supreme will can thus be seen either as a process unfolding in time, or as a transtemporal act of willful selection. I should note that this idea is an example of the principle of *acintya bhedābheda tattva* which describes the supreme being as simultaneously possessing variegated features and perfect unity.

If the Paramātmā knows the entire space-time situation, then it may seem that the *jīvātmās* cannot have free will. However, by free will we simply mean the actual volition of the transcendental self, as opposed, for example, to the pattern of actions and reactions generated by neurons in the brain. The conscious self exerts his free will when material events, starting with events in the brain, occur in accordance with his desire, even though these events are actually directed by a higher agency.

This model of interaction between the conscious self and the material energy has some simple consequences which may shed light on some of the apparently inexplicable phenomena observed by parapsychologists. Figure 10 shows some data reported by Dean Robert Jahn of the School of Engineering of Princeton University.[21, 22] Jahn and his colleagues have been investigating the apparent ability of many people to mentally influence processes which, according to physical theory, should be happening independently of human volition.

They have conducted an extensive series of experiments using what they call random event generators, or REGs. These are devices in which a physical process, such as electronic noise, is used to generate a stream of +1s and -1s which theoretically occur at random with a probability of 50-50. The running total of the +1s and -1s is registered on a visual display that is observed by a human subject. The subject (who is generally an ordinary person and not a psychic) tries to will the display to change consistently either in the positive direction, or the negative direction.

Theoretically the total of the +1s and -1s should execute a random walk that is centered about a mean of 0, and that wanders on either side of 0 in the manner predicted by statistical theory. However, Jahn and his colleagues have seen that when many people will the display to drift in a particular direction, it will show a tendency to do so which can be highly significant statistically. In this figure, the curve marked PK+ represents the cumulative results of the attempts of many subjects to influence the display in the positive direction, and the curve PK- represents the results of corresponding attempts to influence the display in the negative direction. The curve BL represents the baseline obtained by running the REG in the absence of an observing

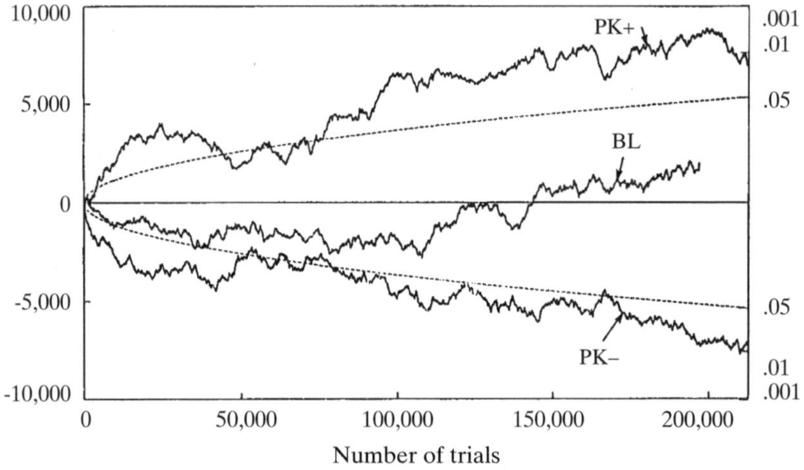

Figure 10—Evidence for observer influence on random physical events reported by Robert Jahn and his colleagues at Princeton University.

subject. The interesting thing to note here is that both the PK+ and the PK- curves tend to remain outside of the parabolic curve representing two standard deviations from the mean for the theoretical random process. Statistically, this is highly unlikely.

In these experiments it appears that the display exhibits unexpected behavior because the random noise source is behaving in an unexpected way. The evidence indicates that the electronic processes linking the source to the display are always functioning normally. This is somewhat disconcerting, since (1) the observing subject has no conscious knowledge of the source or of the electronics linking it to the display, and (2) in some experiments the production of random data by the source takes place some time before the subject participates in the experiment and decides to influence the display in a particular way. This suggests that the random events in the source are occurring abnormally in such a way as to produce subsequent effects that agree with the will of an observer. This seems to be a reversal of the law of cause and effect that is normally assumed to hold true in physical theories.

It is therefore interesting that the model of mind/body interaction that we have been considering provides a simple explanation for this kind of phenomenon. Figure 11 shows how various space-time histories could unfold in the nondeterministic version of classical mechanics, assuming that no constraints are imposed on them other than the laws of nature. In the next figure we see what happens if we add the additional constraint that at time T the history must pass through the interval marked A, which represents a certain group of possible events. Since the laws of physics do not allow unlimited freedom for the paths, they must begin to curve before time T in such a way as to reach A by that time. For example, this anticipatory curving might involve seemingly random events that "just happen" to combine together in the right way to produce some later systematic effect.

On the basis of standard physical theories we wouldn't expect to find this kind of teleological or goal directed behavior. However, if we suppose that A represents certain events desired by an individual at time T, and that the Paramātmā shapes the history of events in accordance with this desire and the laws of physics, then it follows that such teleological behavior of matter should take place. It is possible for the the overall space-time history to be selected in such a way that

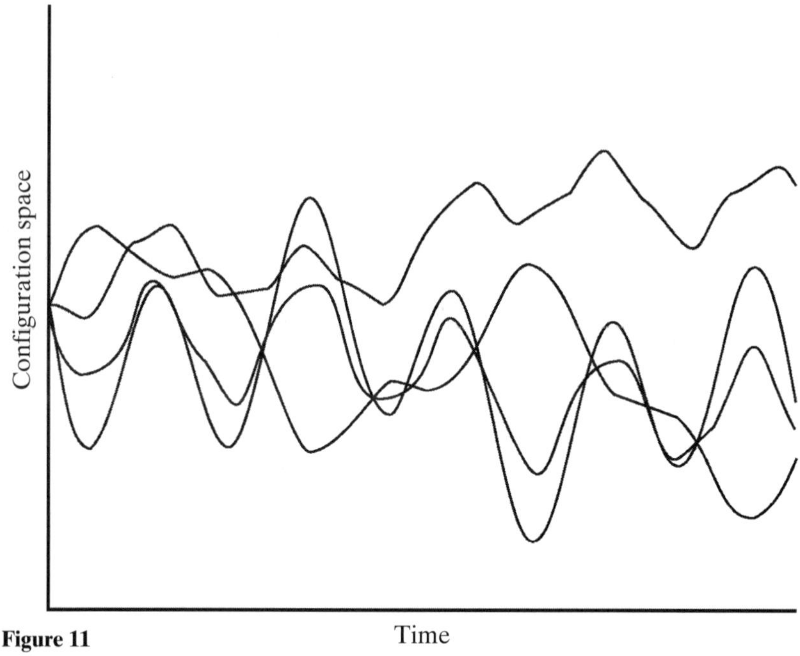

Figure 11

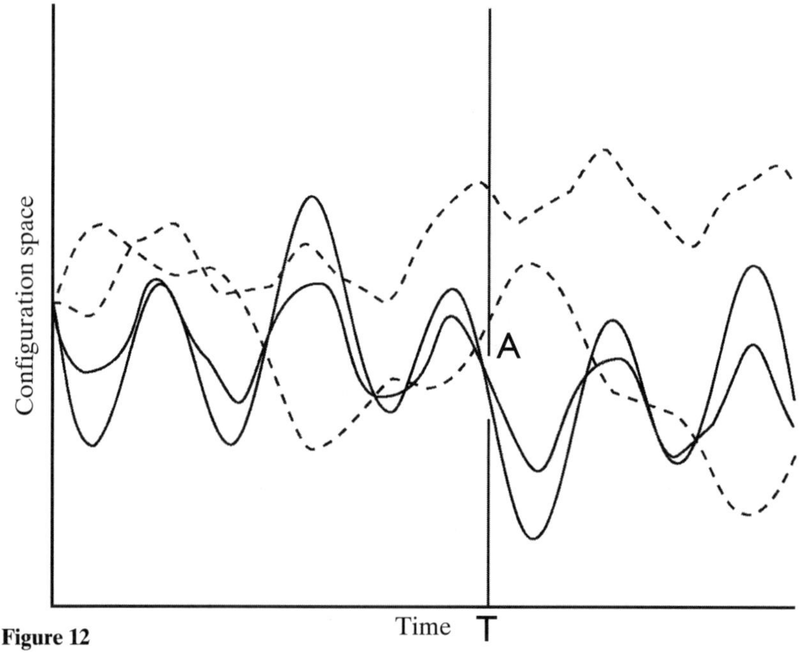

Figure 12

it generally satisfies the laws of physics, but in some regions exhibits statistically unexpected goal directed behavior. This can be done by selecting the history in accordance with both the nondeterministic physical laws and rules prescribing the occurrence of certain events (such as A) at certain times (such as T).

Using mathematical imagination we can perform this selection by restricting the set of all physically acceptable paths to smaller and smaller classes satisfying the various additional prescriptions. For the Paramātmā this mathematical process of sorting through infinitely many possibilities is carried out effortlessly through the exercise of unlimited transcendental intelligence. Thus the gross physical laws, the subtle laws of karma, and the desires of the *jīvātmās* present a vast array of partially conflicting criteria, and the Paramātmā guides the course of events by reconciling all of these criteria in accordance with His will.

I should note that the space-time history can be selected in such a way that two events at different places are correlated, even though a signal propagating at the speed of light would not have time to link one event with the other. This might seem to violate the theory of relativity, but actually it does not since this theory only restricts the development of correlations which propagate by cause and effect within space-time. In general, the unifying superconsciousness of the Paramātmā is not contradicted by the limits on space-time interactions imposed by the theory of relativity.

Conclusions

To sum up, the main purpose of this chapter was to show that from Newton's time to the present, scientific knowledge of physical laws has always been compatible with the idea that the course of natural events is directed by the will of a transcendental supreme being. Our scientific knowledge has also been compatible with the idea that the conscious self is not merely an epiphemenon of brain mechanisms, but is a nonphysical entity that can interact with the brain. Ideas of this kind are compatible with our knowledge of physics due to the fact that the physical laws that have thus far been affirmed by empirical research can be interpreted as nondeterministic laws applying to an objectively real material energy.

By going through this analysis we have only demonstrated a possibility. We have not proven anything. But in view of the history of the past three hundred years, this might be a good possibility to keep in mind. The understanding of nature as a machine has resulted in much technological progress, but now we find people throughout the world abandoning traditional ways of life to join in a struggle for technical supremacy—a struggle that culminates in the construction of more and more deadly machines of mass destruction.

It can be argued that this trend of modern civilization has been strongly encouraged by scientific theories that appear to contradict any philosophy of life other than materialism. It may be very difficult to change this dangerous trend. But an essential ingredient for such a change could be the wide dissemination of a valid approach to scientific knowledge that allows for a tangible spiritual dimension to human life, and is compatible with the ancient understanding that mankind is dependent on a transcendental supreme being. Such an approach opens up the possibility of directing human energy towards higher spiritual goals, and of providing a solid ethical basis for the conduct of our material affairs.

REFERENCES

1. Haugland, J., ed., 1981, *Mind Design*, Cambridge, Mass.: MIT Press, p. 3.
2. Wigner, E. P., 1970, "Physics and the Explanation of Life," *Found. of Phys.* 1, 35.
3. Stapp, H. P., 1985, "Consciousness and Values in the Quantum Universe," *Found. of Phys.* 15, 35.
4. Costa de Beauregard, O., 1976, "Time Symmetry and Interpretation of Quantum Mechanics," *Found. of Phys.* 6, 539.
5. Mattuck, R. D. and Walker, E. H., 1979, "The Action of Consciousness on Matter: A Quantum Mechanical Theory of Psychokinesis," in *The Iceland Papers,* Puharich, A., ed., Essentia Research Associates, pp. 111–159.
6. Capra, F., 1975, *The Tao of Physics*, Berkeley: Shambala.
7. Bohm, D., 1981, *Wholeness and the Implicate Order*, London ; Boston: Routledge and Kegan Paul.
8. Henon, M., 1983, in *Proceedings of the Summer School "Chaotic*

Behavior of Deterministic Systems" (Les Houches, July 1981), Iooss, G., Helleman, R. H. G., Stora, R., eds., North-Holland.

9. Jaki, S., 1970, *The Relevance of Physics*, Chicago: Univ. of Chicago Press, p. 119.
10. Jaki, S., op. cit.
11. Thompson, R., 1985, "A Trans-temporal Approach to the Laws of Physics," submitted to *Found. of Phys.*. Although I never pursued the publication of this technical paper, a formulation of quantum mechanics which serves the same purpose was published in 1990 by M. Gill-Mann and J. B. Hartle, 1990, "Quantum Mechanics in the Light of Quantum Cosmology" in *Complexity, Entropy, and the Physics of Information,* Vol. 8, Zurek, W. H., ed., Redwood City, CA: Addison-Wesley Pub. Co., pp. 425–58.
12. von Neumann, J., 1955, *Mathematical Foundations of Quantum Mechanics,* Princeton, N.J.: Princeton Univ. Press.
13. Wigner.
14. DeWitt, B. S. and Graham, N., 1973, *The Many-Worlds Interpretation of Quantum Mechanics,* Princeton, N.J.: Princeton Univ. Press, p. 153.
15. Bohm, D. and Hiley, B. J., 1984, "Measurement Understood Through the Quantum Potential Approach," *Found. of Phys.* 14, 255.
16. Feynman, R. P. and Hibbs, A. R., 1965, *Quantum Mechanics and Path Integrals*, New York: McGraw Hill.
17. Feynman, R. P., 1948, "Space-Time Approach to Non-Relativistic Quantum Mechanics," *Rev. of Mod. Phys.* 20, 367.
18. Thompson.
19. Bhaktivedanta Swami Prabhupada, A. C., 1983, *Bhagavad-gītā As It Is*, Los Angeles: Bhaktivedanta Book Trust.
20. Bhakti Siddhanta Saraswati Thakur, 1958, *Shri Brahma Samhita*, Sree Gaudiya Math.
21. Jahn, R. G. and Dunne, B. J., 1984, *An REG Experiment with Large Data Base Capability, III: Operator Related Anomalies*, School of Engineering/Applied Science, Princeton: Princeton Univ.
22. Dunne, B. J., Jahn, R. G. and Nelson, R. D., 1985, *Princeton Engineering Anomalies Research*, School of Engineering/Applied Science, Princeton, N.J.: Princeton Univ.

2

On God and Science

In a book review in *Scientific American,* Harvard evolutionist Stephen Jay Gould points out that many scientists see no contradiction between traditional religious beliefs and the world view of modern science. Noting that many evolutionists have been devout Christians, he concludes, "Either half my colleagues are enormously stupid, or else the science of Darwinism is fully compatible with conventional religious beliefs—and equally compatible with atheism, thus proving that the two great realms of nature's factuality and the source of human morality do not strongly overlap."[1]

The question of whether or not science and religion are compatible frequently comes up, and Gould himself points out that he is dealing with it for the "umpteenth millionth time." It is a question to which people are prone to give muddled answers. Definitions of God and God's modes of action in the world seem highly elastic, and the desire to combine scientific theories with religious doctrines has impelled many sophisticated people to stretch both to the limit. In the end, something has to give.

To help us locate the snapping point, let's look at what a few scientists have said about God.

Dr. John A. O'Keefe, a NASA astronomer and a practicing Catholic, has said, "Among biologists, the feeling has been since Darwin that all of the intricate craftsmanship of life is an accident, which arose because of the operation of natural selection on the chemicals of the earth's shell. This is quite true. . . ."[2]

O'Keefe accepts that life developed on earth entirely through physical processes of the kind envisioned by Darwin. He stresses, however, that many features of the laws of physics have just the right values to allow for life as we know it. He concludes from this that God created the universe for man to live in—more precisely, God did this at the moment of the big bang, when the universe and its physical laws sprang out of nothing.

To support this idea, O'Keefe quotes Pope Pius XII, who said in his address to the Pontifical Academy of Science in 1951:

> In fact, it would seem that present-day science, with one sweeping step back across millions of centuries, has succeeded in bearing witness to the primordial Fiat lux ["Let there be light"] uttered at the moment when, along with matter, there burst forth from nothing a sea of light and radiation, while the particles of chemical elements split and formed into millions of galaxies.[3]

Now this might seem a reasonable union of religion and science. God creates the universe in a brief moment; then everything runs according to accepted scientific principles. Of the universe's fifteen-billion-year history, the first tiny fraction of a second is to be kept aside as sacred ground, roped off from scientific scrutiny. Will scientists agree not to trespass on this sacred territory?

Certainly not. Stephen Hawking, holder of Isaac Newton's chair at Cambridge University, once attended a conference on cosmology organized by Jesuits in the Vatican. The conference ended with an audience with the Pope. Hawking recalls:

> He told us that it was all right to study the evolution of the universe after the big bang, but we should not inquire into the big bang itself because that was the moment of Creation and therefore the work of God. I was glad then that he did not know the subject of the talk I had just given at the conference—the possibility that space-time was finite but had no boundary, which means that it had no beginning, no moment of Creation.[4]

Whether or not Hawking's theory wins acceptance, this episode shows that science cannot allow any aspect of objective reality to lie outside its domain. We can get further insight into this by considering the views of Owen Gingerich of the Harvard Smithsonian Center for Astrophysics. In a lecture on modern cosmogony and Biblical creation, Gingerich also interpreted the big bang as God's act of creation. He went on to say that we are created in the image of God and that within us lies "a divine creative spark, a touch of the infinite consciousness, and conscience."[5]

What is this "divine spark"? Gingerich's words suggest that it is spiritual and gives rise to objectively observable behavior involving conscience. But mainstream science rejects the idea of a nonphysical conscious entity that influences matter. Could "divine spark" be just another name for the brain, with its behavioral programming wired in by genetic and cultural evolution? If this is what Gingerich meant, he certainly chose misleading words to express it.

Freeman Dyson of Princeton's Institute for Advanced Studies arrived at ideas similar to those of Gingerich's, but from a non-Christian perspective.

> I do not claim that the architecture of the universe proves the existence of God. I claim only that the architecture of the universe is consistent with the hypothesis that mind plays an essential role in its functioning. . . . Some of us may be willing to entertain the hypothesis that there exists a universal mind or world soul which underlies the manifestations of mind that we observe. . . . The existence of a world soul is a question that belongs to religion and not to science.[6]

Dyson fully accepts Darwin's theory of chance variation and natural selection. But he also explicitly grants mind an active role in the universe: "Our consciousness is not just a passive epiphenomenon carried along by chemical events in our brains, but an active agent forcing the molecular complexes to make choices between one quantum state and another."[7] He also feels that the universe may, in a sense, have known we were coming and made preparations for our arrival.[8]

Dyson is verging on scientific heresy, and he cannot escape from this charge simply by saying he is talking about religion and not science. Quantum mechanics ties together chance and the conscious observer. Dyson uses this as a loophole through which to introduce mind into the phenomena of nature. But if random quantum events follow quantum statistics as calculated by the laws of physics, then mind has no choice but to go along with the flow as a passive epiphenomenon. And if mind can make quantum events follow different statistics, then mind violates the laws of physics. Such violations are rejected not only by physicists but also by evolutionists, who definitely do not envision mind-generated happenings playing any significant role in the origin of species.

It would seem that O'Keefe, Gingerich, and Dyson are advancing religious ideas that are scientifically unacceptable. Unacceptable because they propose an extra-scientific story for events that fall in the chosen domain of science: the domain of all real phenomena.

To see what is scientifically acceptable, let us return to the remarks of Stephen Jay Gould. In his review in *Scientific American,* Gould says, "Science treats factual reality, while religion struggles with human morality."[9] We can compare this to a statement by the eminent theologian Rudolf Bultmann: "The idea of God is imperative, not indicative; ethical and not factual."[10]

The point Gould and Bultmann make is that God has nothing to do with facts in the real world. God is involved not with what is but what ought to be, not with the phenomena of the world but people's ethical and moral values.

Of course, a spoken or written statement of what ought to be is part of what is. So if God is out of what is, He cannot be the source of statements about what ought to be. These must simply be human statements, and so must all statements about God. As it's put by Don Cupitt, Cambridge philosopher of religion, "There is no longer anything out there for faith to correspond to, so the only test of faith now is the way it works out in life. The objects of faith, such as God, are seen as guiding spiritual ideals we live by, and not as beings."[11]

This may sound like atheism, and so it is. But we shouldn't stop here. Human religious activity is part of the factual world, and so it also lies within the domain of science. While religious people "struggle with morality," inquisitive scientists struggle to explain man's religious behavior—unique in the animal kingdom—in terms of the Darwinian theory of evolution. This was foreshadowed by a remark made by Darwin himself in his early notes: "Love of the deity effect of organization, oh you materialist!"[12] Religious ideas, including love of God, must arise from the structure and conditioning of the brain, and these in turn must arise through genetic and cultural evolution. Darwin himself never tried to develop these ideas extensively, but in recent years sociobiologists such as Edward O. Wilson have.[13]

So is the science of Darwinism fully compatible with conventional religious beliefs? That depends on one's conventions. If by God you mean a real spiritual being who controls natural phenomena, even to a slight degree, then Darwinism utterly rejects your idea—not because science empirically disproves it, but because the idea goes against the fundamental scientific program of explaining all phenomena through the laws of physics. Religious beliefs are compatible with Darwinism only if they hold that God is simply a human idea having something to do with moral imperatives. But if this is what you believe, then instead of having religious beliefs, you have "scientific" beliefs about religion.

Judging from the theistic ideas of O'Keefe, Gingerich, and Dyson, many far-from-stupid scientists do believe in God and Darwinism. But in their efforts to combine truly incompatible ideas, they succumb to enormously muddled thinking. And so they commit scientific heresy in spite of themselves. If one is at all interested in knowledge of God, one should recognize that such knowledge is not compatible with mainstream science, and in particular not with Darwinism.

REFERENCES

1. Gould, Stephen Jay, 1992, "Impeaching a Self-Appointed Judge," *Scientific American,* July, p. 119.
2. Jastrow, Robert, 1978, *God and the Astronomer,* New York: Warner Books, Inc., p. 138.
3. Jastrow, pp. 141–2.
4. Hawking, Stephen, 1988, *A Brief History of Time,* New York: Bantam Books, p. 116.
5. Gingerich, Owen, 1982, "Let There Be Light: Modern Cosmogony and Biblical Creation," an abridgement of the Dwight Lecture given at the University of Penna. in 1982, pp. 9–10.
6. Dyson, Freeman, 1979, *Disturbing the Universe,* New York: Harper & Row, pp. 251–52.
7. Dyson, p. 249.
8. Dyson, p. 250.
9. Gould, p. 120.
10. Cupitt, Don, 1985, *Only Human,* London: SCM Press, Ltd., p. 212.
11. Cupitt, p. 202.
12. Paul H. Barrett, et. al., eds., 1987, *Charles Darwin's Notebooks,* 1836–1844, Ithaca, N.Y.: Cornell University Press, p. 291.
13. Wilson, Edward O., 1978, *On Human Nature,* Cambridge, Mass.: Harvard University Press.

3

Does God Go Against The Laws of Nature?

Ernan McMullin, a physicist, philosopher, and Catholic priest in the Department of Philosophy at Notre Dame University, has given careful thought to the relation between religion and modern science. In the introduction to his book *Evolution and Creation,* he offers some advice he calls "valuable direction for the contemporary Christian":

> When an apparent conflict arises between a strongly supported scientific theory and some item of Christian doctrine, the Christian ought to look very carefully to the credentials of the doctrine. It may well be that when he does so, the scientific understanding will enable the doctrine to be reformulated in a more adequate way.[1]

McMullin applies this advice to the question of how the Christian doctrine of creation is to be reconciled with the neo-Darwinian theory of evolution. Many Christian creationists have argued that divine creation is a supernatural process that cannot be understood in terms of known physical principles. But McMullin presents an alternative scenario in which creation is seen as a process of evolution proceeding according to natural laws.

He bases this scenario on ideas expressed by the early church father Augustine. Augustine maintained that Genesis in the Bible refers to a process of instantaneous creation in which God implants "seed principles" in formless matter. These seed principles are not final created forms. Rather, they contain the potential to gradually manifest these forms.

McMullin grants that Augustine thought each created form would develop from its own seed principle. The idea that one type of organism would evolve from another was foreign to him. But McMullin points out that Augustine's idea can be readily adapted to modern evolutionary thinking. The seed principles can be thought of as the laws of nature God imposed on formless matter at the moment of creation (the Big Bang). Since God is omniscient and omnipotent, He can create laws that bring about the gradual manifestation of all created forms in the universe, including human beings.

These gradual evolutionary developments are simply the unfolding of Gods original plan, and they do not require any further "divine interventions" that would violate God's natural laws. Thus McMullin is able to formulate an idea of evolutionary creation that agrees fully with modern science and "complements Christian belief."[2]

Can McMullin's approach be applied to reconcile the *Bhagavad-gītā* with modern science? Of course, the topic of evolution is touchy and controversial. So we may be wise at first to just consider the idea that nature runs by divinely created natural laws. Let us see if the *Bhagavad-gītā* supports this idea.

In the *Bhagavad-gītā* (9.8) Kṛṣṇa says, "The whole cosmic order is under Me. Under My will it is automatically manifested again and again, and under My will it is annihilated at the end." Here Kṛṣṇa says that material nature (*prakṛti*) is manifested automatically (*avaśam*). Kṛṣṇa also says (13.30), *prakṛtyaiva ca karmāṇi kriyamāṇāni sarvaśaḥ*. This means that material activities are in all respects carried out by material nature (*prakṛti*). This also suggests that *prakṛti* runs automatically, an idea given further support by the nearly identical statement (3.27) *prakṛteḥ kriyamāṇāni guṇaiḥ karmāṇi sarvaśaḥ*. Kṛṣṇa also says (13.20) that the transformations of matter and of living beings are both products of material nature.

All in all, then, one might argue that the *Bhagavad-gītā* agrees with the modern scientific conclusion that all material phenomena run according to the laws of nature. These phenomena are divinely directed in the sense that the laws of nature are created and sustained by God.

One might further suggest that God never engages in any kind of "divine intervention," for then He would break His own laws (and violate the conclusions of science). From McMullin's observations, one might gather that we'd be wise to understand the *Bhagavad-gītā* in this way. After all, if we think that God sometimes breaks the laws of nature, when does He do that? Certainly He doesn't seem to do it during the scientific experiments that demonstrate the natural laws.

If we think God breaks the laws of nature, He must do it when scientists aren't looking.

This means we are trying to fit God into the gaps in our scientific knowledge. McMullin warns, "Making God a 'God of the gaps' is a risky business. Gap-closing is the *business* of science. To rest belief in God on the presence of gaps in the explanatory chain is to pit religion *against* science."[3]

If we invoke a "God of the gaps," then we are asking for embarrassment when science fills the gaps and shows that we are fools. To show the inevitable results of this kind of folly, McMullin cites a remark by Augustine:

> If those not bound by the authority of the Scriptures find a Christian mistaken in a field which they themselves know well and hear him base foolish opinions on the Scriptures, how are they going to believe the Scriptures regarding the resurrection of the dead? [How can they believe the Scriptures] when they think that the pages of Scripture are full of falsehoods regarding facts which they themselves have learnt from experience and light of reason?[4]

We can rephrase this by asking, "How are people going to believe in the scriptures of Kṛṣṇa consciousness if devotees tell them that these scriptures are full of statements contrary to modern science?" Augustine has raised a good point, and McMullin responds to it by calling him "the man of good sense."[5]

But there might be a problem here. What if your scriptures really do make statements contrary to modern science? How far can you go in scriptural reinterpretation and reformulation? To see what I mean, let's consider some further statements from the *Bhagavad-gītā.*

First of all, is it valid to interpret *prakṛti* as material nature in the sense that physical scientists understand this term? Kṛṣṇa says, "Earth, water, fire, air, ether, mind, intelligence and false ego—all together these eight constitute My separated material energies." (Bg. 7.4) Now modern science certainly accepts earth, water, fire, and air as forms of material energy, and ether might be so accepted if we were to identify it as Einstein's curved space-time continuum. But modern physics makes no reference to mind, intelligence, and false ego as separate material energies.

Careful study shows that the *Bhagavad-gītā* and the *Śrīmad-*

Bhāgavatam portray mind, intelligence, and false ego as material energies not made from earth, water, fire, air, and ether. According to these texts, the mind comes up with thoughts, which govern the behavior of the body. This means the physical body is influenced by a type of energy, called mind (*manas*), unknown to modern science.

So even if the *Bhagavad-gītā* is saying that material phenomena run automatically by the laws of nature, we must recognize that the *Gītā's* laws of nature are quite different from modern physicists' laws. If the *Bhagavad-gītā* is right, then thinking is not just a product of brain action. Rather, it involves the action of a kind of energy that science doesn't know about.

This could be true, because there is an enormous gap in our scientific understanding of the brain. Why should we suppose that if science ever fills this gap it will fill it with the kind of physical theory of brain action that many scientists now favor? Scientists generally believe that the brain controls the mind. But a theory may emerge in which the mind controls the brain.

Another point is that according to the *Bhagavad-gītā,* God does intervene in the course of natural events. The transformations of matter by natural law are only partly automatic, like the workings of a computer interfacing with a human operator.

The *Bhagavad-gītā* (13.23) defines the role of the Supersoul as follows: "In this body there is another, a transcendental enjoyer, who is the Lord, the supreme proprietor, who exists as the overseer and permitter, and who is known as the Supersoul." The words overseer (*upadraṣṭā*) and permitter (*anumantā*) indicate that the Supersoul is in charge of the activities of each person. This means that the Supersoul's decisions determine the behavior of the person's physical body.

It follows that the human body does *not* strictly follow the laws of physics. If it did, the Supersoul's role as controller would be a mockery, because His decisions would always have to accord with a system of differential equations.

Nor can we say that the Supersoul exerts control by directing the random events of quantum theory. Quantum mechanical randomness must always follow quantum statistics, and this means that it must appear noisy and chaotic, like the clicks made by a Geiger counter near a radioactive substance. Of course, the Supersoul can create random effects if He wants to. But to say that the Supersoul must always act in the chaotic fashion dictated by quantum statistics would be to contradict His position as overseer and permitter.

In the *Bhagavad-gītā* (15.15) Kṛṣṇa says, "I am seated in everyone's heart, and from Me come remembrance, knowledge and forgetfulness." Here one might conceivably argue that Kṛṣṇa simply set matter in motion at the time of creation in such a way as to provide remembrance, knowledge, and forgetfulness for all the sentient beings who would later develop.

But this interpretation strains hard against *Bhagavad-gītā* 10.10: "To those who are constantly devoted to serving Me with love, I give the understanding by which they can come to Me." This indicates that Kṛṣṇa gives personal attention to individuals.

Commenting on this verse, Śrīla Prabhupāda writes that Kṛṣṇa gives instructions from within so that one "may ultimately come to Him without difficulty." Of course, when a person receives these instructions, the result is that the person's behavior changes.

In other words, Kṛṣṇa specifically reciprocates with each person in an observable way that cannot be accounted for by any impersonal system of physical laws. This conclusion is also supported by *Bhagavad-gītā* 10.11: "To show them special mercy, I, dwelling in their hearts, destroy with the shining lamp of knowledge the darkness born of ignorance."

McMullin raises the question, "If Nature is complete in its own order, if there are no barriers to the reach of science, does not belief in a Creator drop away as superfluous?"[6] Many intelligent people may feel inclined to reply that if Nature truly is complete in its own order, then belief in the Creator as described in *Bhagavad-gītā* ought to drop away.

But why should we think that the order of nature, as envisioned by contemporary scientists, is complete? If science does succeed in filling the many gaps that exist in our current knowledge, a radically new and unexpected picture of reality may emerge. It may be the business of scientists to fill gaps, but scientists are certainly not obliged to fill them with the ideas current at one moment in history.

Just as nineteenth-century physicists had no idea of the quantum mechanical theory of the atom, so present-day scientists can have no idea of the science of mind that may develop in the future. And if science someday makes enormous progress and scientists begin to acquire the scientific knowledge of Brahmā (the creator), they may then be able to see clearly how God intervenes creatively in the phenomena of nature.

REFERENCES

1. McMullin, Ernan, ed., 1985, *Evolution and Creation,* Notre Dame: University of Notre Dame Press, p. 2.
2. McMullin, p. 38.
3. McMullin, p. 35.
4. McMullin, p. 48.
5. McMullin, p. 48.
6. McMullin, Ernan, 1987, "The Impact of the Theory of Evolution on Western Religious Thought," *Synthesis of Science and Religion, Critical Essays and Dialogues,* T. D. Singh and Ravi Gomatam, eds., San Francisco: Bhaktivedanta Institute, p. 82.

4

Rational "Mythology"*

In Vivekananda Swami's famous lecture on Hinduism at the Parliament of Religions in 1893, he began by outlining some of the salient features of traditional Hinduism. He mentioned karma, reincarnation, and the problem of evil in the material world. He went on to explain that the solution to this problem depends on seeking refuge in God. God is that one "by whose command the wind blows, the fire burns, the clouds rain, and death stalks upon the earth."[1] He is the source of strength and the support of the universe. He is everywhere, pure, almighty, and all-merciful. And we are related to God as a child to a father or mother and as a friend to a beloved friend.

Vivekananda said that we are to worship God through unselfish love, and he pointed out that the way to achieving love of God was "fully developed and taught by Krishna, whom the Hindus believe to have been God incarnate on earth."[2] Through love we are to perfect ourselves, reach God, see God, and enjoy bliss with God. On this, he said, all Hindus are agreed.[3]

But he went on to say that in the final stage of realization, God is seen to be impersonal Brahman. The individual then ends separate existence by realizing his identity with Brahman. Making an analogy with physical science, he said, "Physics would stop when it would be able to fulfill its services in discovering one energy of which all the others are but manifestations, and the science of religion [would] become perfect when it would discover. . . . One who is the only Soul of which all souls are but delusive manifestations."[4]

The Pros and Cons of Pure Monism

Vivekananda's strictly monistic concept of God has a long history. The idea has always been linked with the rational, speculative

---

*Can a rational person accept the stories of the *Purāṇas* as literally true? Presented at the Parliament of the World's Religions, Chicago, 1993.

approach to reality. For example, in the fifth century B.C., the Greek philosopher Parmenides concluded by speculative arguments that "only One Thing can possibly exist and that this One Thing is uncreated, unchangeable, indestructible, and immovable. Plurality, creation, change, destruction, and motion are mere appearances."[5]

Parmenides argued that the One must have no parts distinct from one another, for otherwise it would be not One but many. Thus he concluded that the One must be a sphere of perfectly uniform substance. But even a sphere has an inside and an outside, and so it is marked by duality, not oneness. The idea of absolute oneness, or pure monism, may seem alluring, but it requires us to give up all conceivable attributes and finally give up thought itself.

Vivekananda Swami

Vivekananda recognized this problem, and he argued that in the Hindu religion specific forms of gods and goddesses serve as symbols to help us visualize the inconceivable. Thus he said, "The Hindus have discovered that the absolute can only be realized, or thought of, or stated, through the relative, and the images, crosses, and crescents are simply so many symbols, so many pegs to hang the spiritual ideas on."[6]

The idea of religious imagery as a symbol for the unthinkable Absolute sometimes turns out useful in the modern age. Vivekananda was born in Calcutta in 1863 as Narendranath Datta, and he grew up during the high noon of British dominance in India. During this period, European rationalism, based on the famous French Enlightenment, made a strong impact on India. Reformers like Rammohan Roy and Devendranath Tagore founded the Brahmo Samaj in an effort to revise Hinduism and make it compatible with modern Western thinking.[7] This effort required the solving of two problems: (1) the problem of religious plurality and (2) the problem of the clash between modern science and old religious beliefs.

The old philosophy of pure monism, or *advaita,* is well suited to solve these problems. First of all, if religious imagery has only a symbolic meaning that refers to something inconceivable, then many different systems of symbols should work equally well. In this way, all major religious systems can be reconciled. This was Vivekananda's idea, and he greatly stressed the equality of all religions.

Likewise, if religious imagery is simply symbolic, then there is no question of a conflict between religion and science. A religious story that seems to conflict with established scientific facts can simply be interpreted as a symbolic clue pointing to the One beyond the grasp of the finite scientific mind. Vivekananda also mentioned that the stark simplicity of the impersonal Brahman fits with the simplicity sought by physicists in their hoped-for Grand Unified Theory of nature.

Devendranath Tagore

But in pure monism, what becomes of love of God, or indeed, love of anyone? If the ultimate reality is pure oneness, and personal existence is illusory, then love is also illusory. Love requires two, and not just two of anything. Two persons are needed for a relationship of love. If such relationships do have spiritual reality, then at least two spiritual persons must eternally exist. In traditional Hindu thought, there are, in fact, two categories of eternal persons: (1) the *jīva* souls that live in individual material bodies and (2) the original Supreme Personality of Godhead and His countless spiritual expansions. As Vivekananda pointed out, Hindus believe that the Supreme Being incarnated on earth as Kṛṣṇa, who expounded on the ways of loving devotional reciprocation between Himself and individual *jīva* souls.

Unfortunately, after making this point, Vivekananda rejected both Kṛṣṇa and the individual soul as illusory. In his monistic approach to religion, all conceivable features of the Absolute are ruled out. Beingness, knowledge, and bliss are three, and they must be discarded from the One as earthbound misconceptions. The same is true of the might and mercy of the Lord. Likewise, if the real truth is absolute oneness, all personal relationships of admiration, friendship, parental love, or conjugal love must be given up as delusions.

The Vaiṣṇava Alternative Given by Bhaktivinoda Ṭhākura

It is natural then to ask if some other solution is available to the problems posed when modern rational thought meets the multiplicity of religious systems. To explore this, I now turn to the life of Bhaktivinoda Ṭhākura, a contemporary of Swami Vivekananda.

Bhaktivinoda Ṭhākura was born in 1838 as Kedaranath Datta in the Nadia district of West Bengal. As a young man he acquired an English education, and he used to exchange thoughts on literary and spiritual topics with Devendranath Tagore, the Brahmo Samaj leader and Vivekananda's early teacher. In due course he studied law, and for many years he supported his family as a magistrate in the British court system.

Bhaktivinoda Ṭhākura

Bhaktivinoda deeply studied the religious thought of his day. He scrutinized the works of European philosophers, and he was greatly impressed with the devotional teachings of Jesus Christ. At first, his Western education inclined him to look down on the Vaiṣṇava literature of devotional service to Kṛṣṇa. Indeed, he wrote that the *Bhāgavata,* one of the main texts describing Kṛṣṇa, "seemed like a repository of ideas scarcely adopted to the nineteenth century."[8]

But at a certain point he ran across a work about the great Vaiṣṇava reformer Lord Caitanya, and he was able to obtain the commentary Caitanya had given on the *Bhāgavata* to the *advaita* Vedāntists of Benares. This created in him a great love for the devotional teachings of Kṛṣṇa as presented by Caitanya.[9] In due course he achieved an exalted state of spiritual realization by following Caitanya's teachings, and he wrote many books presenting those teachings to people both in India and abroad.

Lord Caitanya

A Historical Interlude

Before we go into Bhaktivinoda Ṭhākura's spiritual teachings, let me give an explicit idea of the intellectual climate in which he was operating in late nineteenth-century Bengal. To do this, I will quote a passage from the writings of Sir William Jones, a jurist who worked for the British East India company and was the first president of the Asiatic Society of Bengal. In an article on Hindu chronology written in 1788, Jones gave the following account of the close of Dvāpara-yuga, the Third Age of the *Purāṇas* and the *Mahābhārata:*

> I cannot leave the third Indian age, in which the virtues and vices of mankind are said to have been equal, without observing, that even the close of it is manifestly fabulous and poetical, with hardly more *appearance* of historical truth, than the tale of *Troy,* or of the *Argonauts;* for Yudhishthir, it seems, was the son of Dherma, the *Genius of Justice;* Bhima of Pavan, or the *God of Wind;* Arjun of Indra, or the *Firmament;* Nacul and Sahadeva of the Cumars, the Castor and Pollux of *India;* and Bhishma, their reputed great uncle, was the child of Ganga, or the Ganges, by Santanu, whose brother Devapi is supposed to be still alive in the city of Calapa; all which fictions may be charming embellishments of an heroick poem, but are just as absurd in civil History, as the descent of two royal families from the Sun and the Moon.[10]

What Jones is referring to here is the story in the *Mahābhārata* of events in India at the time of Kṛṣṇa's advent. According to Hindu tradition, these events took place about five thousand years ago, when the Dvāpara-yuga gave way to the present epoch, called the Kali-yuga. Yudhiṣṭhira, Arjuna, Bhīma, Nakula, and Sahadeva are the five Pāṇḍava brothers who figured in many of Kṛṣṇa's pastimes.

We can see from Jones's comments that he does not regard the story of the Pāṇḍavas as true history. Why not? For many of us, the problem is that the story contains elements simply not credible to a person trained in the modern rational viewpoint. We know that people don't descend from demigods. All documents putting forth such nonsense are rejected by responsible historians, so objective historical accounts hold no such absurdities. Such things never happened, and our history books abundantly confirm this.

Sir William Jones

Sir William Jones was clearly thinking along these lines, but he was not exactly a modern rationalist. Jones was a Christian who believed fully in the Mosaic chronology of the Bible. The table to the right shows how Jones attempted to reconstruct Hindu chronology to bring it in line with Christian views.[11] Jones, it seems, was able to scorn Hindu myths as absurd while at the same time accepting as true the supernatural events of the Bible.

It is perhaps poetic justice that the same scornful treatment Jones applied to the *Mahābhārata* was soon applied to the Bible. During Jones's lifetime, the "higher" scientific criticism of the Bible was being developed in Germany, and it was unleashed in England in the mid-nineteenth century. In 1860, the Anglican theologians Benjamin Jowett and Baden Powell stole attention from Darwin's newly published book *On the Origin of Species* by a controversial essay that rejected miracles, on scientific grounds.[12] The Darwinists and the higher Biblical critics quickly joined forces, and Darwin's supporter Thomas Huxley began quoting German Biblical scholars in his essays on the interpretation of Genesis.[13] As the nineteenth century drew to a close, rational, scientific skepticism became the only acceptable path for a scholar or intellectual in any respectable field of study.

The Bhāgavata

Bhaktivinoda Ṭhākura was confronted with this hostile intellectual climate in his efforts to present spiritual knowledge to the young

Reconstruction of Hindu Chronology
by Sir William Jones

Occidental History	Hindu History	Years from 1788 A.D.	Date
Adam	Menu I, Age I	5794	4006B.C.
Noah	Menu II	4737	2949
Deluge		4138	2350
Nimrod	Hiranyacasipu, Age II	4006	2218
Bel	Bali	3892	2104
	Rama, Age II	3817	2029
	Noah's death	3787	1999
	Pradyota	2817	1029
	Buddha, Age IV	2815	1027
	Nanda	2487	699
	Balin	1937	149
	Vicramaditya	1844	56
	Devapada	1811	23
Christ		1787	1A.D.
	Narayanpala	1721	67
	Saca	1709	79
Walid		1080	708
Mahmud		786	1002
Shengez		548	1250
Taimur		39	1397
Babur		276	1512
Nadirshah		49	1739

Ages I, II, III, and IV are Satya-, Treta-, Dvapara-, and Kali-yugas.
Menu I is Svayambhuva Manu. Menu II is Vaivasvata Manu.

Bengali intellectuals of his day. After drinking in from their British teachers the ideas of William Jones and other Western orientalists, these young people were not at all inclined to give credence to old myths. How then could the teachings of Kṛṣṇa on love of God be presented? Bhaktivinoda Ṭhākura judiciously chose to give a partial picture of the truth that would introduce important spiritual ideas without invoking rejection due to deep-seated prejudices.

In a lecture delivered in Dinajpur, West Bengal, in 1869, he focused on the *Bhāgavata,* or *Bhāgavata Purāṇa,* as the preeminent text on the nature of the Supreme and the means of realizing our relation with the Supreme. Rejecting pure monism as a useless idea, he held that God is an eternal person. Thus he said, "The *Bhāgavata* has . . . a Transcendental, Personal, All-intelligent, Active, absolutely Free, Holy, Good, All-powerful, Omnipresent, Just and Merciful and supremely Spiritual Deity without a second, creating, preserving all that is in the universe."[14] The highest object of the soul, he went on to say, is to "serve that Infinite Being for ever spiritually in the activity of Absolute Love."[15]

Bhaktivinoda described the material world as the product of *māyā.* Here *māyā* means not illusion but the eternal energy of the Supreme that He uses to bewilder souls who desire to live outside of harmony with Him. The creation of the material world through *māyā* is actually an aspect of the Lord's mercy, since He thereby allows independent-minded souls to act in a world from which God is apparently absent.

All these ideas are taken from the *Bhāgavata* without modification. But in describing what the *Bhāgavata* says about the details of the material universe, Bhaktivinoda Ṭhākura adopted an indirect approach. Thus he said,

> In the common-place books of the Hindu religion in which the *Raja* and *Tama Gunas* have been described as the ways of religion, we find description of a local heaven and a local hell; the heaven is as beautiful as anything on earth and the Hell as ghastly as any picture of evil. . . . The religion of the *Bhagavat* is free from such a poetic imagination. Indeed, in some of the chapters we meet with descriptions of these hells and heavens, and accounts of curious tales, but we have been warned in some place in the book, not to accept them as real facts, but to treat them

> as inventions to overawe the wicked and to improve the simple and the ignorant.[16]

In fact, the *Bhāgavata* does ascribe reality to hells and heavens and their inhabitants. It describes in great detail the higher planetary systems and the various demigods who live there, including Brahmā, Śiva, and Indra. Not only does the *Bhāgavata* say that these beings are real, but it gives them an important role in the creation and maintenance of the universe. It also gives them a role in many of Kṛṣṇa's manifest pastimes (*līlās*) within the material world. For example, in the story of the lifting of Govardhana Hill, it is Indra who creates a devastating storm when Kṛṣṇa insults him by interfering with a sacrifice in his honor.

Bhaktivinoda Ṭhākura chose to sidestep these "mythological" aspects of the *Bhāgavata* in an effort to reach an audience of intellectuals whose mundane education ruled out such myths as absurd fantasy. Indeed, he went even further. In 1880 he published a treatise entitled *Śrī Kṛṣṇa Saṁhitā* in which he elaborately explained the philosophy of Kṛṣṇa consciousness.[17] In this book he also put forth a reconstruction of Indian history similar to the one introduced by Sir William Jones to bring Hindu chronology into line with the Mosaic timetable of the Bible. This involved converting demigods and Manus into human kings and reducing their total span of history to a few thousand earthly years.

I should point out clearly that Bhaktivinoda Ṭhākura did not personally accept the modified version of the *Bhāgavata* he presented to the Bengali intellectuals. He actually accepted the so-called myths of the *Bhāgavata* as true, and he presented them as such in many of his writings. For example, in his book *Jaiva Dharma,* Bhaktivinoda said this:

> I have said that the Vaishnava religion came into being as soon as the creatures came into existence. Brahma was the first Vaishnava. Sriman Mahadeva is also a Vaishnava. The ancient Prajapaties are all Vaishnavas. Sri Narada Goswami, who is the fancy-born child of Brahma, is a Vaishnava. . . . You have seen the Vaishnava religion of the beginning of the creation. Then again when Gods, men, demons, etc., have been separately described, we get Prahlada and Dhruva from the very start. . . . Manu's sons and Prahlada are all grandsons of Prajapati,

> Kashyapa. . . . There is no doubt about it . . . that the pure Vaishnava religion began with the beginning of history. Then the kings of the solar and lunar dynasties and all great and famous sages and hermits became devotees of Vishnu.[18]

This passage was written in response to challengers who argued that Vaiṣṇava *dharma* is a recent development. The passage takes it for granted that beings such as Brahmā, Mahādeva, Nārada, and Prahlāda literally exist as described in the *śāstras,* or Vedic scriptures. Many similar examples can be found in Bhaktivinoda Ṭhākura's writings.

Now, if Bhaktivinoda Ṭhākura accepted the literal truth of the *śāstras,* how could he justify making presentations in which he denied it? His grand-disciple Śrīla A. C. Bhaktivedanta Swami Prabhupāda has pointed out that there is a precedent for making such indirect presentations of *śāstra.* An interpretation of a text that adheres directly to the dictionary definitions of its words is called *mukhya-vṛtti,* and an imaginary or indirect interpretation is called *lakṣaṇā-vṛtti* or *gauṇa-vṛtti.* Śrīla Prabhupāda pointed out, "Sometimes . . . as a matter of necessity, Vedic literature is described in terms of the *lakṣaṇā-vṛtti* or *gauṇa-vṛtti,* but one should not accept such explanations as permanent truths."[19] In general, one should understand *śāstra* in terms of *mukhya-vṛtti.*

The Theology of Visions

One might grant that Bhaktivinoda Ṭhākura was justified in modifying the *śāstras* to reach out to intellectuals trained to scorn old myths. But serious questions can still be raised: What is the scope for making such a presentation of religion today, and to what extent can such a presentation be regarded as true? Is the mythological material in the Hindu *śāstras* unimportant, so that one might present it as true to people who believe in it and false to people who disbelieve? Or should we accept from modern knowledge that Hindu myths really are false and try to formulate a philosophy that preserves the essential idea of love of God while dispensing with superannuated ideas?

To answer these questions, let us see how we would have to reformulate Vaiṣṇava philosophy to make it readily acceptable to Western intellectuals in the late twentieth century. To do this we must

William James

deviate to some extent from the prevailing materialistic framework of modern science. Physical scientists tell us that the mind, with all its conscious experiences, is simply a product of the brain. If we accept this, then all religious experience, whether it be the bliss of Brahman or *prema-bhakti,* love of God, is simply hallucinatory. If this is true, we can forget about religion—unless, of course, we like hallucinations.

For an alternative viewpoint, I will turn to the psychologist William James. Although James was a man of the nineteenth century, he was a Western scientist who applied the methods of empirical scientific research to the phenomena of religion. Thus his observations are still relevant today.

As a result of his studies, James reached the following conclusions:

> The further limits of our being plunge, it seems to me, into an altogether other dimension of existence from the sensible and merely "understandable" world. Name it the mystical region, or the supernatural region, whichever you choose. . . . Yet the unseen region in question is not merely ideal, for it produces effects in this world. When we commune with it, work is actually done upon our finite personality, for we are turned into new men, and consequences in the way of conduct follow in the natural world upon our regenerative change. But that which produces effects within another reality must be termed a reality itself, so I feel as if we had no philosophic excuse for calling the unseen or mystical world unreal.[20]

One could take this idea of a mystical or transcendent dimension and arrive at the following version of Vaiṣṇava philosophy: Such a transcendental region does exist, and it is the eternal abode of Kṛṣṇa. Advanced souls can perceive that realm in meditation by the grace of

Lord Kṛṣṇa

Kṛṣṇa, and so they are able to enter into Kṛṣṇa's eternal loving pastimes. But all Purāṇic descriptions of events within the material world have to be understood rationally through modern scientific knowledge. On the whole, the myths in the *Purāṇas* are not literally true. But the stories of Kṛṣṇa's pastimes are not simply fantasy. Rather, they are spiritual transmissions into the meditative minds of great souls, and they refer not to this world but to the purely transcendental domain.

This is a philosophy that might appeal to many, and I will refer to it as the theology of visions. It allows one to retain the idea of love of God, while at the same time avoiding disturbing conflicts between mythological tales and modern knowledge. It also appears implicitly in the work of some modern scholars of religion who study the *bhakti* tradition.

To illustrate this, I will briefly consider an article, "Shrines of the Mind," by David Haberman, Assistant Professor of Religion at Williams College.[21] In this article, Haberman argues that Vraja, the traditional place of Kṛṣṇa's manifest *līlās,* is first and foremost a mental shrine, a realm that can be entered and experienced in meditation.

He argues that the physical Vraja, a tract of land near the North Indian city of Mathurā, has only been a major center for the worship of Kṛṣṇa since the sixteenth century, when the followers of Caitanya Mahāprabhu and other Vaiṣṇavas "rediscovered" the lost sites of Kṛṣṇa's pastimes. In fact, says Haberman, these sites never really existed before the sixteenth century, and so they weren't rediscovered. Rather, they were projected onto the physical landscape of Vraja from the transcendental landscape perceived in meditation.

Haberman gives a number of interpretations of what happens when a person meditates on a mental shrine. These range from the contemplation of imaginary scenes in the ordinary sense to entry into "an eternal transcendent world which is perceptible only to the mind's eye and is reached through meditative technique."[22] Since Haberman seems to lean toward the latter, it could be said that he is hinting at a version of the theology of visions: One can enter into Kṛṣṇa's transcendental world by meditation, but Kṛṣṇa never had any actual pastimes in the physical world. Physical, worldly history followed the lines revealed by modern scholarship. This means that many centuries ago in Vraja there may have been various primitive tribes following animistic cults, but there was no Kṛṣṇa literally lifting Govardhana Hill.

Although this religious theory allows one to avoid certain conflicts with modern scholarship, it does have a number of drawbacks. A few of these are the following:

1. This theory is contrary to Vaiṣṇava tradition, so it calls into question the thinking of the many great souls who have supported the tradition. Since those great souls are the very meditators who have seen visions of Kṛṣṇa, how can those visions be real? In other words, why should persons who see the absolute realm believe in the truth of myths that even worldly scholars see to be false?
2. This theory doesn't explain why the worship of Kṛṣṇa should be a recent affair, as scholars claim. If there is an eternal realm of Kṛṣṇa that can be accessed by meditation, why did people begin to access it only recently?
3. What does this theory say about the multiplicity of religions? Are the visions reported in other religious traditions real? If not, then why is it that Vaiṣṇava visions alone are real? If so, then are there many transcendental realms, one for each religion? Or is it that people see in one transcendental realm whatever they are looking for?
4. This theory greatly limits the power of God. If God only appears in visions, what becomes of His role as the creator and controller of the universe? If we let modern science explain the material world, God's role is whittled down to practically nothing.
5. The theology of visions can easily be transformed into a purely psychological theory of religious experience. After all, this is the

view that will be overwhelmingly favored by psychologists, neuroscientists, and physical scientists of all varieties.

In view of objections (1) through (4), objection (5) is almost unavoidable. We are left with a totally mundane theory that explains religion away. In the case of Kṛṣṇa's *līlās,* this line of thinking leads us to especially unpleasant conclusions. Thus Haberman describes meditation on Kṛṣṇa *līlā* as follows: "The desired end is a religious voyeurism and vicarious enjoyment said to produce infinite bliss."[23] Such sad conclusions are avoided in the more balanced approach taken by traditional Vaiṣṇavas, who stress Kṛṣṇa's roles as the supreme creator and the performer of humanly impossible pastimes on earth.

Shifting the Boundary Between Myth and Science

Yet if we start from the theology of visions and proceed in the inductive manner of scholars, we can see how it *could* serve as a steppingstone toward a more satisfactory theory. A starting point for developing such a theory can be a story related by Haberman about the Vaiṣṇava saint Narottama Dāsa Ṭhākura.[24]

It seems that Narottama was once meditating on boiling milk for Rādhā and Kṛṣṇa. When the milk boiled over in his meditation, he took the vessel off the fire with his bare hands and got burned in the process. When Narottama awoke from his meditation, he discovered that his hands were actually burned.

There are many stories like this, and I will briefly mention two more. In the second story, Śrīnivāsa Ācārya, a contemporary of Narottama Dāsa Ṭhākura, was meditating on fanning Lord Caitanya. In Śrīnivāsa's meditation, Lord Caitanya placed His garland around Śrīnivāsa's neck. When Śrīnivāsa awoke from meditation, the unusually fragrant garland was actually there, around his neck.[25]

In the third story a Vaiṣṇava saint named Duḥkhī Kṛṣṇa Dāsa was sweeping the site of Kṛṣṇa's *rāsa* dance in Vraja. He found a remarkable golden anklet and hid it, since he thought that it was very important. Later, an old lady came to him and asked for the anklet. It turned out that the old lady was really Lalitā, one of the transcendental maidservants of Rādhā and Kṛṣṇa. The lady finally revealed that the anklet belonged to Rādhā Herself, and then she disclosed her true form as Lalitā.[26]

What are we to make of such stories? The story of the burned hands might be accepted by many scholars. After all, it is well known that Catholics meditating on the crucifixion of Christ sometimes develop stigmata, in which the wounds of Christ appear on their hands and feet. If meditation can somehow cause bleeding wounds, then maybe it can also cause burns.

The story of the miraculous garland goes one step further. Here a tangible object is said to materialize. This may seem fantastic, but it turns out that there is an extensive literature on materialization. For example, Stephen Braude, a professor of philosophy at the University of Maryland, has argued that many cases of alleged materializations produced by spirit mediums are backed up by solid empirical evidence that deserves serious study.[27] If materializations by spiritualists might be factual, why not materializations of beautiful garlands by saintly persons?

This brings us to the third story. Although this story seems "far out," there are many similar stories in which a transcendent person seems to step into our material continuum, perform some action, and then disappear. Another example would be the story from *Caitanya-caritāmṛta* in which Kṛṣṇa, as a small boy, approached the saint Mādhavendra Purī, gave him a pot of milk, and then mysteriously disappeared. Mādhavendra Purī drank the milk, thus showing that it was tangible. Later that night he had a dream in which Kṛṣṇa revealed the location of the Gopāla Deity, which had originally been installed by Kṛṣṇa's grandson Vajra and had been hidden during a Muslim attack.[28]

The stories of the burned hand, the miraculous garland, and the transcendental visits are progressively harder and harder to accept from a conventional scientific standpoint. But it is hard to see how to draw a line between such stories that might possibly be true and ones that definitely cannot. And all the stories seem to hint at energetic exchanges between spiritual and material energy that might add an important new chapter to our scientific knowledge, if only they could be properly studied.

When we study a body of empirical evidence, we always evaluate it within our limiting assumptions. In the end, the conclusions we derive from the evidence may reflect our limiting assumptions as much as they reflect the evidence itself. If the assumptions change, the conclusions will also change, even though the evidence stays the same.

Consider what might happen if all the available evidence about the history of human experience were to be studied not through nineteenth-century rationalism but through a new science in which spiritual transformations of matter were considered a real possibility. The result might be a completely different picture of the past from the one now accepted by scholars.

For one thing, the objections that Sir William Jones expressed about the story of the Pāṇḍava brothers might not seem so weighty. If higher beings can step into our continuum from another realm, then humans might well descend from such beings. The new picture of the past might prove much more compatible with traditional spiritual teachings than the one that now prevails.

In the late twentieth century there were signs that a broader approach to science might be developing. In the days of Vivekananda and Bhaktivinoda Ṭhākura, mechanistic, reductionistic science appeared to be marching unimpeded from triumph to triumph, and many people believed that it would soon find explanations for everything. But in the late twentieth century this triumphant march had been checked on many different fronts.

For example, physics in the 1890s looked like a closed subject, but in the early decades of the twentieth century it entered a phase of paradox and mystery with the development of relativity theory and quantum mechanics. The mysteries of quantum mechanics continue to inspire scientists to contemplate ideas that would have seemed outrageously mystical at the turn of the century.[29, 30, 31]

But now physics has encountered an even more serious obstacle. The bold architects of universal physical theories are now realizing that these theories can never be adequately tested by experiment.[32] Thus the Harvard physicist Howard Georgi characterized modern theoretical physics as "recreational mathematical theology."[33]

In the mid-twentieth century, computer scientists believed they were on the verge of proving that thought is mechanical, thereby fulfilling La Mettrie's eighteenth-century dream of man as a machine. But in more recent years, even though computers have become more and more powerful, the dream of simulating human intelligence has seemed to recede further and further into the future.

With the discovery of the DNA spiral helix by Watson and Crick in 1953, many scientists thought that the ultimate secret of life had been revealed. Since then, molecular biologists have had tremendous success in shedding light on the mechanisms of living cells. But as molecular biology unveils the incredible complexity of these high-precision mechanisms, the goal of explaining the origin of life seems progressively more difficult to attain.[34]

These are just a few of the many areas in which the program of mechanistic reductionism seemed to be reaching ultimate limits as the twentieth century drew to a close. Perhaps as a result of these developments, many professional scientists are now showing a willingness to consider theoretical ideas and areas of research that have traditionally been taboo.

For example, we now find organizations of professional scientists who openly study phenomena lying on the edge between physical science and the realms of mysticism and the paranormal. Examples are the International Association for New Science (IANS), the Society for Scientific Exploration (SSE), the Institute of Noetic Sciences (IONS), and the International Society for the Study of Subtle Energies and Energy Medicine (ISSSEEM). These all sponsor regular scientific conferences.

Some of the phenomena these groups study seem similar to the "mythical" phenomena so often reported in old religious texts and in recent accounts of religious experiences. A synergistic interaction between scholars of religion and these new scientific organizations might prove to be a valuable source of new insights for both groups of researchers.

The Direct Presentation of Vaiṣṇava Teachings

We have discussed how Bhaktivinoda Ṭhākura found it necessary to present a modified version of the Vaiṣṇava teachings to young Bengali intellectuals at the high noon of British political and ideological imperialism. But as the sun began to set on the British empire, his son and successor Śrīla Bhaktisiddhānta Sarasvatī began a vigorous program of directly presenting the Vaiṣṇava conclusions throughout India. This program was taken abroad by his disciple Śrīla A. C. Bhaktivedanta Swami Prabhupāda, who boldly celebrated the ancient Rathayātrā festival of Jagannātha Purī in London's Trafalgar Square.

In the changing climate of scientific opinion in the late twentieth century, the time may have come to openly introduce the traditional teachings of *bhakti* to the world's intellectual communities. The once jarring conflicts between rationalism and traditional religion may progressively fade as science matures and becomes open to the study of mystical phenomena. This opens up the possibility of an approach to religion that is intellectually acceptable and at the same time satisfies the soul's inner desire for love in a transcendental relationship.

This leaves us with one possible objection. Could it be that the Vaiṣṇava teachings, with their specific emphasis on Kṛṣṇa as the Supreme, are guilty of sectarian disregard for other religious traditions? The answer is that, of course, any doctrine can be put forward in a narrow, sectarian way. But as Bhaktivinoda Ṭhākura pointed out in his essay on the *Bhāgavata,* the Vaiṣṇava teachings are inherently broad-minded and acknowledge the value of all religious systems.

The following prayer shows the approach to other religions taken in the *Bhāgavata:*

> O my Lord, Your devotees can see You through the ears by the process of bona fide hearing, and thus their hearts become cleansed, and You take Your seat there. You are so merciful to Your devotees that You manifest Yourself in the particular eternal form of transcendence in which they always think of You.[35]

This verse states that God appears to His devoted worshipers in many different forms, depending on their desires. These forms include the *avatāras* of Kṛṣṇa described in traditional Vaiṣṇava texts, but are not limited to those forms. Indeed, it is said that the expansions of the Supreme Personality of Godhead are uncountable, and they cannot be fully described in the finite scriptures of any one religious community.

The following verse gives some idea of the different religious communities in the universe, as described by the *Bhāgavata:*

> From the forefathers headed by Bhṛgu Muni and other sons of Brahmā appeared many children and descendants, who assumed different forms

> as demigods, demons, human beings, Guhyakas, Siddhas, Gandharvas, Vidyādharas, Cāraṇas, Kindevas, Kinnaras, Nāgas, Kimpuruṣas, and so on. All of the many universal species, along with their respective leaders, appeared with different natures and desires generated from the three modes of material nature. Therefore, because of the different characteristics of the living entities within the universe, there are a great many Vedic rituals, mantras, and rewards.[36]

This statement is explicitly "mythological," and one can well imagine how Sir William Jones might have reacted to it. But it offers a grand picture of countless races and societies within the universe, all given religious methods suitable for their particular natures. Here the word "Vedic" cannot be limited to particular Sanskrit texts that now exist in India. Rather, it refers to the sum total of religious systems revealed by the infinite Supreme God for the sake of elevating countless societies of divinely created beings.

As always, the distinguishing feature of the Vaiṣṇava teachings is that God is a real person and His variegated creation is also real. Thus the Vaiṣṇava approach to religious liberality is to regard all genuine religions as real divine revelations. Likewise, the Vaiṣṇava teachings

Śrīla Bhaktisiddhānta Sarasvatī

Bhaktivedanta Swami Prabhupāda

of love of God aim to set in place a relationship of loving service between the real individual soul and the Supreme Personality of Godhead, the performer of real transcendental pastimes.

REFERENCES

1. Vivekananda, 1963, pp. 10–11.
2. Vivekananda, 1963, p. 11.
3. Vivekananda, 1963, p. 13.
4. Vivckananda, 1963, p. 14.
5. Jordan, 1987, p. 27.
6. Vivekananda, 1963, p. 17.
7. Majumdar, 1965.
8. Thakur Bhaktivinod, 1986, p. 5.
9. Thakur Bhaktivinod, 1986, p. 6.
10. Jones, 1799, p. 302.
11. Jones, 1799, p. 313.
12. Moore, 1986, p. 334.
13. Moore, 1986, p. 344.
14. Thakur Bhaktivinod, 1986, p. 30.
15. Thakur Bhaktivinod, 1986, p. 30.
16. Thakur Bhaktivinod, 1986, pp. 24–25.
17. Rūpa-vilāsa dāsa, 1989, pp. 138–39.
18. Thakur Bhakti Vinod, 1975, pp. 155–56.
19. Bhaktivedanta Swami Prabhupāda, 1975, *Ādi-līlā,* Vol. 2, p. 95.
20. James, 1982, pp. 515–16.
21. Haberman, 1993.
22. Haberman, 1993, p. 31.
23. Haberman, 1993, p. 26.
24. Haberman, 1993, p. 33.
25. Rosen, 1991, pp. 63–64.
26. Rosen, 1991, pp. 119–39.
27. Braude, 1986.
28. Bhaktivedanta Swami Prabhupāda, 1975, *Madhya-līlā,* Vol. 2, pp. 12–19.
29. Bohm, 1980.
30. Penrose, 1989.
31. Jahn and Dunne, 1987.

32. Weinberg, 1992.
33. Crease and Mann, 1986, p. 414.
34. Horgan, 1991.
35. Bhaktivedanta Swami Prabhupāda, 1987, text 3.9.11.
36. Hridayananda Goswami, 1982, text 11.14.5–7.

BIBLIOGRAPHY

Bhaktivedanta Swami Prabhupāda, A. C., 1975, *Śrī Caitanya-caritāmṛta, Ādi-līlā,* Vol. 2, Los Angeles: Bhaktivedanta Book Trust.

Bhaktivedanta Swami Prabhupāda, A. C., 1975, *Śrī Caitanya-caritāmṛta, Madhya-līlā,* Vol. 2, Los Angeles: Bhaktivedanta Book Trust.

Bhaktivedanta Swami Prabhupāda, A. C., 1987, *Śrīmad Bhāgavatam,* Third Canto - Part One, Los Angeles: Bhaktivedanta Book Trust.

Bohm, David, 1980, *Wholeness and the Implicate Order,* London: Routledge & Kegan Paul.

Braude, Stephen, 1986, *The Limits of Influence,* New York: Routledge.

Crease, Robert and Mann, Charles, 1986, *The Second Creation,* New York: Macmillan.

Haberman, David, 1993, "Shrines of the Mind," *Journal of Vaiṣṇava Studies,* Vol. 1, No. 3.

Horgan, John, 1991, "In the Beginning . . . ," *Scientific American,* February.

Hridayananda dāsa Goswami, 1982, *Śrīmad Bhāgavatam,* Eleventh Canto - Part Three, Los Angeles: Bhaktivedanta Book Trust.

Jahn, Robert and Dunne, Brenda, 1987, *Margins of Reality,* San Diego: Harcourt Brace Jovanovich.

James, William, 1982, *The Varieties of Religious Experience*, New York: Penguin Books.

Jones, William, 1799, *The Works of Sir William Jones,* Vol. I, London: Printed for G. G. and J. Robinson, Pater-Noster-Row and R. H. Evans, No. 26, Pall-Mall.

Jordan, James N., 1987, *Western Philosophy: From Antiquity to the Middle Ages,* New York: Macmillan.

Majumdar, R. C., 1965, *Svami Vivekananda: A Historical Review,* Calcutta: General Printers and Publishers, Ltd.

Moore, James R., 1986, "Geologists and Interpreters of Genesis in the Nineteenth Century," *God and Nature,* eds. David Lindberg and Ronald Numbers, Berkeley: University of California Press.

Penrose, Roger, 1989, *The Emperor's New Mind,* Oxford: Oxford Univ. Press.

Rosen, Steven, 1991, *The Lives of the Vaishnava Saints: Shrinivas Acharya, Narottam Das Thakur, Shyamananda Pandit,* Brooklyn, New York: Folk Books.

Rūpa-vilāsa dāsa, 1989, *The Seventh Goswami,* Washington: New Jaipur Press.

Thakur, Sri Srila Bhakti Vinode, 1975, *Jaiva Dharma,* Madras: Sree Gaudiya Math.

Thakur, Shrila Bhaktivinod, 1986, *The Bhagavat: Its Philosophy, Its Ethics & Its Theology,* Nabadwip: Shri Goudiya Samiti.

Vivekananda, Swami, 1963, *Selections from Svami Vivekananda,* Calcutta: Advaita Ashrama.

Weinberg, Steven, 1992, *Dreams of a Final Theory,* New York: Pantheon Books.

5

The Miracle of the Milk

On September 21, 1995, Hindu communities all over the world were electrified by news of temple deities accepting offerings of milk. According to the stories, when deities of Gaṇeśa, Lord Śiva, and others were offered spoonfuls of milk, the milk would mysteriously disappear. It seemed that the deities were showing their divine power by mystically drinking the milk.

In India, "The gatekeeper of the Birla Temple reported that at least 55,000 have visited the temple and they spoonfed about 125 litres of milk." In America, "Thousands of awe-struck worshipers have swarmed into Hindu temples in Richmond Hill and Oakville to witness the remarkable phenomenon of milk-drinking statues that has baffled religious observers around the world." In one London temple, "a deity of Ganeshji was reported to have swallowed 3,000 pints."

Inevitably, there were skeptical rebuttals. Devotees in India discovered that if one touches a spoon filled with milk to the side of a smooth object, the milk will be drawn to the object by capillary attraction and will flow down from the point of contact in a thin stream. People who don't notice the stream of milk could imagine that the milk is literally disappearing before their eyes. The milk would not accumulate in a noticeable pool because it would be carried away bit by bit on the clothing and bodies of throngs of worshipers, or it would simply flow down a drain at the foot of the Deity. According to the debunkers, people were accepting a miracle simply on the basis of mass hysteria triggered by a simple misperception.

What is the truth? It is hard to say from few second-hand reports what really happened on September 21. But it is clear that as a social phenomenon the miracle of the milk is significant. Miracles and rumors of miracles clearly have a profound impact on human thinking. To make a few general observations about miracles, therefore, seems worthwhile.

Miracles and Nature

The word miracle comes from the Latin word *mira,* which means "to wonder at." Miracles are wondrous events that seem to surpass the laws of nature and are therefore ascribed to a divine or supernatural cause. Miracles have traditionally been seen as evidence for the reality of divine power, and they have served as an inspiration for religious faith. At the same time, miracles have also served as a focus for skepticism and doubt.

For most people the "laws of nature" are simply the regular patterns of events perceived through ordinary experience. For example, in ordinary experience a fluid such as milk always retains the same volume and appearance unless affected by heat, chemical action, or living organisms. One certainly doesn't expect to see milk disappear when brought into contact with a stone or metal statue. If it does disappear, this suggests that some higher power is involved. One could then invoke religious doctrines concerning God and demigods to explain the unexpected phenomenon: the event confirms the doctrines.

Unfortunately, other explanations for many alleged miracles are also possible. Human beings are subject to four defects: our senses are imperfect, we tend to make mistakes, we fall into delusion, and we have an inherent tendency to cheat.

If an unusual event occurs, the defects of our senses can easily give rise to many false reports of similar events. For example, let us suppose that milk really did disappear when offered in some temple on September 21. As word of this wonder spread, people elsewhere could easily be deluded by the capillary effect later pointed out by skeptics. This delusion would generate more stories, and the cheating propensity would induce some people to exaggerate or even outright lie.

The ultimate result is that genuine miracles, if they really do occur, will tend to be surrounded by a cloud of false reports. The false reports will vastly outnumber the genuine and create an atmosphere of skepticism. Since miracles are often taken as proof of religious doctrines, doubts about miracles give rise to doubts about the doctrines.

Yogis and Siddhis

Although miracles apparently violate natural law, they can nonetheless be seen as manifestations of *higher* natural laws. Thus the fourth-century Christian patriarch St. Augustine wrote, "Miracles do not happen in contradiction to nature, but only in contradiction to that which is known to us in nature."[1]

According to the *Śrīmad-Bhāgavatam,* powers known as *siddhis* include the ability to nullify gravity (*laghimā*), change the size of one's body (*aṇimā* and *mahimā*), and acquire objects at a distance (*prāpti*).[2] These *siddhis* are considered naturally existing, and a mystic yogi can acquire them.

Śrīla Prabhupāda points out that with *prāpti-siddhi,* "not only can the perfect mystic yogi touch the moon planet, but he can extend his hand anywhere and take whatever he likes. He may be sitting thousands of miles away from a certain place, and if he likes he can take fruit from a garden there."[3] When the yogi takes the fruit from a distance, a person sitting in the garden would see the fruit mysteriously disappear.

A yogi might also cause milk to disappear mysteriously—without the direct intervention of a demigod such as Gaṇeśa. I do not say that this is how the miracle of the milk got started. But as a general rule, many wonderful phenomena that might be attributed to a divine agency can also be caused in material ways involving ordinary living beings. This is important to understand, since miracles tend to confirm religious faith.

To perform mystical feats, a person does not have to be highly elevated in yoga. Śrīla Prabhupāda discouraged his disciples from taking an interest in miracles, because many unscrupulous persons have attracted and cheated people by a display of mystic powers.

The typical pattern in India is that a person will begin to exhibit genuine mystic powers. When praised by naive followers, he then develops an inflated ego and presents himself as a divine incarnation. In many instances the person later loses his powers, and he then resorts to cheap tricks in an effort to live up to his followers' expectations. This, of course, provides a great opportunity for skeptics, who seize upon these cases to show the foolishness of religion.

The Paranormal

The mysterious disappearance of objects is sometimes linked to quite ordinary people who may have never practiced yoga. In poltergeist cases, unusual events tend to occur in the presence of a so-called target person. These events include spontaneous fires, mysterious sounds, unexplained movement of objects, and things' mysteriously appearing and disappearing. Traditionally, these phenomena have been attributed to ghosts. (The word poltergeist is German for "noisy ghost.") But some parapsychologists have argued that these phenomena are actually caused by the subconscious mind of the target person.

The parapsychologist Ian Stevenson has given an example of a poltergeist case from India that involves disappearing food.[4] It seems that a woman named Radhika from the village of Degaon, south of Bombay, had the reputation in the village of being a sorceress. Food mysteriously disappearing in the village was turning up in Radhika's dwelling. The villagers thought she was stealing food by mystical means and offered to provide her with food if she would stop.

Stevenson's informant, one Swami Krishnanand, decided to put Radhika's abilities to the test. In one instance, "Swami Krishnanand . . . pointed to a *lota* [a small pot] which he held in his hand and to a man who was milking a cow some distance away, and asked to have some of the milk put into the *lota*. Instantly the *lota* became filled with milk and at the same time the milker noticed that his own vessel had less, rather than more, milk in it. He looked up astonished."[5] Radhika believed that these effects were due to a discarnate spirit that was allied with her, and Stevenson was inclined to favor this interpretation.

There are many accounts of this nature, and if any of them are true, it follows that many miracles may be real even though not due to the direct action of God or the highly placed servants of God known as demigods. But are any of these accounts true? This brings us to the modern scientific treatment of miracles.

Science and Miracles

The modern scientific approach can be traced back to the development of mathematical physics by Isaac Newton in the seventeenth century. Newton introduced the strict mathematical formulation of the laws of nature known as the "laws of physics." Scientists highly value the laws of physics because by experimental measurements one can confirm the laws with great accuracy.

The laws of physics have undergone a number of revolutionary transformations since Newton's day, but they have always been completely incompatible with the kind of miraculous events I have been discussing. In particular, the law of conservation of energy does not allow for a macroscopic object to disappear without moving from point to point through three-dimensional space.[6] A miracle, in modern scientific terms, is something that is impossible because it violates the laws of physics.

The eighteenth-century Scottish philosopher David Hume offered a criterion for evaluating miracles that is still widely accepted. He declared, "No testimony is sufficient to establish a miracle unless the testimony be of such a kind that its falsehood would be more miraculous than the fact which it endeavours to establish."[7]

This dictum shows that the validity of miracles ultimately must be decided by faith. Many scientists will conclude that large numbers of witnesses are lying rather than accept that a major violation of the laws of physics has taken place. For such scientists, miracles are ruled out. For others, the laws of physics are not sacrosanct, and the combined testimony of many responsible observers is enough to suggest that we still have much to learn about nature's laws.

Śrī Caitanya's Miracles

The points I have made so far might suggest that miraculous events should not be granted a serious role in religion. But this is not correct, as we can see by considering the role of miracles in the Gauḍīya Vaiṣṇava tradition.

The pastimes of Lord Caitanya are filled with miraculous events. Lord Caitanya revived the dead son of Śrīvāsa Ṭhākura and healed sick persons such as the leper Vāsudeva and the son-in-law of Sārvabhauma Bhaṭṭācārya, who was dying of cholera. Lord Caitanya revealed visions of His transcendental form to Sārvabhauma Bhaṭṭācārya and Rāmānanda Rāya, and He influenced the Māyāvādī *sannyāsīs* of Benares by manifesting a brilliant effulgence after entering their assembly. Lord Caitanya would sometimes mysteriously exit locked rooms, and He appeared in several *kīrtana* (chanting) parties at once during the Rathayātrā in Jagannātha Purī.

There are at least three instances in which Lord Caitanya made food disappear by eating from a distant place. While living in Jagannātha Purī, in the state of Orissa, He would sometimes mystically visit the home of His mother, Śacīmātā, in Bengal and eat the food she cooked for Him. He also mystically traveled from Jagannātha Purī to eat the offerings of Nṛsiṁhānanda Brahmacārī, also living in Bengal. During the chipped-rice festival He invisibly visited Lord Nityānanda, who fed Him morsels of chipped rice. Most of the assembled devotees could not understand what Lord Nityānanda was doing, but some were able to see that Lord Caitanya was present.

The wonderful actions of Lord Caitanya clearly play an important role in the *Caitanya-caritāmṛta,* written by Kṛṣṇadāsa Kavirāja Gosvāmī shortly after Lord Caitanya's departure. After describing how Lord Caitanya ate the offerings of Nṛsiṁhānanda Brahmacārī, Kṛṣṇadāsa Kavirāja cites other examples of Lord Caitanya's mystically appearing in the presence of His devotees. Kṛṣṇadāsa concludes by saying, "Thus I have described the appearance of Śrī Caitanya Mahāprabhu. Anyone who hears about these pastimes can understand the transcendental opulence of the Lord."[8]

Miracles as Evidence

This sounds very much as though Lord Caitanya's miraculous activities are being presented as evidence proving His transcendental nature. In a sense this is true, but there are important distinctions to make between the miracles of Lord Caitanya and miracles described in popular accounts.

First of all, the miracles described in the *Caitanya-caritāmṛta* have been accepted by higher authorities—in this case Kṛṣṇadāsa Kavirāja and his gurus Raghunātha Dāsa Gosvāmī and Svarūpa Dāmodara. One of the drawbacks of miracle accounts is that they are typically transmitted by ordinary people, forced to evaluate them on the basis of imperfect information. This results in the acceptance of false accounts as genuine, and it may also result in the rejection of genuine miracles. But this problem is avoided if the miracle accounts are presented by higher authorities who are competent to evaluate them and who have reliable sources of information. In this case, Raghunātha Dāsa Gosvāmī and Svarūpa Dāmodara were highly qualified observers who directly witnessed many of Lord Caitanya's pastimes and were well acquainted with other witnesses.

For people in general, accepting miracle accounts from higher authorities reduces the problem of how to evaluate miracles to the deeper problem of how to decide who is a bona fide guru. Since the bona fide guru appears in disciplic succession, people are aided in solving this problem by established spiritual institutions and canonical texts. Although ascertaining who is a genuine spiritual authority may be difficult, it is easier than trying to sort out miracle stories one by one.

Another point is that Kṛṣṇadāsa Kavirāja was not trying to demonstrate that because Lord Caitanya exhibited mystic powers He is transcendental. Mystic powers are common attributes of practically all beings above the level of modern humans (and of some who are subhuman), and such powers play a natural role in spiritual pastimes. Gurus such as Śrīla Prabhupāda who discourage interest in miracles are simply trying to protect people from the depredations of mystical cheaters.

Lord Caitanya's activities are significant not because they involve mystic *siddhis* per se, but because they exhibit the transcendental loving reciprocation between the Lord and His devotees. Perhaps an intuitive longing for this reciprocation plays a part in attracting people so strongly to accounts of miracles.

REFERENCES

1. Augustine, *Against Faustus the Manichee,* Book 29, Chapter 2.
2. Hridayananda dāsa Goswami, 1982, *Śrīmad-Bhāgavatam,* Canto 11, Chapter 15, Los Angeles: Bhaktivedanta Book Trust.
3. Bhaktivedanta Swami Prabhupāda, A. C., 1985, *The Nectar of Devotion,* Los Angeles: Bhaktivedanta Book Trust, pp. 11–12.
4. Stevenson, Ian, 1972, "Are Poltergeists Living or Are They Dead?" *The Journal of the American Society for Psychical Research,* Vol. 66, No. 3, July.
5. Stevenson, p. 243.

6. Subatomic particles can do this by a process known as quantum-mechanical tunneling. A macroscopic object is one that is much larger than an atom, and for such objects, quantum-mechanical tunneling is ruled out.
7. Hume, David, 1902, "An Enquiry Concerning Human Understanding," in *Enquiries Concerning the Human Understanding and Concerning the Principles of Morals,* Second Edition, ed. L.A. Sleby-bigge, Oxford, pp. 115–116.
8. Bhaktivedanta Swami Prabhupāda, 1975, A. C., *Śrī Caitanya-caritāmṛta, Antya-līlā,* Vol. 1, Los Angeles: Bhaktivedanta BookTrust, text 2.83.

6

Challenges Facing Science and Religion

In the Vaiṣṇava tradition of India, God is defined as Brahman, Paramātmā, and Bhagavān: the unlimited light of pure being underlying nature, the Lord within the heart, and the supreme transcendental Person. In Christian tradition, a similar idea can be found in the Trinity of Father, Son, and Holy Spirit. In both traditions the emphasis is on God's personal nature. As a transcendental person, God controls nature on a grand scale, He acts within history, and He deals with people on an individual level.

This concept of God has been central to the lives of large numbers of people over many centuries, but at the present time it is not intellectually respectable. To be sure, it is often said that there is no conflict between science and religion. But this statement is true only if one makes a drastic redefinition of traditional concepts of God.

Consider the following conversation, which took place in 1959, between astronomer Harlow Shapley and biologist Julian Huxley:

Shapley: And in that famous address in 1951 the Pope went along with evolution.
Huxley: He still said there must be a God who is somehow responsible in some way, didn't he?
Shapley: Well, he didn't deny God, no. And you don't either.
Huxley: I certainly do.
Shapley: Oh, no. If you defined God, you wouldn't.
Huxley: Now don't go into semantics.
Shapley: You're not an atheist, Julian; you're an agnostic.
Huxley: I am an atheist, in the only correct sense, that I don't believe in a supernatural being who influences natural events.

The success of modern science depends on our ability to create mechanistic models of natural phenomena in which all natural causes

Above: Science and religion both claim to describe the world we live in. From the standpoint of religion, the world is an emanation of divine energy, full of life and meaning. From the scientific standpoint, the world is given by a pattern of data, prescribed by mathematical relationships. How can these two world views be reconciled?

are represented by formulas and numbers. Since God cannot be reduced to formulas, God has to be decoupled from nature. At most, God can be admitted as the ultimate cause of the laws used in scientific models. As physicist Steven Weinberg put it, "The only way that any sort of science can proceed is to assume that there is no divine intervention and see how far one can get with this assumption."

The elimination of God from nature begins with the rejection of stories that seem obviously contrary to natural laws—stories about

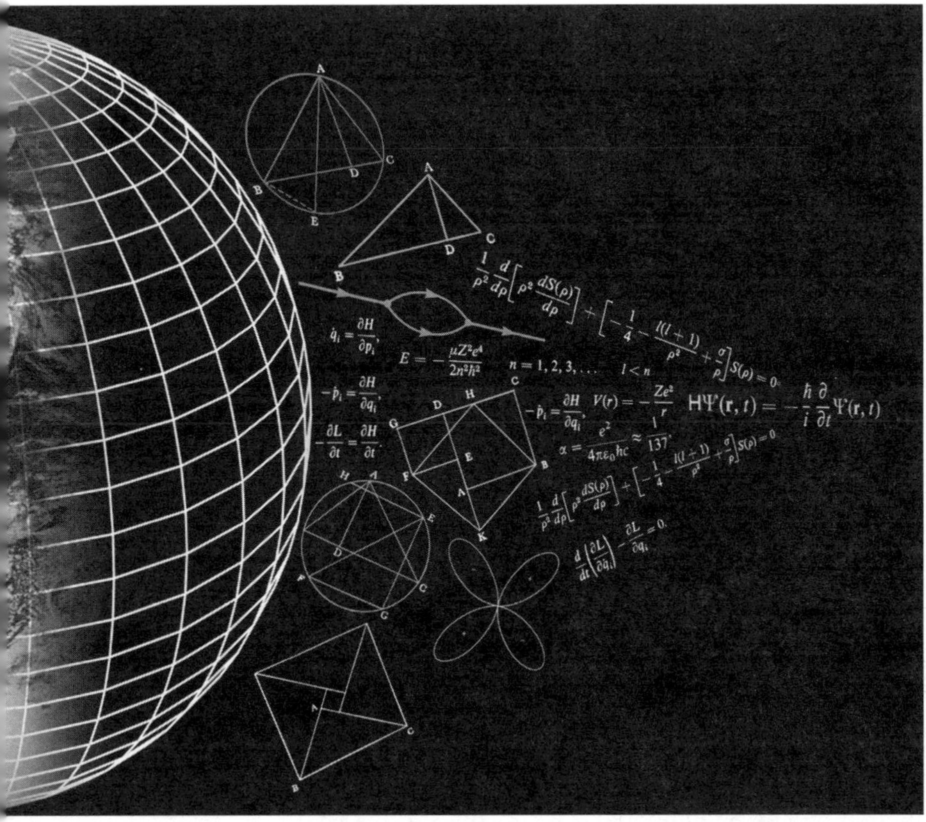

the lifting of mountains (Kṛṣṇa) or the parting of seas (Jehovah). At first, this elimination can be seen as a rational reform in which the dross of superstition is removed and the way is paved for a deeper spiritual understanding. An attractive approach is to make a distinction between the rational and the transcendental. One treats the rational domain according to the methods and findings of science, while positing a transcendental domain lying beyond reason and accessible only to higher, spiritual states of consciousness. The transcendental domain can be approached only through faith, acceptance of revealed knowledge, and submissive obedience to higher spiritual authority.

This approach to religion and science can be a useful rhetorical strategy, and it may be satisfactory for a rare person who truly lives on a high transcendental platform and directly knows what is transcendental. But for others, it suffers from the difficulty that it is hard to make a clear distinction between the rational and transcendental domains. How do we draw the line?

If we hold the line at a particular part of the intellectual landscape, we will come in conflict with science, which will insist on extending its established theoretical picture. If we let the line be completely flexible, we will find that nothing relevant to the world of our experience remains on the transcendental side. This lends weight to the perspective that the transcendental is strictly *anirvacanīyam,* having no impact whatsoever on our words or our actions. But this is a far cry from traditional conceptions of God as a supreme personality (with both describable and indescribable aspects) who takes an interest in individual lives.

On surveying the issues involving science and religion, my overwhelming impression is that there is much that we do not know. I therefore think that it is premature to try to draw a clear-cut line between science and religion. Rather, we should realize that there is a broad gray area in which much further exploration needs to be done.

In the theoretical domains claimed by science, many fundamental questions remain. In the empirical study of nature, and especially in the study of human life, much data begs for an explanation and has not been assimilated into the scientific world view. In the field of religion there are likewise many unanswered questions.

I will briefly discuss some important issues involving science and religion, and point out questions that need to be addressed.

God and the Laws of Physics

Sir Isaac Newton is a good starting point. Newton's great contribution was to introduce a system of mathematical laws that could be verified with quantitative precision. In so doing, he created a domain of natural law that inevitably came into territorial conflict with the domain of divine action.

Newton himself believed that God is active in this world, and he was criticized by the philosopher Wilhelm Leibniz for his proposal that God makes periodic adjustments in the motion of matter. But the basic thrust of Newton's system of physics was to limit God's action to the enforcement of unchanging laws imposed at the time of creation.

The mathematical form of Newton's laws made this nearly unavoidable. A set of deterministic differential equations define the motion of material particles. Even if something is thought to exist outside the collection of material particles, there appears to be no way for it to influence their motion, and Newton's famous divine adjustments therefore appear awkward and unnatural.

But the key word here is "appears." In recent years it has been discovered that in many situations, Newton's equations give rise to a phenomenon known as deterministic chaos. This means that arbitrarily small changes in the motion of Newtonian particles are quickly amplified to produce large changes. It doesn't matter how small the changes are. If you make the changes a millionth as large or a million-millionth as large, they quickly amplify to produce big effects.

It has also been discovered that deterministic chaos gives engineers a practical opportunity to systematically control chaotic systems by making tiny adjustments. The implication is that God could readily control nature by introducing adjustments far smaller than anything we could ever hope to measure. Could this be a way for God to exercise divine control over a semi-autonomous natural world?

The Special Theory of Relativity

Early in the twentieth century, Albert Einstein introduced fundamental changes into classical, Newtonian physics with his celebrated special theory of relativity. This theory yields the famous formula $E = mc^2$, which was demonstrated by the release of atomic energy. But apart from this, relativity theory has few practical consequences, since it predicts measurable effects differing from classical physics only for objects with velocities approaching the speed of light.

But Einstein's theory has profound philosophical implications. In the equations called Lorentz transformations, it allows time to be mapped into space and space to be mapped into time. This means that time and space must have the same geometric nature. Time, including past, present, and future, must exist as an extended continuum, just as space does. All events have their place in this continuum, and the passage of time is an illusion.

Einstein went so far as to use this idea to console a widow. When his friend Besso died, Einstein wrote to Besso's wife, saying, "Michael has preceded me a little in leaving this strange world. This is not important. For us who are convinced physicists, the distinction between past, present, and future is only an illusion, however persistent."

Einstein believed that the passage of time is an illusion. The life of an individual exists timelessly as a fixed, space-time worm (shown above Einstein's head) that has a fertilized egg on one end and a deceased body on the other. This raises questions about the existence of free will.

This idea has serious consequences for the nature of consciousness. It seems, at first glance, to negate the idea of free will and to imply that everything is determined. It also raises the question of how even the illusion of time's passage arises in a world in which time is a static geometric coordinate. What is it that experiences the illusion? If all events are just blips in an existing continuum, what room is there for an experiencer who moves through events in temporal order?

If these fundamental questions can be resolved, the further question arises whether or not an existing past and future can somehow be perceived by an experiencer not strictly bound to a shifting present moment. This brings to mind Christian ideas of prophecy and the Purāṇic idea of *tri-kāla-jña,* or knowledge of past, present, and future. Like Newton's theory, Einstein's theory at first seems to restrict the scope of religion. But on further thought, it shows potential for giving us deeper insights into traditional theological ideas.

Quantum Physics

Quantum physics constitutes a great departure from the deterministic theories of classical physics and relativity. As such, it has sometimes been heralded as the gateway to a new synthesis of science and religion that will reintroduce spirit and consciousness into the world of matter. But this turns out to be easier said than done.

Quantum mechanics allows events to take place in two fundamental ways. First, there is the Schrödinger equation, which determines how the state of a physical system changes continuously with the passage of time. The Schrödinger equation is a partial differential equation fully as deterministic as any of its cousins in classical physics. There is no scope here for spirit to influence matter, except possibly through the technique mentioned above of controlling deterministic chaos. (This is a touchy issue: It turns out that the Schrödinger equation may be less prone to creating chaos than Newton's equations.)

The second process of change is the famous quantum jump, sometimes called "collapse of the wave function." This happens purely by causeless chance. The system suddenly changes freely to a new state, and the only restriction on the change is that it must satisfy statistics encoded into the old state of the system. Since chance events are not determined, they might seem to provide a loophole for the control of matter by spirit. Unfortunately, this idea runs into a conflict with statistical laws.

For example, consider a series of clicks in a Geiger-counter tube triggered by the decay of radioactive atoms. According to quantum mechanics, these clicks occur at random. So could they express an intelligent message projected into matter by spirit? If the message contained more than one or two words, it would strongly violate the laws of probability theory. If we try to reconcile spiritual and physical causation in this way, we are forced to modify the accepted meaning of chance in quantum mechanics, and this entails a fundamental modification of quantum mechanics itself.

Henry Stapp is one physicist who has suggested that quantum mechanical randomness might be different from what we normally think of as chance. To Stapp, the idea that quantum choices come randomly out of nowhere should be seen as an "admission of contemporary ignorance, not as a satisfactory final word." Stapp seeks a possibility that agrees with all scientific data but lies somewhere between "pure chance" and "pure determinism." He concludes: "I think such a possibility is open, but to give this logical possibility a nonspeculative foundation will require enlarging the boundaries of scientific knowledge."

Although Stapp is primarily concerned with individual consciousness, scientists such as William Pollard and Donald Mackay have seen chance as a loophole for introducing divine control into the world of physics. Pollard's idea was summed up neatly by the physicist-priest John Polkinghorne: "Will not God's power to act as the cause of uncaused quantum events (always cleverly respecting the statistical regularities which are reflections of his faithfulness) give him a chance to play a manipulative role in a scientifically regular world?" Polkinghorne dismissed this idea as contrived, saying that "Houdini-like wrigglings" are required to insert control signals from mind or God into the straitjacket of physical processes.

The lesson of quantum mechanics seems to be that we must either discard the idea that spirit influences matter or be prepared to develop a new physics that includes some kind of spirit-matter interface. The latter program is far from easy to carry out, but we may find many rewarding insights if we make the attempt.

The Brain and Consciousness

In the scientific world, the theories of physics provide the basis for the life sciences and for our understanding of mind and consciousness. Thus Nobel laureate Francis Crick has recently announced what he calls the Astonishing Hypothesis. He claims, "You, your joys and your sorrows, your memories and your ambitions, your sense of personal identity and free will, are in fact no more than the behavior of a vast assembly of nerve cells and their associated molecules."

In one sense, this should be called the Standard Hypothesis. With a few exceptions, such as Sir John Eccles, neuroscientists take it for granted that mind and consciousness can be fully understood in terms of physical brain processes.

Yet contemporary brain research does have an astonishing feature. Thus far, no one has been able to even suggest an intelligible connection between physiochemical processes and the qualities of perception (called "qualia") that make up conscious experience. Thus Crick admits, "I have said almost nothing about qualia—the redness of red—except to brush it to one side and hope for the best."

In his book *Consciousness Explained,* the philosopher Daniel Dennett deals with qualia by denying their existence. He gives many examples suggesting that consciousness is an illusion, and that what really happens in the brain is quite different from what we imagine as our conscious experience. But we may ask: How can illusion (false awareness) arise without the prior existence of awareness? Could it be that there is an *ātmā,* or soul, linked with the bodily machine, and could it be that qualia are functions of this nonphysical entity?

Life after Death

In the *Bhagavad-gītā,* Kṛṣṇa refers to the body as a machine occupied by the soul and guided by the Lord in the heart. In contrast, both modern science and some schools of Christian thought have embraced the idea of the living being as a pure machine. Physicists such as John Polkinghorne propose that the self survives death through a process of physical reconstruction. Thus Polkinghorne says of the atoms that make up our bodies: "It is the pattern that they form which constitutes the physical expression of our continuing personality. There seems to be no difficulty in conceiving of that pattern, dissolved at death, being recreated in another environment in an act of resurrection."

By implicitly accepting Crick's astonishing hypothesis, Polkinghorne is able to suggest a scientific model of the Christian doctrine of resurrection. But if conscious self identity is distinct from the brain, as I proposed above, then survival after death must involve more than just the pattern of atoms in the body. The *Bhagavad-gītā,* of course, presents the idea of transmigration, in which the personality is carried by the soul and subtle mind from one body to another.

It is remarkable that there is a great deal of empirical evidence suggesting that transmigration may actually take place. The psychiatrist Ian Stevenson has studied thousands of cases in which a young child seems to spontaneously remember a previous life, without having had the opportunity to learn about that life by ordinary means of communication. Stevenson has shown that skills, interests, phobias, and other personality traits tend to show continuity from one life to another. He has also studied cases in which children have birthmarks corresponding to wounds causing death in their previous life.

Stevenson's work has been replicated by other researchers. It does appear to place transmigration in the arena of phenomena that might prove scientifically verifiable. Of course, this gives rise to the question of how transmigration works and what it has to do with the known laws of physics. The question also arises of whether "past life memories" of the kind studied by Stevenson may be an underlying cause for the acceptance of transmigration in various religious traditions.

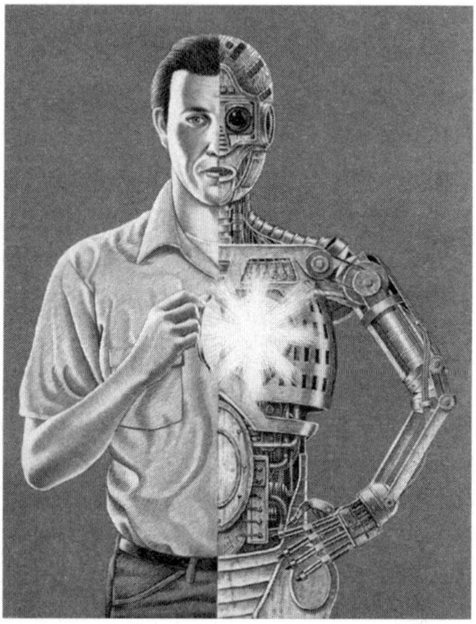

Is a human being a pure machine, working according to the laws of physics, or a spiritual entity interacting with a physical body?

Near Death Experiences

NDEs provide another example of empirical evidence pertaining to the possible survival of the conscious self after death. NDEs are generally reported in connection with life-threatening physical traumas such as heart attacks, but they also resemble the spontaneous so-called mystical visions of people in a normal state of health. In addition, shamans, yogis, and mystics in many traditions have sought to deliberately separate the perceiving self from the body and travel in an out-of-body state.

Typical NDEs involve an autoscopic and a transcendental phase. In the autoscopic phase, the subject sees his or her body from outside the body. In this phase, the person may remember seeing things that should have been invisible to the body's physical eyes, and this may be interpreted as evidence of a non-ordinary state of consciousness.

In the transcendental phase, the subject often reports entering into another world, typically characterized by brilliant light, beautiful scenery, and a sense of universal knowledge. The subject may encounter other persons, ranging from effulgent religious figures to departed relatives.

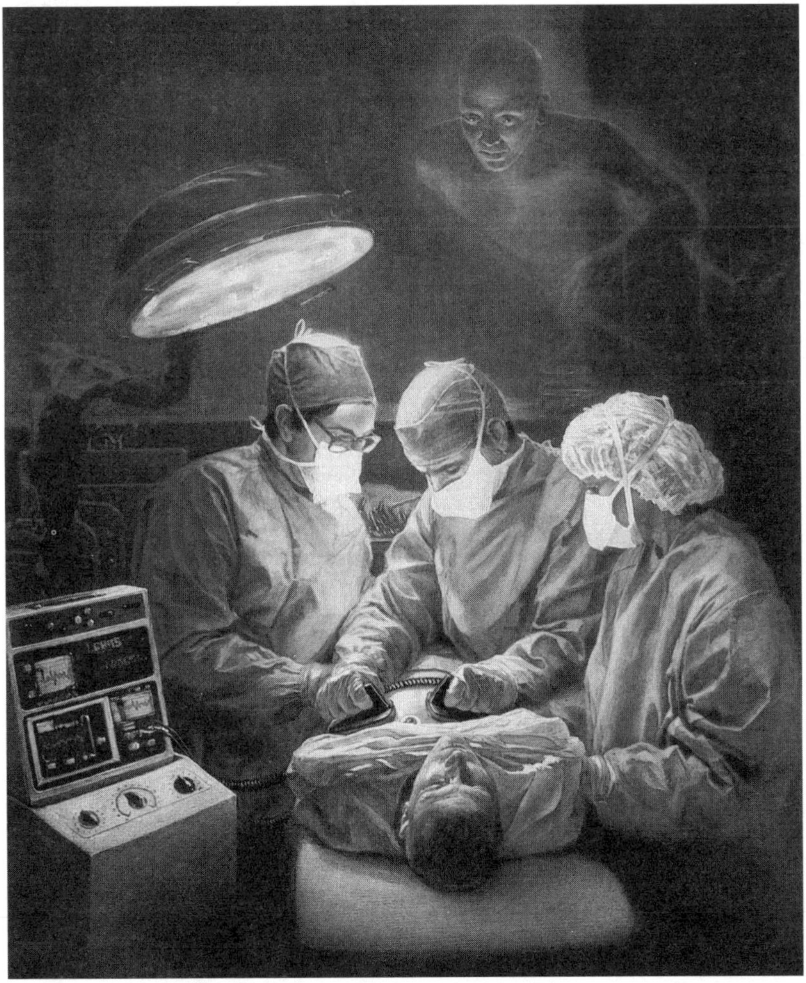

Persons medically near death have sometimes reported seeing their bodies from a vantage point outside the body. In some cases, they have accurately described events that occurred when their brains and physical sense organs should not have been in working order.

People reporting NDEs often seem transformed in a positive spiritual way by the experience. Clearly such experiences are highly relevant to our understanding of religion. On the one hand, NDEs may seem to verify religious traditions. On the other, it can be argued that religious traditions have been strongly influenced by this kind of experience, whatever its underlying cause may be.

In the nineteenth century, the psychologist William James made a study of religious experience that led him to the conviction that our immediate world of sensations and physical laws is part of a larger reality. He proposed that "the world of our present consciousness is only one out of many worlds of consciousness that exist, and that these other worlds must contain experiences which have a meaning for our life also; and that although in the main their experiences and those of this world keep discrete, yet the two become continuous at certain points, and higher energies filter in."

The NDE evidence shows that we have much to learn about such possible contacts with other worlds. For example, Satwant Pasricha and Ian Stevenson have published a report of sixteen near-death accounts from India. In these cases, the subject typically reports being taken away from his sickbed by horrible-looking persons who convey him into the presence of a judge. The judge then reprimands the subject's captors, saying, "Why did you bring the wrong man? Take him back!" The person is then returned to his home, where he wakes up bearing physical marks corresponding to his otherworldly experience.

These Indian cases seem to follow a different pattern from NDEs reported in the West, and one might be tempted to conclude that all such experiences are culturally conditioned fantasies. Pasricha and Stevenson note that their Indian subjects naturally identify their captors with the Yamadūtas of classical Hinduism. But they also point out that the experiences may be real, and that people in different societies may be subject to different kinds of experience on the boundary between life and death.

Extraordinary Events

Religious traditions in both India and the West are filled with stories of extraordinary encounters between humans and various kinds of beings, ranging from angels, demigods, and avatars to demons and evil spirits. Today, of course, it is customary to consign these stories to the mythological side of religion, since we know that such beings do not exist. We tend to assume, on the most charitable level, that such stories may have been created for the sake of conveying moral and spiritual lessons to a community of naive believers with an appetite for tall tales.

But the concept of God as a historical actor in Judeo-Christian tradition (Jehovah) and in Vaiṣṇava tradition (Kṛṣṇa) depends on the truth of extraordinary stories. If we relegate all of these stories to fantasy and myth, then the role of God in these traditions is drastically changed.

But how do we know that extraordinary events and beings are unreal? Most of us go through life without experiencing such things, and it is natural to extrapolate from our own experience when evaluating events lying outside that experience. Then again, the known laws of physics seem to rule out many reported extraordinary events.

If we look at the available empirical evidence, however, we find many extraordinary events being reported today by ordinary people. Consider, for example, the notorious UFO abductions, in which people claim to be carried off by odd-looking humanoid beings who subject them to apparent medical procedures. Since thousands of people report these experiences, they constitute an important social phenomenon that demands an explanation.

The first explanation that comes to mind is that these people are crazy. But several psychological studies have indicated that mental imbalance does not explain the abduction phenomenon. For example, psychologist Nicholas Spanos and his colleagues at Carleton University in Canada published a study in *The Journal of Abnormal Psychology* showing that UFO experiencers' scores on tests of psychological health were as high as or higher than those of members of control groups.

John Mack, M.D., a professor of psychiatry at the Harvard Medical School, has published a study of alien abduction encounters in which he argues that these experiences are in some sense real. He remarks: "To acknowledge that the universe (or universes) contains beings that enter our world and effect us as powerfully as the alien entities seem able to do would require an expansion of our notions of reality that all too radically undermines Western scientific and philosophical ideology." Mack heads an academic research group called Program for Extraordinary Experience Research that has pursued discussions of alien abductions in peer-reviewed psychological journals such as *Psychological Inquiry.*

The alien abduction phenomenon is clearly difficult to explain, whatever its true nature may be. It is also relevant to the understanding of religion. If we carefully compare contemporary UFO experiences with the mystical experiences reported in various religious

In religious traditions, we find many stories of extraordinary events—accounts of interactions between this world and a higher spiritual dimension, and these stories remain enigmatic from a scientific perspective. In the story above, Duhkhi Kṛṣṇadāsa found a mysterious golden anklet while sweeping a sacred area in Vṛndāvana. An old woman came to claim the anklet, and finally revealed herself as an inhabitant of the spiritual world. On the opposite page is illustrated the story of Kṛṣṇa lifting Govardhana Hill. Are the extraordinary elements in these stories always fictitious? The modern view of reality banishes such stories from physical reality. However, before we drastically revise the religious traditions, we should consider that future developments in science may render many extraordinary events acceptable.

traditions, we find a continuum characterized by both common traits and significant differences.

The similarities include the reported tendency of alien beings to communicate telepathically, to move by levitation, to pass through solid matter, and to appear and disappear mysteriously, often accompanied by inexplicable aureoles of light. These and other reported powers correspond to the mystic *siddhis* of the *Purāṇas* and to the charisms of Roman Catholic tradition. It seems that extraordinary encounters tend to follow lawful patterns that show up repeatedly all over the world, even though they violate the norms of ordinary experience. This suggests that common causal factors lie behind these experiences.

The differences mainly concern the identity of the reported beings. UFO aliens per se play no part in major religious traditions, though they may show some links with classical Christian demonology. The angels, *devas,* and saintly beings of one tradition are different from those of another, although sometimes there is apparent overlap.

This gives rise to many questions. Are extraordinary experiences simply generated within the mind according to cultural conditioning? Or are systems of belief within different cultures conditioned by an agency or agencies responsible for extraordinary experiences?

One possible answer is that there is a divine control system within the universe that maintains administrative divisions for different religions, while tolerating partly independent groups that pursue their own agendas. The angels and demons of traditional Christianity immediately come to mind.

The *Bhāgavata Purāṇa* (*Śrīmad-Bhāgavatam* 11.14.5–7) explicitly refers to a system that provides for many religions. It states: "All of the many universal species, along with their respective leaders, appeared with different natures and desires generated from the three modes of material nature. Therefore, because of the different characteristics of the living entities within the universe, there are a great many Vedic rituals, mantras, and rewards." This statement gives a very general meaning to the word "Vedic," which here seems to encompass all religions in the universe.

If the idea of a universal system of beings seems too extravagant, we can consider the possibility of explaining different extraordinary experiences as internally generated hallucinations. But what is a hallucination?

The psychologist Raymond Moody, M.D., published a study in which psychologically normal people sought visions of departed relatives by gazing into a mirror under carefully controlled circumstances. The project was inspired by extensive traditions about visions induced by gazing into crystals, mirrors, water, and other reflective surfaces. Moody reported that in some cases people had extremely vivid visions in which a person—generally a deceased relative—seemed to step out of the mirror in solid, 3D form and engage in an extended conversation. Hallucinations? Perhaps, but we have much to learn about what hallucinations really are and what causes them.

The Vaiṣṇavas' story of Duhkhī Kṛṣṇadāsa illustrates how visions can contribute to a religious tradition. Very briefly, the story recounts how Duhkhī Kṛṣṇadāsa found a golden anklet while sweeping a sacred area in Vṛndāvana, Kṛṣṇa's traditional birthplace in India. He hid the anklet, but was later met by an old woman who asked for it, claiming that it had been lost by her daughter. After some conversation, the old woman revealed her beautiful form as Lalitā, one of the *gopīs* serving Kṛṣṇa's eternal consort, Rādhārāṇī. After Duhkhī Kṛṣṇadāsa gave her the anklet, which turned out to be Rādhārāṇī's, Lalitā mysteriously disappeared. Later, Duhkhī Kṛṣṇadāsa's guru received this story with skepticism, and in the course of trying to convince him, Duhkhī Kṛṣṇadāsa again met Lalitā. This time, however, he met her by entering into her world through meditation.

Stories of this kind play an important role in many religious traditions. From a scientific perspective, we have a long way to go before we can begin to understand them.

The Fossil Record

We now turn from the discussion of present-day phenomena to the historical sciences, such as geology and evolutionary biology. It is here that some of the greatest conflicts have taken place between science and religion.

In the early nineteenth century, the developing science of geology began to reveal a very strange picture of the history of life on the earth. In its current form, the story begins with the formation of the earth about 4.5 billion years ago. After less than a billion years, life appeared in the form of bacteria and algae. This state of affairs persisted until about 500 to 600 million years ago, with the appearance of peculiar marine life forms, such as the Ediacara fauna and the creatures of the Burgess Shale. A wide variety of more familiar marine creatures appeared in the subsequent Cambrian period, and life began to seriously invade the land in the Devonian, about 400 million years ago. There followed the age of Carboniferous coal swamps, the age of early reptiles, and then some 150 million years of dinosaurs. After the dinosaurs mysteriously died out, the age of mammals prevailed for some 65 million years up to the present. Humans of modern form appeared at the very end of this period, no more than about 100,000 years ago.

This story does not explicitly appear in the sacred books of any religion, as far as I am aware. Some Christian creationists deny it altogether and advocate a young earth, based on Mosaic chronology, which dates the creation of the earth to about 6,000 to 10,000 years ago. Other creationists prefer to reconcile the Bible with geology by interpreting the days of creation in Genesis as long ages. And some propose the existence of races of humans or semi-humans that preceded the recent appearance of Adam and Eve.

In Hinduism, the immensity of geological time does not pose a problem. Hindu chronology, as defined in the *Purāṇas,* is based on several major time intervals similar to those of the geologists. These are the *divya yuga* of 4,320,000 years, the *manvantara* of about 307 million years, and the *kalpa* of 4,320,000,000 years. Astronomer Carl Sagan remarked, "The Hindu religion is the only one of the world's great faiths . . . in which the time scales correspond, no doubt by accident, to those of modern scientific cosmology."

But whether this similarity is accidental or not, the Hindu account of what happened in the past is quite different from the geological story. It refers almost exclusively to the activities of superhuman beings who themselves live for millions or hundreds of millions of years. The Purāṇic stories hardly seem to refer to the earth as we know it at all, and it may well be that they were intended to refer to a higher, celestial realm.

Darwin's Theory

Scientists interpret the fossil record as the history of the gradual development of life according to the neo-Darwinian theory of evolution. I will refer to this briefly as Darwin's theory, but it was actually developed after the second World War as a synthesis of Mendelian genetics and Darwin's original ideas.

Darwin's theory is based entirely on the laws of physics and blind chance. In the words of Darwinian theorist Richard Dawkins, it attributes the origin of living species to a "blind watchmaker," completely devoid of intelligence, foresight, or purpose. For this reason, it has been strongly rejected by many conservative Christians, who take it that life was created by Divine Providence.

But other Christian groups, such as the Roman Catholics and the liberal Protestants, profess to find no difficulty in seeing Darwinian evolution as God's method of creation. Some say that God is a strict Darwinian who simply stood by transcendentally and let evolution produce worshipers in the fullness of time. Others compromise by proposing guided evolution, in which God gently nudges the Darwinian process in the desired direction. This, of course, is not accepted by mainstream science.

In principle, there is no reason why Darwinian evolution could not be God's method of creating species. In practice, however, the theory of evolution itself throws up obstacles against this. Among all

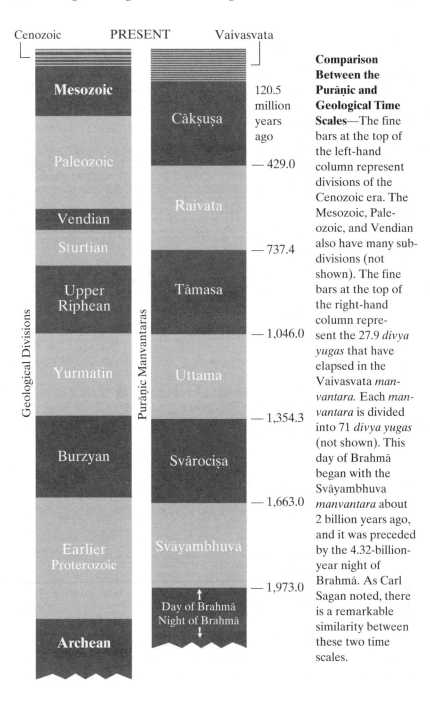

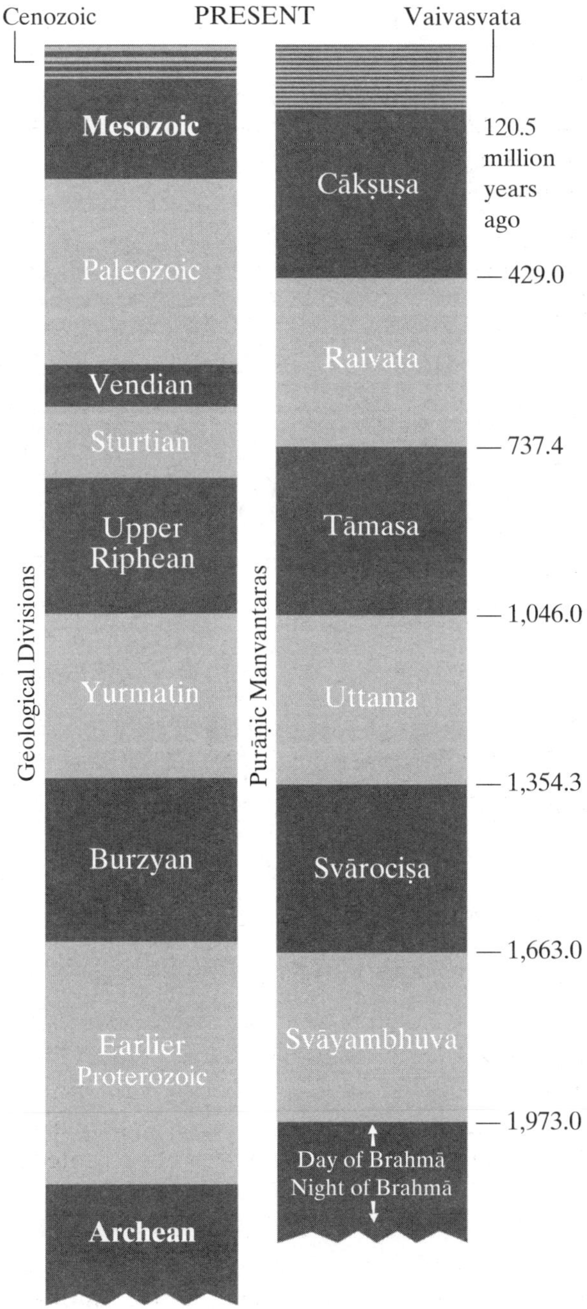

Comparison Between the Purāṇic and Geological Time Scales—The fine bars at the top of the left-hand column represent divisions of the Cenozoic era. The Mesozoic, Paleozoic, and Vendian also have many subdivisions (not shown). The fine bars at the top of the right-hand column represent the 27.9 *divya yugas* that have elapsed in the Vaivasvata *manvantara.* Each *manvantara* is divided into 71 *divya yugas* (not shown). This day of Brahmā began with the Svāyambhuva *manvantara* about 2 billion years ago, and it was preceded by the 4.32-billion-year night of Brahmā. As Carl Sagan noted, there is a remarkable similarity between these two time scales.

"We never may be able to trace the steps by which the organization of the eye passed from simpler stages to more perfect, preserving its relations—the wonderful power of adaptation given to organization. This is really perhaps the greatest difficulty to the whole theory." (Darwin's *Notes on Transmutation*)

of today's scientific theories, the neo-Darwinian theory of evolution is perhaps the easiest to criticize from a theoretical scientific point of view.

From its very inception, Darwin's theory has not been able to explain in detail how complex organs such as brains or eyes come into being. The general idea is that organs develop by a series of tiny steps. For example, the eye is said to begin as a light-sensitive spot. The spot turns into a pit and thus develops directional sensitivity through shadowing. The pit closes over to form a pinhole camera, and then translucent skin forms a crude lens that collects and focuses light. Gradually, features and improvements are added, until we have the eye of an eagle.

The problem is that this is simply a "just so" story that we are asked to accept on faith. It cannot be verified as we verify Newton's theory by calculating a planetary orbit and then observing that the planet actually follows the orbit. The eye is simply too complex, and the more we study it, the more complex we find it to be.

With the recent development of biochemistry, the task of explaining the origin of complex organs and functions has become even more daunting. In Darwin's day, the living cell seemed to be a simple bag of chemicals. Now it is seen to be a high-precision molecular machine far more complex than our most advanced computers.

The biochemist Michael Behe (who is not a creationist) has published a book arguing that the findings of biochemistry are extremely difficult to explain by Darwin's theory. He points out that even

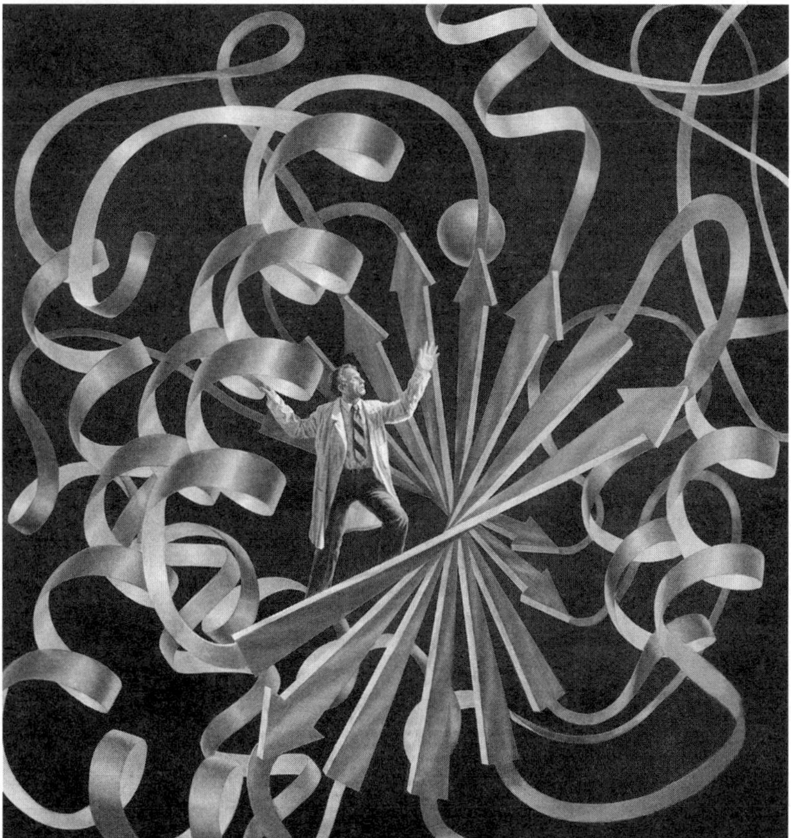

Here the structure of a protein molecule in a living cell is represented by an arrangement of coils and curved arrows. The intricacy of these molecules and the precision of their interactions have caused some biochemists to doubt that Darwinian processes could fully account for their origin.

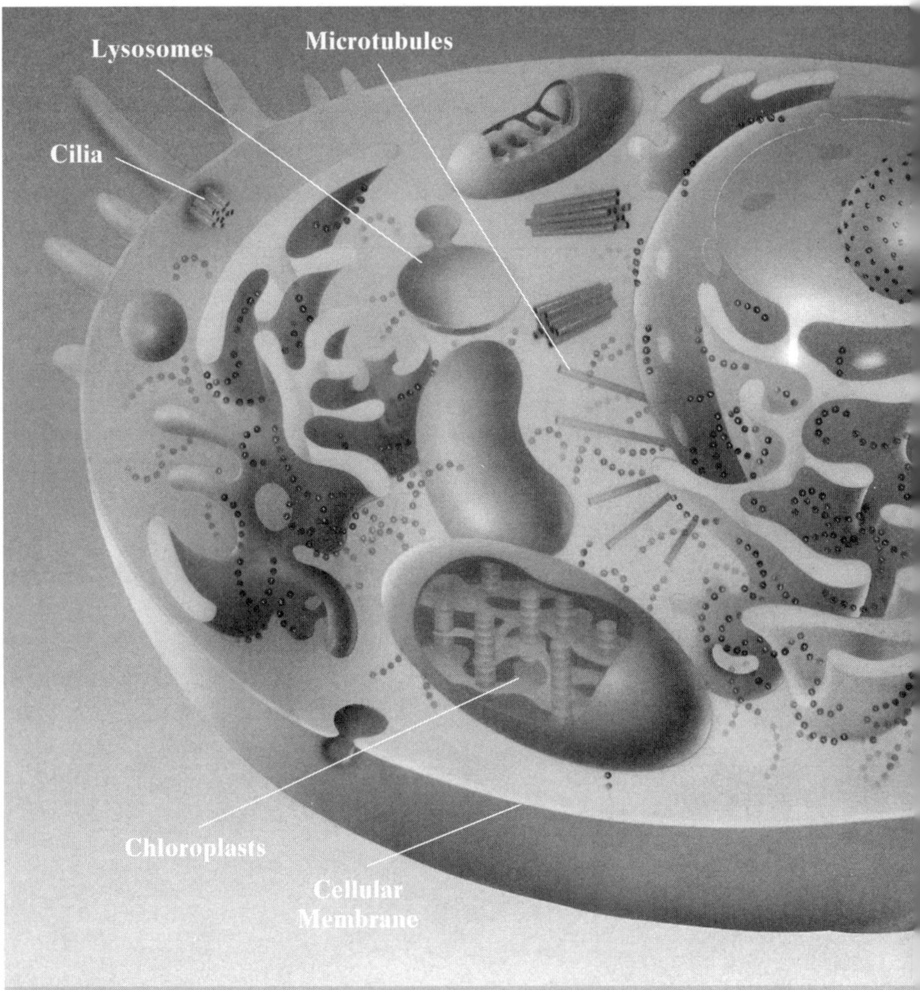

In Darwin's time living cells were regarded as simple bags of chemicals that could have arisen spontaneously from organic compounds. However, it is now clear that cells contain intricate biochemical machinery. The steps by which this machinery may have originated are unknown and difficult to imagine. Thus it is no longer justifiable to simply take it for granted that living cells have evolved from chemicals by physical processes. Some important structures of typical plant

Illustration by Śrīnivāsa Dāsa

and animal cells are depicted at left. The **ribosomes** manufacture protein molecules by following blueprints encoded in messenger RNA. Although they appear here as mere dots, the ribosomes have a complex structure. The **endoplasmic reticulum** consists of a complex of membranes that form internal compartments used in the synthesis and transport of various compounds produced by the cell. The **nucleus** contains the hereditary material, DNA, which carries instructions for the operation and perpetuation of the cellular machinery. Complex molecular processes are involved in replicating the DNA. The **nucleolus** is a factory for the partial manufacture of ribosomes. The **microtubules** form a complex latticework that gives form to the cell and enables it to systematically move and change shape. Some cells possess **cilia**, whiplike structures that execute a swimming stroke through the action of an internal arrangement of sliding rods. **Lysosomes** contain enzymes that break down unwanted material within the cell. The **chloroplasts** found in plant cells are complex chemical factories that carry out photosynthesis—the storage of solar energy in the form of sugar molecules. The **cellular membrane** is equipped with many complex protein molecules that regulate the passage of molecules into and out of the cell and act as sensors informing the cell of external conditions. The **mitochondria** are chemical factories that generate energy for the cell through the controlled breakdown of food molecules.

though scientists have taken an interest in the origin of bio-molecular systems, nothing has been published in the scientific literature that really comes to grips with how evolution is supposed to work on the molecular level. This absence of published work indicates an absence of scientific ideas about molecular evolution.

Of course, one can argue that vague evolutionary stories should be accepted if they cannot be decisively disproven. Darwinian evolution can be shown to work in many simple cases. It is consistent with the solidly established theories of physics, and it saves these theories from the onslaught of supernatural doctrines of creation.

The crux of the matter is this: Does everything in nature work strictly according to impersonal mathematical laws, or is there a spirit-matter interface? If there is, then the drawbacks of Darwinian theory may eventually be overcome by reintroducing purpose and intelligent design into nature.

Conclusion

Although traditions of personal theism are ruled out by the spirit of modern science, they are not refuted decisively by the still-evolving theories of physics. Indeed, even some of the extraordinary phenomena connected with theistic teachings may eventually find confirmation as physical and biological sciences come to grips with perplexing forms of human experience. This may provide the key to understanding how matter interacts with consciousness.

These developments may take a great deal of time. At present, our ignorance is overwhelming, but this is a hopeful sign, since the expansion of knowledge also expands the boundary between the known and the unknown. The main danger we should avoid is to block the advancement of knowledge by prematurely imposing final conclusions, either from the side of scientific rationalism or from the side of religious dogmatism.

PHYSICS

7

High Technology and The Ground of Being

In the United States and the former Soviet Union, scientists competed to perfect optical phase conjugation—a process that can reverse the motion of a beam of light, causing an image scrambled by an irregular medium (such as frosted glass) to return to its original, undistorted form. They hoped to use reversed light beams to focus laser weapons on enemy missiles.

At Syracuse University an eminent physicist appeared before a large audience. A professor of religion introduced him as the man who may save the world from the fragmentation of modern Western thinking and bring people to a platform of transcendental wholeness. The physicist then began expounding metaphysical ideas based on physics and Eastern philosophy.

Although it may seem surprising, the military research work and the university lecture share a common foundation in a fundamental feature of the laws of physics. To understand how this is so, let us first consider optical phase conjugation.

The application of the technology of optical phase conjugation to "star wars" weapons systems is still in the conceptual stage, but the unscrambling of light that has passed through frosted glass has actually been demonstrated.

In a typical experiment, light is reflected from an object and passes through frosted glass, causing the light beam to distort in a complicated way. The beam then reflects from a device called a phase conjugate mirror, which reverses the distorted beam and passes it back through the frosted glass. When the light enters an observer's eye, he perceives a clear, undistorted image of the original object instead of a garbled blur, which he would see if the image were reflected back through the glass by an ordinary mirror.

As the reflected beam leaves the phase conjugate mirror, it has the curious properties that (1) it encodes information for the original image in a distorted, unrecognizable form, and (2) as time passes, the apparently random distortion is reduced, and the information contained by the beam becomes clearly manifest. Normally we would expect to see just the opposite—a pattern containing meaningful information will gradually degrade until the information is irretrievably lost.

According to classical physical theory, however, the laws of physical dynamics are reversible, and thus it is possible in theory for any physical process to run backward and recreate an earlier state of affairs from its later end product. This implies that information is never actually lost as a result of physical transformations, and in principle it might be possible to again extract the information from the cosmic energy background. The restoration of a garbled image by a phase conjugate mirror seems to provide an example of this.

While the phase conjugate mirror example shows an apparently random pattern being produced by letting an orderly pattern degrade by natural processes, random patterns can also be produced in other ways. In some techniques of optical phase conjugation, one adds to the reflecting beam a predistorted image—of a face, for example—that was not present when the beam first passed through the clouded glass. As the beam retraces its path, the face undistorts and becomes clearly visible (see Figure 1).

This example of research in optical phase conjugation has bearing on metaphysical questions. Could it be that the universal background of random electromagnetic noise incorporates patterns that are imposed on the physical medium by a transcendental source of order, and which are programed to naturally generate orderly forms and sequences of events?

The Implicate Order

As it turns out, the fact that dispersed information can give rise to localized organization has been used as the cornerstone for a comprehensive metaphysical world view. This is the theory of the implicate order, devised by David Bohm—the physicist who spoke at Syracuse University.

Bohm generally illustrates his ideas with an apparatus consisting of two concentric cylinders with the space in between filled with a vis-

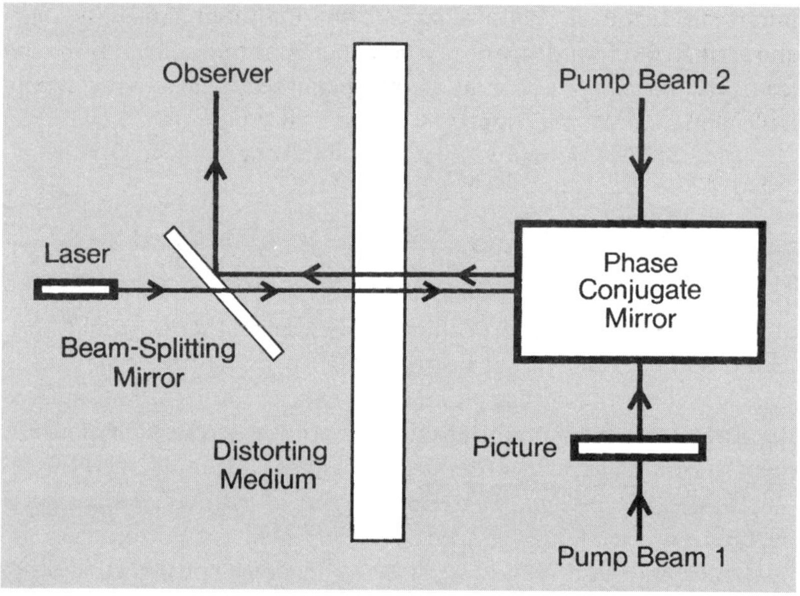

Figure 1—A diagram of apparatus for sending an image through a distorting medium such as a pane of frosted glass or a cloud. Light from the laser (at left) first passes through the distorting medium and stores in the phase conjugate mirror (right) information encoding that medium's particular pattern of distortion. The first pump beam of the phase conjugate mirror passes through a transparency of the image to be transmitted and is combined with the distortion information encoded in the phase conjugate mirror. The result is a predistorted beam that moves to the left through the distorting medium, emerges on the other side, and carries to the observer (top left) a sharp image of the picture being transmitted.

cous fluid such as glycerine. If a drop of ink is placed on the surface of the fluid and the outer cylinder is slowly rotated, the drop will be drawn out into a long, thin strand that ultimately will become invisible. If the outer cylinder is then slowly rotated in the opposite direction, the stretching out of the drop will be reversed, and at a certain time the drop will again become briefly visible. Then it will again stretch out and disappear as the rotation of the cylinder continues.

We can see that this is another example of how information for an organized structure—in this case the drop of ink—can be dispersed throughout a physical medium in an unrecognizable form and then recovered through a physical transformation that restores the original structure. Bohm would say that the dispersed ink drop has become enfolded in the fluid, and that when it reappears, it has become unfolded.

From this example we can understand Bohm's world view by two steps. In the first step, we imagine that all phenomena in the universe are enfolded in an ultimate physical substrate—the ground of all being—which Bohm calls the "implicate order." As processes of physical transformation occur in this substrate, successive enfolded patterns unfold and emerge in explicit form, manifesting the "explicate order" of our ordinary experience.

The second step in understanding Bohm's world view is to understand his conception of the implicate order as a unified whole consisting of apparently distinguishable parts. According to Bohm, although the parts seem distinct, each part is identical with the whole since it includes, or "enfolds," the whole. To Bohm the most important characteristic of ultimate reality is undifferentiated wholeness. Although he accepts the existence of distinct parts as an aspect of the explicate order, he regards it as incorrect to suppose that, on a fundamental level, reality is actually made up of distinct parts.

The intuitive basis behind this idea of wholeness is that when information is enfolded into a physical system, it tends to become distributed uniformly throughout the system.

For example, when a drop of ink is enfolded into the glycerine, the pattern of ink from which the drop can later be recovered stretches out over a broad area. If we could somehow remove the ink from all parts of this pattern except for a small region, then we would find that a dim image of the original drop could be restored, or unfolded, from the ink in this region alone. Thus, in one sense, the enfolded drop has been distributed over many different parts of the glycerine at once.

This leads to the idea of a continuum in which all patterns ever manifest in any part are represented equally in all parts. Speaking loosely one can say that the whole of the continuum in both space and time is present in any small part of the continuum. By invoking quantum mechanical undefinability, which holds that a particle such as an electron must be defined simultaneously as a particle and a wave, one can then leap from this idea to the idea of a unified entity encompassing all space and time, in which each part not merely represents the whole but contains the whole and is thus identical to it.

This is Bohm's implicate order. Although it is partly based on physics, it also clearly involves ideas that are quite alien to traditional physical science. In fact, Bohm's implicate order represents an attempt to build a bridge between physics and a metaphysical system some call the "perennial philosophy."

The essence of the perennial philosophy is that reality consists of a hierarchy of levels ranging from gross matter through mind, intelligence, and ego, and culminating in an all-encompassing transcendent state of absolute oneness. Many cultures have expounded such philosophies, and the most highly developed examples include Buddhism, the *advaita-vedānta* philosophy of India, Sufism, Taoism, and Christian mysticism.

Though Bohm does not explicitly say so in his books, it is clear from published conversations that he is trying to create a synthesis of physics and the particular form of *advaita-vedānta* expounded by the Indian philosopher Krishnamurti, whose teachings Bohm greatly admires. Thus Bohm's implicate order is motivated by metaphysical ideas extending far beyond the limits of his reasoning about physics.

The idea that "unfolded" information can give rise to observable organized form is based both on physical theory and practical examples, such as the phase conjugate mirror. But the idea that the parts of the implicate order actually include the whole does not arise naturally from these sources of inspiration, and indeed it is very difficult, if not impossible, to formulate this idea mathematically.

Where, then, does this idea ultimately come from? Bohm speaks of insight that comes from beyond manifest thought, and that may even originate from a level transcending the implicate order. He emphasizes, however, that human thought cannot grasp the unmanifest, and he stresses the danger of becoming deluded by false insights. But if human thought is not an adequate instrument for gaining knowledge of the unmanifest, then how will we be able to distinguish between true and false "insights"?

As we have indicated, Bohm's ideas come from the Indian philosophical system of *advaita-vedānta,* which forms one school of thought within a diverse body of tradition generally known as Hinduism. According to this tradition, transcendental knowledge can be reliably attained through the mutual reinforcement of two forms of revelation; internal and external.

The external revelation is expressed in scriptures, or *śāstras,* which descend to the human level through a chain of enlightened beings, and which originate from a transcendental, supremely intelligent source. The general term for this body of revealed knowledge is *Veda.*

The internal revelation is directly transmitted into the consciousness of a spiritual aspirant from the same supreme intelligence that introduced the Vedic *śāstras* into the material realm. This corresponds to Bohm's idea of insight originating from a source beyond the implicate order. In the Vedic system, however, this insight is corroborated by the *śāstras,* which are directly accessible to the external mind and senses. By accepting the guidance of the *śāstras,* a spiritual aspirant is able to discriminate between genuine and spurious spiritual insight. We suggest that Bohm's metaphysical system is incomplete without some form of explicit external revelation.

If one is going to seriously seek transcendental knowledge, one should at least theoretically accept that (1) the ultimate transcendental source of this knowledge is able to communicate with human beings, and (2) records of genuine communications of this kind do exist in human society. If this is not so, then one has little hope of understanding that which lies utterly beyond the grasp of the mind and senses.

One might therefore seriously consider the perennial notion that a supreme intelligence, known in the West as God, may be the source of the organized information that gives rise to our manifest world. Bohm, in fact, comes very close to admitting the possibility of a sentient supreme being. However, in line with the philosophy of *advaita-vedānta,* he finally turns away from this idea, declaring, "There's nothing we can do with that."

Simultaneous Oneness and Difference

It is interesting to note that the Vedic *śāstra* entitled *Brahma-saṁhitā* gives a very clear description of Bohm's idea of a whole that is fully contained in each of its parts. Ironically, this is part of a series of prayers to God as a supreme person:

> He is an undifferentiated entity, as there is no distinction between potency and the possessor thereof. In His work of creation of millions of worlds, His potency remains inseparable. All the universes exist in Him, and He is present in His fullness in every one of the atoms that are scattered throughout the universe, at one and the same time. Such is the primeval Lord whom I adore (*Brahma-saṁhitā* 5.35).

One might object that the human mind acting on its own could not possibly demonstrate the truth of the personal conception of the supreme whole. Therefore, one should adopt a more cautious conception that is abstract and impersonal. The point can be made, however, that *any* conception of the Absolute generated by the finite mind is as mundane as any other, including both personal and impersonal conceptions. One then may as well forego all metaphysical speculation and restrict one's attention entirely to the manifest world of interacting material energies.

But if one does want to introduce ideas about the Absolute derived from revealed knowledge, then the Vedic literatures give concrete indication of how direct realization of this knowledge can be attained. Although the Supreme Lord is inaccessible to the mundane mind, the Lord will reveal Himself to persons who surrender to Him and serve Him with love. This, of course, is also a perennial philosophical conclusion.

Back to Physics

We have seen that key aspects of Bohm's world view are based indirectly on traditional sources of revealed transcendental knowledge. One might ask, however, what part of his philosophy of the implicate order can be based exclusively on physical observation and theory.

We suggest that this is limited to the observation that macroscopic forms can arise by physical transformations from patterns of minute fluctuations that look like random noise. These patterns may appear in many forms, ranging from light waves to distributions of nuclear magnetic fields. The patterns are not necessarily spread throughout all space, but patterns that will later give rise to distinct macroscopic events may coexist in the same volume of space.

We can use these observations to show another way in which a link can be established between physics and metaphysics. Our proposed link is derived from the Vedic literature *Śrīmad-Bhāgavatam.* It is the idea that the material creation is brought about and maintained through the injection of divinely ordered sound vibrations into a primordial material substrate called *pradhāna.*

According to this idea, the *pradhāna* is an eternally existing energy of the supreme that is capable of manifesting material space and time, the material elements, and their various possible combinations. Left to itself the *pradhāna* would manifest none of these things, but it does so under the influence of intelligently directed sound vibrations generated by the Supreme Lord.

Here the word sound is a translation of the Sanskrit word *śabda.* Since the *pradhāna* is even more subtle than space as we know it, this *śabda* does not refer to ordinary sound, consisting of vibrations propagating through gross matter. We will therefore interpret "sound"

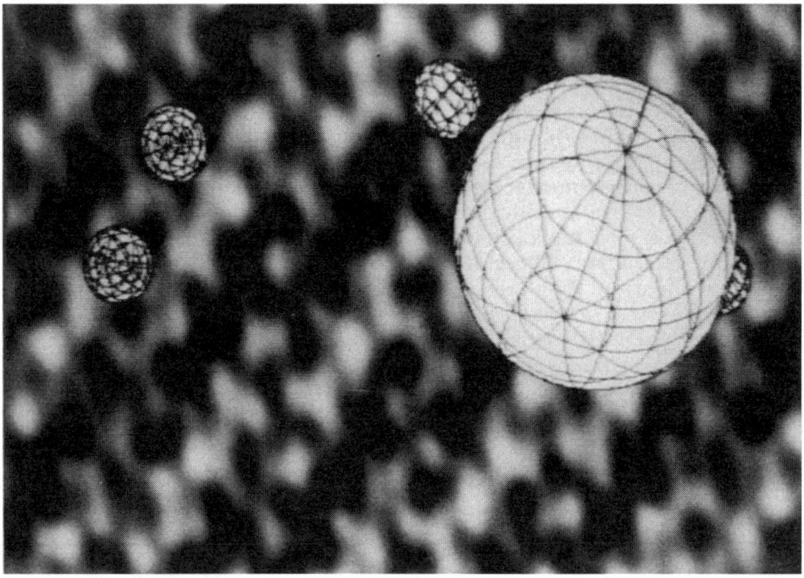

Figure 2—The creation of space from transcendental sound vibration. According to Vedic literature, transcendental sound vibrations propagating through a subtle medium (background) generate universal globes having the properties of space as we know it. Similar ideas are being contemplated by architects of the grand unified theories of modern physics.

here to mean any type of propagating vibration, however subtle.

The creation of the material universes by sound (see Figures 2 and 3) involves (1) the generation of material space and time, (2) the systematic building up of the subtle and gross material elements, (3) the organization of these elements into worlds of living beings, and, finally, (4) the continued maintenance and direction of these worlds.

Optical phase conjugation provides an analogy to this picture of the relation between material and transcendental levels of existence. Consider an arrangement in which pictures are being transmitted through a sheet of frosted glass. An observer on the receiving side would see successive images emerging from the glass screen, but he would not be able to see the transmitting persons and apparatus on the other side.

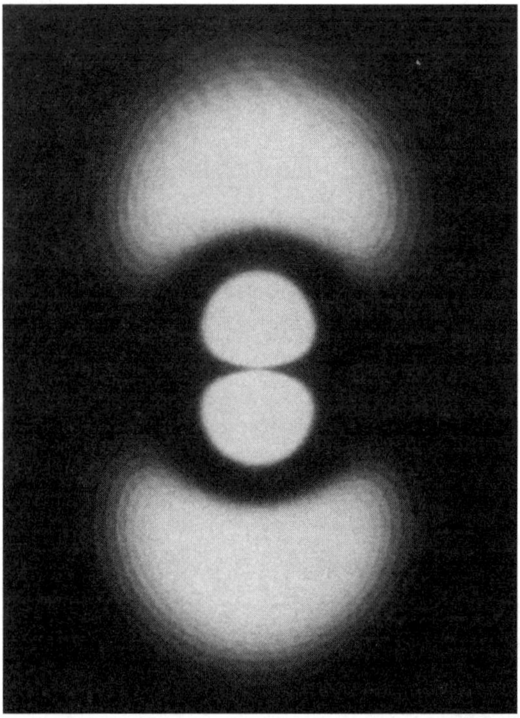

Figure 3—The generation of matter. According to Vedic literature, after the manifestation of space, various forms of gross and subtle matter are generated from transcendental sound vibration. In essence, matter is a transformation of sound vibration. This is reminiscent of modern physics. In this figure we see a hydrogen atom, which in quantum mechanics is represented as a vibrational pattern.

Similarly, according to the Vedic conception, the material energy serves as a veil of illusion, or *māyā,* that prevents living beings in the material realm from directly perceiving God. God is actually in direct control of the material energy, but He is manipulating it in such a way that His presence is hidden, and complex patterns of events seem to unfold simply by material action and reaction.

Let us suppose for the moment that organized wave patterns are continually being injected into the known physical continuum from subtler levels of physical reality. Such patterns will appear to be random, especially if they encode information for many different macroscopic forms and sequences of events. For this reason they will be difficult to distinguish from purely random patterns by experimental observation.

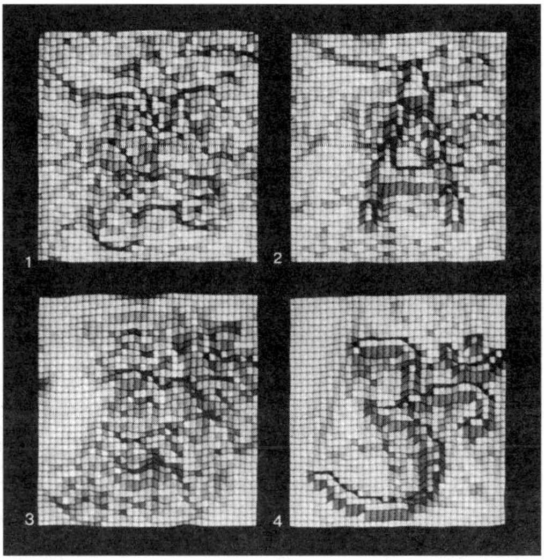

Figure 4—The manifestation of organized form from intelligently directed wave patterns. In frame 1 we see an elastic medium capable of transmitting waves (the surface of a pond is an example). The wave pattern in frame 1 seems chaotic, but in frame 2, which shows the wave pattern after a time interval has elapsed, we see that a letter *A* has emerged. In frame 3, representing a slightly later time, this form has disappeared. Still later, in frame 4, a pattern appears representing the symbol *Aum.* Actually, the information for both the *A* and the *Aum* was encoded in the wave pattern of frame 1.

Thus much of the random noise that surrounds us may consist of information for patterns that will "unfold" in the future to produce macroscopic results, while the rest consists of the "enfolded" or "refolded" remnants of past macroscopic patterns. If a pattern of microscopic vibrations *does* unfold to produce an organized macroscopic effect, then this will make a very striking impression if it can be observed.

To indicate the possibilities for such an event, we can give an example based on the idea of a wave field. The surface of a pond is a simple example of such a field.

The first frame in Figure 4 shows the wave field in an apparently chaotic state of motion. However, this pattern of waves contains hidden information. The successive frames show the motion of the waves (according to the wave equation) as time passes. In frame 2 we see that a letter *A* has appeared in the field. This form quickly takes shape and dissipates, and it is replaced in frame 4 by the similar rapid appearance and disappearance of the symbol ॐ (*Aum*). Actually the information for both symbols is present in all four frames of the figure.

The Theory of Evolution

Natural history is an area in which the hypothesis of unfolding of subtle information has relevant applications. Since the mid-nineteenth century, the prevailing scientific viewpoint has been that the origin of living species can be explained by Darwin's theory of evolution by natural selection and random variation. But there have always been prominent dissenters from this view.

In the nineteenth century Alfred Russell Wallace, the co-inventor of Darwin's theory, felt that the action of some higher intelligence was required to account for such biological phenomena as the human brain. A similar point is made by Bohm, who feels that "natural selection is not the whole story, but rather that evolution is a sign of the creative intelligence of matter." As we have pointed out, Bohm regards this intelligence as emanating either from his implicate order or from beyond.

In the theory of creation by sound vibration that we are considering here, it is to be expected that the forms of living organisms could be generated or modified through the effects of organized wave patterns transmitted into the physical realm by the supreme intelligent being. This will also be difficult to either demonstrate or disprove empirically, because of the incompleteness of the fossil record and the presumed rarity of radical transformations of species.

When evaluating a possible transformation of this kind, there will always be the problem of making sure that the transformation is not a result of ordinary physical cause and effect. To do this effectively would require detailed knowledge about the transformation, which would be very difficult to obtain.

Actually both the theory of creation by sound vibration and the Darwinian theory of evolution are extremely difficult to test empirically. On the physical level both theories are dealing with phenomena that are extremely complex and are not subject to experimental manipulation.

The theory of creation by sound vibration involves transcendental levels of reality not accessible to the mundane senses, and thus in one way it is more unverifiable than the purely physical Darwinian theory. However, if a purely physical theory turns out to be empirically unverifiable, then there is nothing further one can do to be sure about it. In contrast, a theory that posits a supreme intelligent being opens up the possibility that further knowledge may be gained by internal and external revelation brought about by the will of that being. Of course, the dynamics of obtaining such knowledge are different from those of empirical, experimental science and mathematical analysis. Instead of forcing nature to disclose its secrets, one surrenders to the Supreme Lord in a humble spirit and pursues a path of spiritual discipline and divine service.

This approach to knowledge and to life also constitutes one of the great perennial philosophies of mankind, but it has tended to be eclipsed in this age of scientific empiricism. To obtain the fruits of this path to knowledge, one must be willing to follow it, and one will be inclined to do this only if one thinks the world view on which it is based might possibly be true. Establishing this possibility constitutes the ultimate justification for constructing theories, such as the one considered here, linking physics and metaphysics.

8

Paradoxes of Time and Space

Imagine that a man travels into outer space on a rocket at near the speed of light and then returns to earth. According to Einstein's theory of relativity, the man will find he has not aged as much as his identical twin brother who stayed home. Time will have passed more slowly on the rapidly moving rocket than on the slow-moving earth. This disparity in the passage of time is often called time dilation.

This story of the twins is called the twin paradox, since it runs contrary to our expectations. Yet a simple diagram can easily show how it works.

The key to understanding the aging of the twins is Einstein's postulate that no matter how fast a person is traveling, if he measures the speed of a beam of light it will always be the same. In principle, then, we could make a clock by having a beam of light bounce back and forth between two mirrors mounted in frames at a fixed distance from one another. Since light always goes at the same speed, the time a pulse of light takes to make one complete bounce from one mirror to the other and back will always be the same. So we can measure the passage of time by counting complete bounces.

In the graph, distance is plotted on the horizontal axis and the passage of time on the vertical. The scale of the two axes is chosen so that light moves one unit of distance (186,000 miles) in one unit of time (1 second). Thus the path of a beam of light is a line with a slope of +1 or -1. Two stationary mirrors leave parallel vertical lines as time passes. A pulse of light bouncing back and forth between the two mirrors leaves a zig-zag path, and in this diagram we can count 10 complete bounces.

The pair of lines moving right and then left in a V-shape represents the movement of a pair of mirrors that travel first to the right and then to the left. The zig-zag line between these two V-shaped lines represents the path of a light pulse bouncing between the two moving mirrors. We can count nearly 7 complete bounces in this case. This means that while an observer standing next to the stationary mirrors experiences that 10 units of time have passed, an observer traveling with the moving mirrors experiences only 7 units of time.

This shows how the twin paradox works. The striking thing about it is that even though the zigs and zags of the light trapped between the moving mirrors seem unequal, an observer moving with the mirrors will see them to be the same. For this to be possible, both space and time on a moving object must transform in a strange way.

Note, by the way, that the horizontal spacing between the two moving mirrors is shown to be smaller than the spacing between the

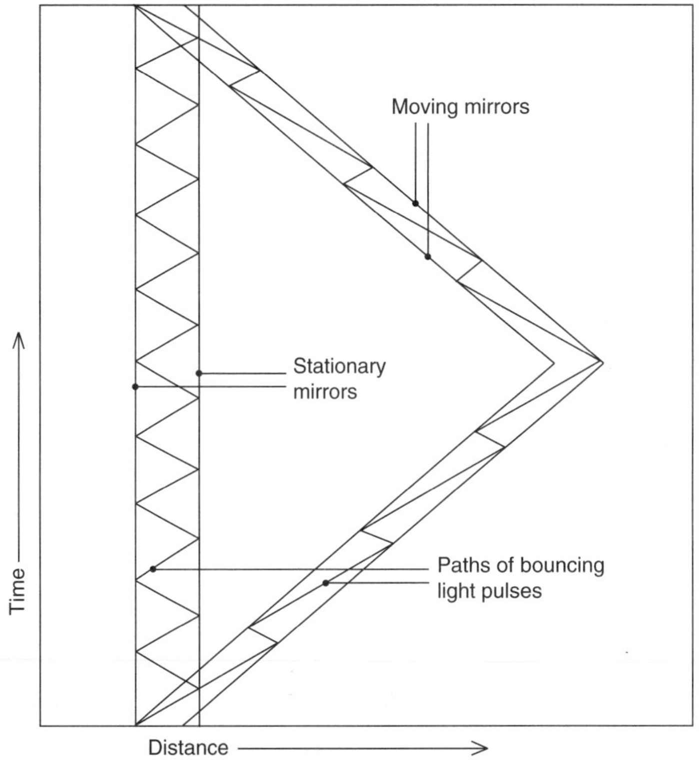

The Twin Paradox in Einstein's Theory of Relativity. The time, as measured by pulses of light bouncing between mirrors, is greater when the mirrors are stationary than it is when they move at close to the speed of light. (See text.)

two stationary mirrors. This is an example of how space transforms with motion. According to Einstein's theory, a moving object will shrink in length by a certain percentage along its line of motion.

Apart from time dilation caused by motion, Einstein also discussed time dilation caused by gravitation. Imagine a beam of light moving up from the surface of the earth. According to the laws of physics, the light must lose energy as it climbs against the pull of gravity. The frequency of a beam of light is proportional to its energy. So as the light climbs upward, its frequency drops.

Now suppose the light is coming from the face of a clock situated on the earth's surface, and that a person in outer space is using this light to see the clock. A person on earth can observe that for every second ticked off by the clock, the light will vibrate through a certain number of cycles. The person observing the clock from outer space will also see that the light vibrates through this many cycles in the time the second hand ticks off one second.

For the observer in outer space, however, the light has a lower frequency than on earth. So he'll see the earth clock running slower than his own clock. Relative to the observer in space, time on earth must be passing more slowly. Calculations show that for a person in outer space, time on the earth's surface would seem to pass only slightly more slowly. But time on a planet with an extremely strong gravitational field would pass very slowly indeed.

According to the theory of relativity, an object with a strong enough gravitational field will be surrounded by an imaginary sphere called the event horizon. As Joe Smith, say at 1:00 p.m. by his own watch, approaches the object in his space ship and passes the event horizon, he won't notice anything unusual. But to an observer watching from a distance, as Joe approaches the event horizon, he will seem to slow down. He will never quite get there, and his watch will never quite reach 1:00 p.m. As the light coming from Joe grows to longer and longer wavelengths, Joe will fade out and gradually become invisible. Objects with such event horizons are known as black holes.

These examples show that modern physics allows for remarkable transformations of space and time. And apparently, similar ideas are found in Vedic literature.

We find an example in the story of a king named Kakudmī, who was able to travel to the world of Brahmā and experience Brahmā's scale of time. Here is the story, as related in the *Śrīmad-Bhāgavatam:*

> Taking his own daughter, Revatī, Kakudmī went to Lord Brahmā in Brahmaloka, which is transcendental to the three modes of material nature, and inquired about a husband for her. When Kakudmī arrived there, Lord Brahmā was engaged in hearing musical performances by the Gandharvas and had not a moment to talk with him. Therefore Kakudmī waited, and at the end of the musical performances he offered his obeisances to Lord Brahmā and thus submitted his long-standing desire. After hearing his words, Lord Brahmā, who is most powerful, laughed loudly and said to Kakudmī, "O King, all those whom you may have decided within the core of your heart to accept as your son-in-law have passed away in the course of time. Twenty-seven *catur-yugas* have already passed. Those upon whom you may have decided are now gone, and so are their sons, grandsons, and other descendants. You cannot even hear about their names.[1]

One *catur-yuga* lasts 4,320,000 years. With this information, we can estimate the rate of time dilation on Brahmaloka. If the concert given by the Gandharvas took about one hour in Brahmā's time scale, then that hour must correspond to 27 times 4,320,000 earth years. It is interesting that this estimate closely matches one for time dilation in another story involving Brahmā.

This is the story of the *brahma-vimohana-līlā,* or the bewilderment of Brahmā by Kṛṣṇa. Several thousand years ago, Kṛṣṇa descended to the earth as an *avatāra* and was playing as a young cowherd boy, tending calves in the forest of Vṛndāvana (south of present-day New Delhi). To test Kṛṣṇa's potency, Brahmā used mystic power to steal Kṛṣṇa's calves and cowherd boyfriends and hide them in suspended animation in a secluded place. He then went away for a year of earthly time to see what would happen.

Kṛṣṇa responded to Brahmā's trick by expanding Himself into identical copies of the calves and boys. So, when Brahmā returned, he saw Kṛṣṇa playing with the boys and calves just as before. Brahmā became bewildered. Checking the boys and calves he had hidden, he found they were indistinguishable from the ones playing with Kṛṣṇa, and he couldn't understand how this was possible. Finally Kṛṣṇa revealed to Brahmā that these latter boys and calves were identical with Himself, and He allowed Brahmā to have a direct vision of the spiritual world.

Now, it turns out that even though Brahmā was absent for one earth year, on his time scale only a moment had passed. The Sanskrit word used here for a moment of time is *truti.*[2] There are various definitions of a *truti,* but the Vedic astronomy text called the *Sūrya-siddhānta* defines a *truti* to be $^{1}/_{33,750}$ of a second.[3] If we accept this figure, then one year on earth corresponds to $^{1}/_{33,750}$ of a second in the time of Brahmā.

As I pointed out, King Kakudmī's visit to Brahmaloka took 27 times 4,320,000 earth years. If we multiply this by $^{1}/_{33,750}$ we find that in Brahmā's time King Kakudmī's visit lasted 3,456 seconds, or just under an hour. This is consistent with the story that the king had to wait for a musical performance to finish before having a brief conversation with Lord Brahmā.

Although the time dilation involved in visits to Brahmaloka is extreme, such large time dilations do arise in the theories of modern physics. For example, suppose that instead of crossing the event horizon of a black hole, Joe Smith simply came close to the event horizon and then went back out into space to rejoin the person observing his journey. If he had come close enough to the event horizon, he would find that although his trip seemed short to him, millions of years had passed, and the observer had died long ago.

It is curious that according to the *Śrīmad-Bhāgavatam* the physical universe is surrounded by a shell, and Brahmaloka is located very close to that shell. The *Bhāgavatam* gives the diameter of this shell as 500 million *yojanas,* which, using the standard figure of 8 miles per *yojana,* comes out to 4 billion miles.

This seems extremely small. In a purport in the *Caitanya-caritāmṛtā,* however, Śrīla Prabhupāda makes the following comment:

> Śrīla Bhaktisiddhānta Sarasvatī Ṭhākura, one of the greatest astrologers of his time, gives information from *Siddhānta Śiromaṇi* that this universe measures 18,712,069,200,000,000 × 8 miles. This is the circumference of this universe. According to some, this is only half the circumference.[4]

Assuming that what is meant is circumference, the diameter of the universe should be 5,956,200,000 million *yojanas,* considerably bigger than 500 million.

What is the meaning of these apparently contradictory figures? I don't know for sure, but it's interesting to consider that transformations of space may take place as one approaches the shell of the universe. The time dilation stories involving Brahmaloka show that transformations of time take place as one approaches the shell, and in the theory of relativity space and time tend to change together.

In the *Mahābhārata* Nārada Muni gives Mahārāja Yudhiṣṭhira a description of the assembly hall of Lord Brahmā on Brahmaloka. He emphasizes that the structure of this hall is impossible to describe, and this seems consistent with the idea that space in Brahmaloka may undergo transformations incomprehensible from our earthly standpoint. Here is his description of Brahmā's hall:

> It is not possible to describe it as it really is, king of the people, for from instant to instant it has another indescribable appearance. I know neither its size nor its structure, Bharata, and never before have I seen such beauty. The hall is very comfortable, king, neither too cold nor too hot; when one enters it, one no longer is hungry, thirsty, or weary. It is as though it is made up of many different shapes, all very colorful and luminous. No pillars support it. It is eternal and knows of no decay. It is self-luminous beyond the moon and sun and the flame-crested fire.[5]

If strange transformations of space do occur in the region of Brahmaloka, then it could be that different scales of distance may be appropriate for describing travel to that region.

Going beyond Brahmaloka, one comes to the shell of the universe, described in Vedic literature as a region of transition from the physical world to the spiritual world. Since the *Bhāgavatam* regards space as we know it as a physical element (called *ākāśa,* or ether), the shell marks the end of distance measurements as we know them, even though the thickness of that shell is described in the *Bhāgavatam* in terms of units of distance. This also suggests that different scales of distance and even different types of distance may be involved in Vedic cosmology.

The shell of the universe also marks the end of time as we know it. According to the Vedic literature, a liberated soul is able to cross the shell of the universe and enter the transcendental region of Vaikuṇṭha, where material time does not exist. Compare this with the idea of Joe Smith's journey through the event horizon of a black hole. Just as Joe passes into a region that, for observers outside the event horizon, is beyond time, the liberated soul passes into a region beyond the time of the physical universe. So in a sense the shell of the universe described in the *Bhāgavatam* might be compared to the event horizon of a black hole.

These comparisons between concepts from the *Bhāgavatam* and concepts from modern physics are crude at best and should be regarded only as metaphors. But they do indicate that some of the strange features of the universe as described in the Vedic literature may be no more "far out" than some of the ideas in accepted theories of modern physics.

REFERENCES

1. Bhaktivedanta Swami Prabhupāda, A. C., 1977, *Śrīmad-Bhāgavatam,* Ninth Canto - Part One, Los Angeles: Bhaktivedanta Book Trust, text 9.3.28–32.
2. Bhaktivedanta Swami Prabhupāda, A. C., 1980, *Śrīmad-Bhāgavatam,* Tenth Canto - Part Three, Los Angeles: Bhaktivedanta Book Trust, text 10.13.40.
3. Sastrin, Bapu Deva, trans., 1860, *Sūrya-siddhānta,* Calcutta: Baptist Mission Press, reprinted in Bibliotheca Indica, New Series No. 1, Hindu Astronomy I, p. 2.
4. Bhaktivedanta Swami Prabhupāda, A. C., 1975, *Śrī Caitanya-caritāmṛta, Madhya-līlā,* Vol. 8, Los Angeles: Bhaktivedanta Book Trust, text 21.84.
5. van Buitenen, J. A. B., trans., 1975, *The Mahābharata,* Books 2 and 3, Chicago: The University of Chicago Press, p. 51.

CONSCIOUSNESS

9

Life: Real and Artificial

In Santa Fe, New Mexico, a group of scientists, mainly from the Los Alamos National Laboratories, held a conference in 1990 on "Artificial Life." The theme of the conference, which I attended, was that the essence of life lies not in biological substance but in patterned organization.

If this idea is valid, the thinking goes, life forms should be able to set themselves up through many different types of material stuff. In particular, life should be able to exist as a pattern of electronic activity in a computer.

The conference organizers, casually dressed, long-haired men in their thirties and early forties, say that artificial, computer-based life forms are developing even now—and may evolve to dominate the earth.

According to this view, the evolutionary role of man is to give birth to silicon-based life patterns that will eventually look back on him as a primitive ancestor. The conference sponsors counseled a broad-minded attitude toward such evolutionary progress: we should transcend parochial anthropocentrism and welcome advanced life in whatever form it may emerge.

However, some attending scientists doubted whether a program running on a computer could be properly thought to be alive. Philosopher Elliott Sober argued that when engineers make a computer simulation of a bridge, no one would think of it as a real bridge: the simulation merely shows a picture in which computations tell us something about bridges. In the same way, when a computer simulates an organism, we see a picture in which computations tell us something about life—we're not seeing life itself.

Tommaso Toffoli, a computer scientist from Massachusetts Institute of Technology, responded to this argument. Suppose, he said, that simulated people were driving in simulated cars on a simulated

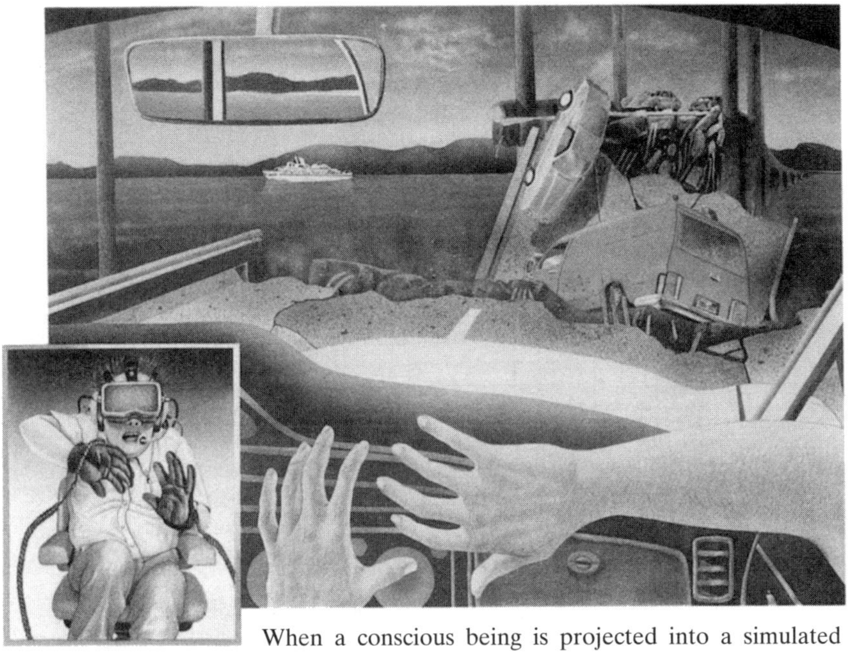

When a conscious being is projected into a simulated world, simulated death can result in real suffering.

bridge. If the bridge were to collapse, the people would fall to their simulated deaths.

The patterns in a faithful simulation match the patterns found in reality: the simulated people cross the simulated bridge just as real people cross a real bridge. And since these patterns, Dr. Toffoli proposed, are the essence of what is happening, we can think of the simulation the same way we think of the original.

In principle, then, if a real material scene can exhibit life, so can a simulation.

In practice, of course, present computers, operating with a few processors, are incapable of matching the patterns of the real world.

But Toffoli suggested that the powerful computers of the future will consist of crystallike arrays of many thousands of microminiature processors, nearly atomic in size, all computing at once. Toffoli described such computers as "programmable matter."

Indeed, we might regard matter itself, with its interacting atomic subunits, as such a computer. According to this idea, life is already a computer simulation running on the "programmable matter" of the universe itself.

Now, if life is but a computer simulation, a series of computational states, then life must be essentially unreal. Words such as "flower," "dog," and "human" are simply names, symbols we attach to patterns of computation. This, in fact, is the Vedic understanding not of life but of the material body. In the Eleventh Canto of *Śrīmad-Bhāgavatam,* Kṛṣṇa says to Uddhāva that the gross and subtle forms of material bodies have no existence of their own; they are only temporary patterns manifested by an eternally existing substrate of reality, called the Absolute Truth.

Kṛṣṇa illustrates this idea with an example: "Gold exists before it is made into gold products, and the gold remains when the products have been destroyed. The gold alone is the reality while used under various names. Similarly, I alone exist before the universe is created and after it is destroyed, and I alone exist while it is maintained. . . ."

> "That which did not exist in the past and will not exist in the future has no existence of its own while it lasts. . . . Whatever is created and revealed by something else is ultimately only that other thing." (*Śrīmad-Bhāgavatam* 11.28.19, 21).

So we can look at the temporary forms of the material universe as patterns in Kṛṣṇa's energy to which various names have been assigned. In essence these patterns in Kṛṣṇa's material energy (*bahiraṅga-śakti*) are the same as the patterns of electrons that form and disappear in the circuitry of a computer during a simulation. So we can view the material universe as the ultimate computer simulation, and Kṛṣṇa as the ultimate simulator.

But seeing the material body as a succession of flickering patterns doesn't mean we should view life the same way. Kṛṣṇa says in *Bhagavad-gītā* (2.20) that the soul, the individual conscious self, eternally exists: "For the soul there is never birth or death. He has not come into being, does not come into being, and will not come into being. He is unborn, eternal, ever-existing, and primeval. He is not slain when the body is slain."

Tommaso Toffoli's simulated people on the simulated bridge lack one main element: consciousness. A series of computations might simulate the changes a person's body undergoes, including those in the brain. But why should patterns of electric current generate the conscious experience of these changes?

We may easily imagine that the patterns of current that make up a machine's computations may flow without conscious awareness. This suggests that if consciousness of the results of these computations exists in the computer, this must be due to some element that our understanding of computers has not yet taken into account.

Here's how some might reply: It may be hard to understand how patterns of computer states could generate consciousness, but we already know that similar patterns generate consciousness in human brains. So why can't this take place in a computer?

The answer is that we don't know in any scientific sense that patterns of brain states do generate consciousness. Resolving how such patterns might do this in brains would be just as hard as figuring out how they might do it in computers.

Bhagavad-gītā provides a simple solution by postulating that consciousness in the material body is due to the presence of an entity fundamentally different from matter. Given the difficulties philosophers and scientists have run into in trying to understand consciousness as patterns of material elements, it is worthwhile thinking about this solution.

If we tentatively adopt this solution, then we may ask: How would the nonmaterial conscious entity be linked to the material body? We can understand how this link might work by returning to Toffoli's story of the simulated bridge.

How could we introduce consciousness into the simulation? One way would be to make a "real-time" simulation, one in which the simulated events take place at the same pace as corresponding events in the real world. (One would simply need a computer which is fast enough.) Then one could put consciousness into the simulation by electronically linking the senses of real, conscious people with the simulated senses of the simulated people. The intentions of the conscious people would move the bodies of the people in the simulated world, and the conscious people would have the experiences the simulated people would have.

Far-fetched? Some people in computer science are already working on it. VPL Research in California is experimenting with "virtual realities" in which a person's eyes, ears, and one hand are hooked up electronically with virtual eyes and ears and a virtual hand in a simulated world. The person looks through "eye-phones," small TV screens placed directly in front of his eyes, and sees as though in the simulated world.

A "data-glove" electronically senses his hand movements, and another device the sense movements of his head; the resulting data control the movements of his simulated hand and head.

Thus the person experiences the simulated world through a simulated body, moves about in that body, and handles simulated objects in that world.

If it is possible to link human consciousness with an unreal, virtual body in a simulated world, why shouldn't it be possible to link spiritual consciousness with similarly unreal bodies in the "real" material world?

The Vedic philosophy known as Sāṅkhya describes the workings of such a communications link. The Third Canto of *Śrīmad-Bhāgavatam* describes Kṛṣṇa's material energy as including an element called "false ego," or *ahaṅkāra,* which serves as the interface between the nonmaterial soul and the material energy. This false ego acts like the eyephones and data gloves that link a human being with a computer running a virtual reality program.

Both the material body as understood in Vedic literature and the simulated body in a computer-generated world are merely temporary patterns in an underlying substrate. But the conscious self—the real essence of the living being—has a substantial reality outside the realm of transient patterns.

In the computer-generated reality this conscious self is a human being not part of the computer system, and in the Vedic philosophy this self is a transcendental entity distinct from matter.

One lesson we can learn from the thoughts and experiments of computer scientists is that such a relationship between the self and the material world is possible. And it just might be our actual situation.

10

The Little Man In the Brain

During a recent television show entitled "Inside Information," neuroscientist V. S. Ramachandran of the University of California at San Diego made some interesting points about how we see. He said that if you ask the man in the street how vision works, he will say there is an image on the retina of the eye. The optic nerve faithfully transmits this image to a screen in the brain, in what we call the visual cortex. And that image is what you see.

Ramachandran pointed out that this explanation leads to a logical fallacy. If you create an image inside the head, then you need another person in the head—a little man in the brain—who looks at that image. Then you have to postulate an even smaller person inside his head to explain how he sees, and so on, *ad infinitum.* This is obvious nonsense, and Ramachandran said that inside the brain there really is no replica of the external world. Rather, there is an abstract, symbolic description of that world. Brain scientists are like cryptographers trying to crack the code the brain uses in perceiving its environment.

So how does perception work? Suppose you are looking at a car traveling down a street. You perceive the shape of the car, its color, and its motion all at once. You may realize at once that it's red, that it's a Volkswagen bug, and that it's slow enough and far enough away so you'll have time to cross the street in front of it.

Research in brain science shows that the brain houses three separate visual systems to see shape, color, and motion. All three systems use information coming down the optic nerves from the eyes, but the systems are distinct both anatomically and functionally. The systems are named after the complex anatomical pathways they occupy in the brain.

The parvo-interblob-pale-stripe system deals with color contrast along borders of objects, but not color per se. It responds to the shapes of objects, but says nothing about their colors. The blob-thin-stripe-V4

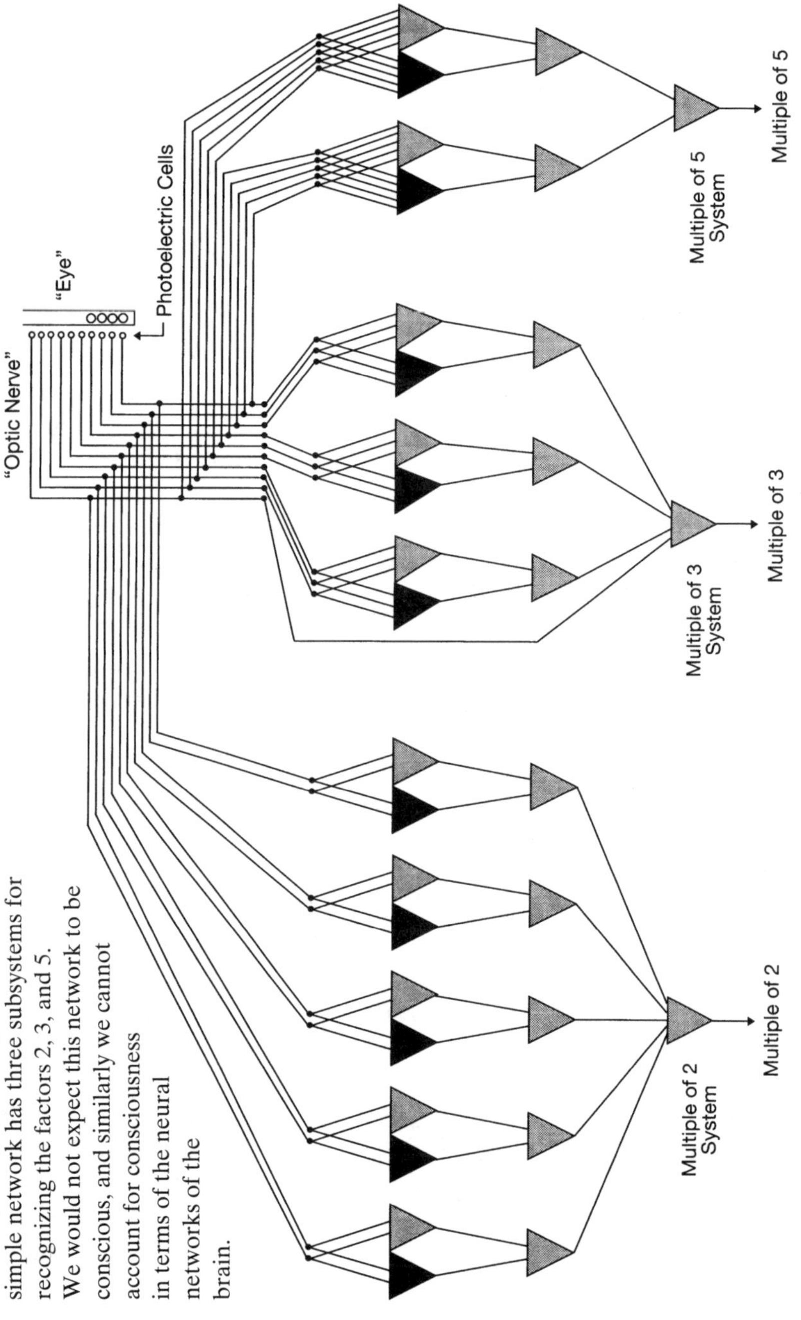

Just as the brain has different subsystems for recognizing different patterns, so this simple network has three subsystems for recognizing the factors 2, 3, and 5. We would not expect this network to be conscious, and similarly we cannot account for consciousness in terms of the neural networks of the brain.

system determines colors and shades of gray, but it has low resolution for shapes. The magno-4B-thick-stripe-MT system tells about movement and depth, but it's colorblind and doesn't react to stationary images.[1] All three systems work together when you see the Volkswagen coming down the street.

To illustrate how such a visual system works, I've devised a simple example with computer logic. The figure on the previous page shows an "eye" consisting of a vertical plastic tube with ten photoelectric cells in a vertical row. The tube has room for one to ten small plastic balls. The photoelectric cells detect the balls. Each output wire from a photocell is "on" if a ball is present in front of the cell, and "off" if a ball is not present.

The ten wires from the cells form a kind of "optic nerve." This nerve divides into three branches leading to three processing systems.

The multiple-of-2 system tells whether the number of balls is odd or even. It works through logic gates, represented by the gray and black triangles. The wires going to the top of a triangle are its input wires, and the wire going down from the triangle's point is its output wire. A gray triangle represents a none-gate. Its output wire is on if none of its input wires are on, and otherwise it is off. A black triangle represents an all-gate. Its output wire is on if all its input wires are on, and not otherwise. The gates in the multiple-of-2 system are arranged so that the final output wire emerging from the bottom of the system is on if the number of balls is even, and off if the number is odd.

Similarly, the gates in the multiple-of-3 system are arranged so that the final output wire is on only if the number of balls is a multiple of 3 (i.e., 3, 6, or 9). In the multiple-of-5 system, the output wire is on only if the number of balls is a multiple of 5 (i.e., 5 or 10).

This network recognizes three distinct features of the number of balls. It does this using three distinct subsystems of gates that operate in parallel, each subsystem using simple logical operations in response to binary information (represented by "on" and "off" or 1 and 0). These sub-systems resemble the brain's subsystems for recognizing the shape, color, and motion of an image. The brain's subsystems use distinct sets of neurons, which also work with binary information. (When a neuron is stimulated, it either fires or it doesn't, with no response in between.)

Our example of a computer network gives some idea of how the brain can process information with which to respond to its environment. Data from the senses, encoded as patterns of nerve impulses, can travel to a wide variety of brain subsystems, where networks of neurons extract various kinds of information. This information can then be combined to yield further information, which in turn can be used to generate brain output.

But can this explain how we see? This view of the brain avoids an infinite regress of little men looking at screens in one another's heads. And it gives us an idea of how the brain can identify complex patterns and respond to them. But it tells us nothing about how we are aware of a Volkswagen coming down the street.

Look again at our computer network model. We could easily build this model out of electrical hardware, and we could hook up the output wires from the three subsystems to colored lights labeled 2, 3, and 5. Suppose we did this, put 6 balls in the tube, and saw lights 2 and 3 turn on, and the light 5 stay off. Would the electrical network be aware that 6 is a multiple of 2 and 3? Is there any reasonable basis for saying the network would be aware of anything?

The answer is no. We can fully understand what the network is doing. We can understand the flows of electrical current within its wires and the operation of its logic gates. But this understanding tells us nothing about whether or not the network is aware of anything. And if someone were to declare that the network actually is conscious of something, we would be at a loss to understand how or why that should be.

This is all well and good with electrical networks. Perhaps they are completely devoid of consciousness. But what about human brains? When I see a Volkswagen coming down the street, I'm having a conscious experience, and I know directly that this is so. I assume that since other people are similar to me, they too have real conscious experiences. Can we understand this phenomenon in terms of networks of neurons in the brain?

The answer seems to be no. Our electrical network could be built using neurons instead of wires. That network would recognize patterns the same way, and we would understand it the same way. The essence of the network lies in the pattern of its logic gates, not in the substance making up these gates. But this means we can't understand consciousness in neural networks any better than in electrical networks.

One might point out that there are more than 10 billion neurons in the cerebral cortex and only a few logic gates in our example. Couldn't it be that consciousness emerges from the interaction of billions of neurons? Perhaps, but how? With billions of logical units in a network, one can certainly handle patterns much more complex than simple columns of 1 to 10 balls. But this tells us nothing about consciousness.

One idea is that consciousness may arise at the level where the brain organizes information from separate systems, like those for shape, color, and motion, and integrates it into one unified gestalt. One problem with this proposal: Does such unification actually occur? To write down a lot of information you need many letters, and if you code the information in patterns of nerve impulses, you need a lot of neurons to store it. No matter how much you try to compress it by careful coding, it remains spread out and not truly unified. The idea of a unified "gestalt" simply takes us back to the original little man who looks at the information and is conscious of it.

The basic fallacy of the little man in the brain argument is that it assumes implicitly that consciousness can be understood in physical terms. One tries to explain consciousness by describing a machine that creates a certain display of information. Then one recognizes that the mere presence of displayed information fails to account for consciousness of that information. Then one proposes another mechanism to interpret the information and finally generate consciousness. When that attempt also fails, one takes refuge in the overwhelming complexity of the brain and says that a consciousness-producing mechanism must be hidden in there somewhere. All we have to do is find it.

One way to escape from the little man fallacy is to forget about consciousness and restrict our attention to the brain's data processing. But this leaves a crucial aspect of life permanently outside the domain of science.

Another way to escape the fallacy is to consider that consciousness just might be due to a nonphysical entity—dare we say a soul?—

that reads the data displays of the brain just as we read the letters of a book.

Although this idea is anathema to scientists who insist that everything must obey known physical laws, it promises to greatly expand the frontiers of science. It could very well be true. And to realize its potential for enriching our scientific understanding, all we have to do is seriously consider it.

REFERENCE

1. Livingstone, Margaret S., 1988, "Art, Illusion and the Visual System," *Scientific American,* January, pp. 78–85.

11

Imitators of Life

Omni: "So then, aren't you artificial life guys playing God?"
Chris Langton: "Well, yeah, in a way I have to admit it."[1]

The dream of creating life is hard to resist. For many years, artificial intelligence seemed a sure way to this goal. Researchers at universities like MIT would regularly claim that within ten years computers would surpass humans in intelligence. But decades passed, and by the 1980s researchers widely conceded that these claims were a bit premature.

Then came artificial life. In 1987 a young scientist named Chris Langton, from Los Alamos National Laboratories, put together in Santa Fe, New Mexico, the first conference on artificial life. The essence of life, he said, is organization transforming by rules, so we can study life effectively through computer simulations. Conference speakers offered studies of computer-simulated "organisms" and "ecosystems." By the widely publicized second conference, in 1990, this new field of scientific study had lots of players.

Their idea was to aim for realistic goals and not have to backpedal like their colleagues in artificial intelligence. As artificial life advocate John Nagle put it, "We need to start low. Where do we get off trying for human-level capabilities when we can't even build an ant?"[2] Of course, ants are formidably complicated. As Nagle admitted, "We just don't know how ants work."[3]

Yet despite the humble start, artificial lifers seem confident that life will one day be embodied in silicon and freed from the constraints of carbon-based wetware. Then evolution will speed along, and human beings will have to confront their evolutionary successors.

At the second artificial life conference some speakers gleefully projected that this might occur within a hundred years. We should accept the inevitable, they said, and give up pride in our ephemeral human body. Others expressed reluctance, or even fear. The reasons for celebrating the replacement of human beings by machines, said conferee Michael Rosenberg, "need to be examined."[4]

The idea that humans may be replaced by superintelligent machines is an old one. So instead of trying to analyze the prospects for artificial life, let me relate some stories from past history. For this I turn to a treatise on machines in ancient India written by a Sanskritist named V. Raghavan.[5]

In Sanskrit a machine is called a *yantra.* As defined by the *Samarańgana Sūtradhara* of King Bhoja in the twelfth century, a *yantra* is a device that "controls and directs, according to a plan, the motions of things that act each according to its own nature."[6] This is close to Langton's definition of life. And in ancient and medieval India mechanical imitations of life were something craftsmen actually built.

Some of their automata were used for divertissements in royal pleasure palaces. These included birds that sang and danced, a dancing elephant, elaborate chronometers with moving ivory figures, and the *gola,* an astronomical instrument with moving planets. The machines were built from common materials in a readily understandable way: "Male and female figures are designed for various kinds of automatic service. Each part of these figures is made and fitted separately, with holes and pins, so that thighs, eyes, neck, hand, wrist, forearm, and fingers can act according to need. The material used is mainly wood, but a leather cover is given to complete the impression of a human being. The movements are managed by a system of poles, pins, and strings attached to rods controlling each limb. Looking into a mirror, playing a lute, and stretching out the hand to touch, give *pan,* sprinkle water, and make obeisance are the acts done by these figures."[7]

This all sounds quite believable, but other machines described may seem less so. These include robots capable of complex independent action.

Many stories in Indian literature tell of a *yantra-puruṣa,* or machine man, that can behave just like a human being. In the Buddhistic *Bhaiṣajya-vastu,* for example, a painter goes to the Yāvana country and visits the home of a *yantrācārya,* or teacher of mechanical engineering. There he meets a machine girl who washes his feet and seems human, until he finds that she cannot speak.[8] In another account, a robot palace guard stands at the gate with a sword, ready to "quickly and quietly kill thieves who break into the palace at night."[9] We even hear of a complete city of mechanical people, presided over by an Oz-like human king who manipulates them from a control center in his palace.[10]

These stories sound like mere products of the imagination, and quite likely this is just what they are. Once one sees a mechanical figure that imitates some human functions, it's easy to imagine robots with human or even superhuman capabilities. This is what modern advocates of artificial life or artificial intelligence are doing. But unlike the old Indian storytellers, they are seriously intent on convincing people that human beings are simply machines, awaiting replacement by superhuman machines in the future.

Ancient Indian thinkers compared the body to a machine. But they understood that a completely nonmaterial entity within the body—the *jīvātmā*—animates the body, endowing it with sentient behavior. The link between the *jīvātmā* and the body was understood to be the Paramātmā, a portion of the Supreme that stays with each living being. Thus in *Bhagavad-gītā* (18.61) Kṛṣṇa says, "The Supreme Lord is situated in everyone's heart, O Arjuna, and is directing the wanderings of all living entities. They are seated in the body as on a machine [*yantra*], made of the material energy."

We can't resist mentioning that Raghavan, the authority on Indian *yantras,* finds the metaphor used in this verse regrettable. He laments that in other countries machines led to a materially focused civilization but in India they only reinforced the idea of God and spirit. Thus, "Even writers who actually dealt with the *yantras,* like Somadeva and Bhoja, saw in the machine operated by an agent an appropriate analogy for the mundane body and senses presided over by the soul." Or an alternative analogy: "the wonderful mechanism of the universe, with its constituent elements and planetary systems, requiring a divine master to keep it in constant revolution."[11]

Sentient Robots

In ancient India, people entertained ideas about advanced mechanical control systems quite different from our modern computerized devices. Let us examine some of these ideas to see if they have any relevance for modern technological thought.

It may come as no surprise that control systems in ancient India were used in military applications, where competition is always intense. In the battle between Kṛṣṇa and Śālva, for example, Śālva's airplane, flown by Dānava soldiers, suddenly became invisible. The technique for invisibility seems not to have blocked the transmission of sound, for the soldiers could still be heard screaming taunts and insults.

Kṛṣṇa then dealt with them as follows: "I quickly laid on an arrow, which killed by seeking out sound, to kill them, and the screeching subsided. All the Dānavas who had been screeching lay dead, killed by the blazing sunlike arrows that were triggered by sound."[12]

These arrows seem similar to modern missiles with infrared sensors and onboard microcomputers that seek out the heat of a jet engine. How did they work?

We can get some idea by considering the weapons used by Arjuna. He got these weapons from various *devas,* so they were known as celestial weapons. They worked through the action of subtly embodied living beings whom Arjuna could directly order from within his mind. Here is a description of how Arjuna prepared himself to use these weapons: "And seated on that excellent car with face turned to the east, the mighty-armed hero, purifying his body and concentrating his soul, recalled to his mind all his weapons. And all the weapons came, and addressing the royal son of Pārtha, said, 'We are here, O illustrious one. We are thy servants, O son of Indra.' And bowing unto them, Pārtha received them into his hands and replied unto them, saying, 'Dwell ye all in my memory.'"[13]

This suggests how the sound-seeking arrows could have worked. They could have been guided by sentient living beings linked to controllable mechanisms built into the arrows. This would mean that the arrows would be examples of artificial life. They would in effect be cyborgs, cybernetic organisms—a fusing of living organisms and machines. But unlike today's hypothetical cyborgs, they would have used features of life that go beyond the realm of gross matter.

According to *Bhagavad-gītā,* the body of a living being consists of two components: the gross body, made of earth, water, fire, air, and ether, and the subtle body, made of mind, intelligence, and false ego. The three components of the subtle body are material elements finer than the gross matter we perceive with our ordinary senses. The *jīvātmā* interacts directly with the subtle body through the agency of the Paramātmā. The subtle body in turn interacts with the gross body through ether, the finest of the gross elements.

If this is true, it should be possible to create a technology of artificial life that directly takes advantage of the properties of the subtle body and the *jīvātmā.* We suggest that this is the kind of technology used in the celestial weapons of Kṛṣṇa and Arjuna. Just as modern computers make cam-and-gearwheel devices old-fashioned, this Vedic technology would leave silicon chips in the dust. Once developed, it would render gross physical technology—with its imagined super-human robots—obsolete.

REFERENCES

1. Langton, Christopher, 1991, "Interview," *Omni,* October, p. 134.
2. Nagle, John, 1990, "Animation, Artificial Life, and Artificial Intelligence from the Bottom, or Some Things to Do with 100 to 1000 MIPS," submitted to the Second Conference on Artificial Life, February, p. 4.
3. Nagle.
4. Rosenberg, Michael, 1990, "Future Imbalance between Man and Machine," submitted to the Second Conference on Artificial Life, February, abstract.
5. Raghavan, V., 1956, "Yantras or Mechanical Contrivances in Ancient India," Transaction No. 10, Bangalore: The Indian Institute of Culture.
6. Raghavan, p. 21.
7. Raghavan, p. 25.
8. Raghavan, p. 5.
9. Raghavan, p. 26.
10. Raghavan, p. 19.
11. Raghavan, p. 32.
12. van Buitenen, J. A. B., trans., 1975, *The Mahabharata,* Books 2 and 3, Chicago: The Univ. of Chicago Press, p. 264.
13. Ganguli, K. M., trans., 1976, *The Mahabharata,* Vol. IV, New Delhi: Munshiram Manoharlal Publishers Pvt. Ltd., p. 78.

12

On Mystic Perfections and Long-Distance Hypnosis

It was 9:00 p.m., April 22, 1886. The four researchers—Ochorowicz, Marillier, Janet, and A. T. Myers—crept quietly through the deserted streets of Le Havre and took up their stations outside the cottage of Madame B. They waited expectantly. Then it happened. "At 9:25," Ochorowicz later wrote, "I saw a shadow appearing at the garden gate: it was she. I hid behind the corner in order to be able to hear without being seen."[1]

At first the woman paused at the gate and went back into the garden. Then at 9:30 she hurried out into the street and began to make her way unsteadily toward the house of Dr. Gibert. The four researchers followed as unobtrusively as possible. They could see she was obviously in a somnambulistic state. Finally she reached Gibert's house, entered, and hurried from room to room until she found him.

This was an experiment in long-distance hypnotic influence. Madame B., a person easily hypnotized, was the subject of many experiments arranged by Professor Pierre Janet and Dr. Gibert, a prominent physician of Le Havre. In these probes they were joined by F. W. H. Myers of the Society for Psychical Research, the physician A. T. Myers, Professor Ochorowicz of the University of Lvov, and M. Marillier of the French Psychological Society.

On this occasion the plan was that Dr. Gibert remain in his study and try to mentally summon Madame B. to leave her cottage and come see him. The cottage was about a kilometer from his house, and neither Madame B. nor any of the people living with her had been told that the experiment would take place. Gibert began issuing his mental commands at 8:55 p.m., and within half an hour she began her journey to his house. F. W. H. Myers wrote that out of twenty-five similar tests, nineteen were equally successful.[2]

This strange story tells of a kind of venture that meets with disapproval both from modern science and from the Vedic literature. The reasons tell us something interesting about both.

Let me begin by discussing how Dr. Gibert's experiment is seen by scientists.

We rarely hear much about people being able to influence others at a distance by mental commands. But many similar experiments have been performed. Here is another example from the late nineteenth century.

One Dr. Dufay was using hypnosis to treat Madame C. for periodic headaches and sickness that the usual medical treatments had failed to relieve. He found he was able to put her to sleep and awaken her by mental commands, sometimes at a distance.

On one occasion when called out of town, he arranged that Madame C.'s husband telegraph him when one of her headaches began and then report any later developments by a second telegram.

One morning at ten o'clock he received a telegram announcing that a headache had begun. So he mentally ordered the woman to sleep, and at four o'clock he ordered her to awaken. The husband telegraphed that she had gone to sleep at ten a.m. and awakened at four. The distance between Dr. Dufay and Madame C. was about 112 kilometers.[3]

Experiments of this kind fall within a field of study that early in the twentieth century was called psychical research and today is more often called parapsychology. This field deals with apparent powers of the human mind that are "paranormal," or hard to explain using accepted physical theories. Distant mental influence is a classic example of such a power.

How most scientists view parapsychology was recently summed up by Dr. James Alcock of Toronto's York University in the journal *Behavioral and Brain Sciences.* He wrote: "Although there has been over a century of formal empirical inquiry, parapsychologists have clearly failed to produce a single reliable demonstration of 'paranormal,' or 'psi,' phenomena. . . . Indeed, parapsychologists have not even succeeded in developing a reasonable definition of paranormal phenomena that does not involve, or imply, some aspect of mind-body dualism."[4]

Here Alcock brings up two important points. The first is that paranormal phenomena have not been reliably demonstrated. The experiments of Dr. Gibert and Dr. Dusart may indeed seem unreliable. They were rather loosely organized and didn't use the strict laboratory protocols we expect in scientific work. But many carefully planned tests of distant influence have been performed in laboratory settings.

For example, take the work done in the 1920s by Professor Leonid Vasiliev of the University of Leningrad. In one series of tests a subject named Fedorova would arrive at Vasiliev's laboratory at about 8 p.m. After about twenty minutes of rest and conversation, she would lie on a bed in a darkened chamber. She was told to keep squeezing a rubber balloon attached to an air tube as long as she was awake, and to stop squeezing it when she began to fall asleep. The air tube was hooked up to an apparatus in the next room that recorded when she would fall asleep and wake up. While in the darkened room, she had no further contact with the experimenters.

When Fedorova entered the room, the experimenter who had been talking with her would signal a colleague, called the sender, who was waiting two rooms away. The sender would then climb into a special lead-lined chamber and open a letter prepared in advance and not yet read by the subject, by the sender, or by the other experimenter. This letter would instruct the sender to do one of three things: (1) stay within the lead-lined chamber and mentally order the subject to go to sleep, (2) stand with his head outside the chamber and issue the same mental commands, or (3) stand with his head outside the chamber and make no commands.

To show the kind of results Vasiliev obtained, here is a list (on the right) of how long it took the subject to go to sleep in twenty-nine runs of this test.[5] The times are in minutes and seconds.

With no mental commands, the average time for the subject to go to sleep comes to 7 minutes and 24 seconds. In contrast, when commands were given inside the chamber the time averaged 4 minutes and 43 seconds. When the commands were issued outside the chamber, the time was 4 minutes and 13 seconds.

It seems the subject was falling asleep faster when a person two rooms away was mentally ordering her to do so.

Vasiliev ran many other carefully organized experiments of this

TIME TO GO TO SLEEP		
without mental suggestion	with mental suggestion from inside chamber	with mental suggestion from outside chamber
7:10	5:10	3:50
4:15	1:25	2:15
4:20	3:40	10:00
8:10	3:40	4:00
6:10	3:55	4:30
14:10	3:15	1:05
6:10	3:05	
7:10	11:00	
6:50	7:35	
14:00		
4:05		

kind, and he reported similar results. In one successful test, mental commands for sleeping and waking were even sent from Sebastopol to Leningrad, a distance of 1,700 kilometers.

Such research, of course, is rejected by scientists like Alcock. The methodology, they will argue, is flawed. In Vasiliev's experiment, neither the subject nor the persons talking with her should know whether a command to sleep will be given. But how do we know that this condition was met? The experimenter talking with the subject might have learned what was in the envelope and cued the subject, either deliberately or inadvertently. This might have influenced how fast the subject fell asleep. Or the subject might have cheated by pretending to doze off faster when the command to sleep was given.

Many scientists will insist that results such as those of Vasiliev must be tossed aside unless the work is iron-clad against fraud. Yet many scientific experiments less cautious of fraud are accepted. Why the stricter standard for parapsychology?

Here we come to Alcock's second point—that paranormal phenomena imply some kind of mind-body dualism.

When Vasiliev started his experiments, he argued that distant transmission of influences from one person to another must work through electromagnetic waves. It must be a kind of radio, in which one brain sends signals to another.

As long as Vasiliev was able to argue this, his research was accepted and funded in the Soviet Union. But his experimental findings soon ruled out the radio hypothesis. For example, with the subject Fedorova the average time before sleep was the same whether the mental commands were sent within the lead-lined chamber or outside it. The chamber was designed to block radio waves, but it seemed to do nothing to halt mental signals.

These and other findings convinced Vasiliev that known forms of radiant energy were not involved in transmitting mental commands. But as soon as this became known, the support for Vasiliev's work was cut off, and remote mental influence was officially condemned in the Soviet Union as "an antisocial idealist fiction about man's supernatural power to perceive phenomena which, considering the time and place, cannot be perceived."[6]

Here too in the West, scientists reject the idea that the mind can do things that violate the known laws of physics. To them, such phenomena must be miracles, and they follow the philosopher David Hume in saying, "No testimony is sufficient to establish a miracle, unless the testimony be of such a kind that its falsehood would be more miraculous, than the fact which it endeavors to establish."[7] Since there is nothing miraculous about fraud, scientists still prefer it as the proper answer for anomalous parapsychological data.

Now, turning from modern science to the Vedic literature, we find a different outlook on the oddities we've been discussing.

According to the *Śrīmad-Bhāgavatam,* there are eight primary *siddhis,* or mystic powers. These ultimately come from the potency of Kṛṣṇa, and since all living beings are Kṛṣṇa's parts and parcels, living beings are potentially able to manifest these powers to a minute degree. From the Vedic point of view, this is completely natural and not at all miraculous.

One of the eight *siddhis,* called *vaśitā,* is described by Śrīla Prabhupāda as follows:

"By this perfection one can bring anyone under his control. This is a kind of hypnotism which is almost irresistible. Sometimes it is found that a yogi who may have attained a little perfection in this *vaśitā* mystic power comes out among the people and speaks all sorts of nonsense, controls their minds, exploits them, takes their money, and then goes away."[8]

This power is similar to the power of distant mental influence studied by Vasiliev and others. But here we find that the natural hypnotic power they studied can, it seems, be made stronger by appropriate techniques of yoga.

The point that yogis who acquire the *vaśitā siddhi* often use it to cheat people fits well with at least one idea of modern science. Scientists tend to think that people claiming this power are mostly cheaters, and the Vedic view agrees. Many psychics use their abilities, alleged or real, to separate foolish people from their money, and this gives a bad name both to psychics and to paranormal phenomena in general.

This brings us to an important Vedic point about the mystic *siddhis*. In the *Uddhava-gītā* section of *Śrīmad-Bhāgavatam* (11.15.33), Kṛṣṇa says, "Learned experts in devotional service state that the mystic perfections of yoga I have mentioned are impediments and a waste of time for one practicing the supreme yoga, by which one achieves all perfection in life directly from Me."

Thus scientists and great devotees both regard mystic *siddhis* as undesirable. For scientists they distract people from "scientific truth," and for devotees they distract one from the path of service to the Supreme Personality of Godhead.

REFERENCES

1. Vasiliev, L. L., 1963, *Experiments in Distant Influence*, London: Wildwood House, p. 211.
2. Vasiliev, p. 213.
3. Myers, F. W. H., 1961, *Human Personality and its Survival of Bodily Death*, New York: University Books, Inc., p. 145.
4. Alcock, James E., 1987, "Parapsychology: Science of the anomalous or search for the soul?" *Behavioral and Brain Science,* p. 553.

5. Vasiliev, p. 144.
6. Vasiliev, pp. xviii, xxiii.
7. Hume, David, 1966, 2nd edition, *Enquiries Concerning the Human Understanding and Concerning the Principles of Morals,* Oxford: Clarendon Press, pp. 115–116.
8. Bhaktivedanta Swami Prabhupada, A. C., 1982, *The Nectar of Devotion,* Los Angeles: The Bhaktivedanta Book Trust, p. 12.

13

Consciousness and The "New Physics"

Although quantum mechanics has been around since before World War II, many scientists refer to it as the new physics. They suggest that it conveys deep insights into the nature of consciousness, insights that confirm the mystical teachings of yogis and herald a new age of enhanced awareness.

But does quantum mechanics (or QM) truly reveal anything about consciousness and its role in nature? A close look at the theory shows that it doesn't. Attempts to analyze the role of "the observer" in QM show that the theory is plagued with persistent conceptual problems. And when we try to bring consciousness into the picture, those problems simply get worse.

To see why this is so, let's consider an idealized experiment, the simple "delayed-choice split-beam experiment" proposed by physicist John Wheeler. As shown in the figure on the next page, this experiment involves a light source, **S**, that fires single photons of light at a half-silvered mirror, **A**. This mirror divides the light equally into two beams, which then reflect from two fully reflective mirrors, **B** and **C**. The two beams mix at a second half-silvered mirror, **D**.

Two photodetectors, **E** and **F**, are mounted on a sliding base so they can be placed in position **(1)** or **(2)**. In position **(1)** the two detectors respond to the light after the beams mix at **D**. With strong monochromatic light, the detectors seem to register the effects of light-wave interference between the two beams. The same thing happens when the light is so weak that photons emerge from the source only one at a time: let many successive photons go through, and one photodetector will count significantly more photon hits than the other. We account for the difference in hitting rates by assuming that each photon splits into two waves, which interfere with one another at **D**.

When placed in position **(2)**, the two photodetectors reveal a curious phenomenon. After a photon emerges from the source, either **E** registers a hit or **F** registers a hit, but not both. So in this arrangement it appears that the photons do not split. Either a photon follows the right-hand path (**SABE**) and hits photodetector **E**, or it follows the left-hand path (**SACF**) and hits detector **F**. We never see both **E** and **F** responding to the same photon.

If this is true, it means the photons are arriving one at a time. How then could they build up an interference pattern at **D**? Interference requires two waves to interfere, and surely this is not possible if the photons must approach **D** one by one, by one path or the other. It seems, then, that QM is saying contradictory things about how the photons behave.

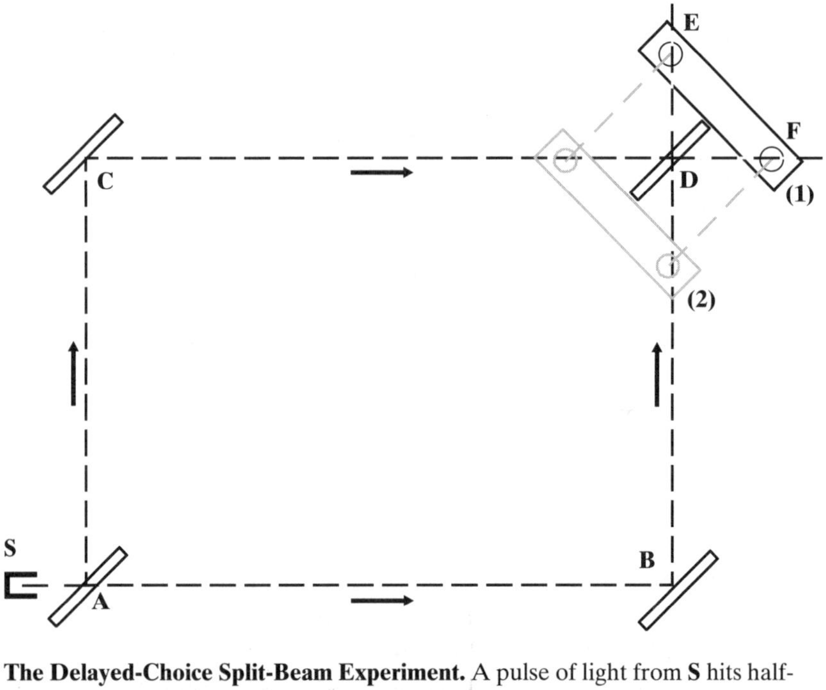

The Delayed-Choice Split-Beam Experiment. A pulse of light from **S** hits half-silvered mirror **A** and splits into two beams, which reflect from fully reflecting mirrors **B** and **C**. Photodetectors **E** and **F** can be placed in position **(1)** or **(2)**. In position **(1)** they record what happens after the beams recombine at **D**, a half-silvered mirror. In position **(2)** they record the beams before they reach **D**.

Niels Bohr, a pioneer quantum physicist, resolved that problem by saying this: If the detectors are in position **(1)** they respond only to light coming through **D**, the two beams interfering with one another. The detectors don't tell us that each photon must follow only one of the two paths. And if the detectors are in position **(2)** they block the photons from reaching **D**, and therefore we see no split photons interfering. So we can suppose that in arrangement **(1)** the photon seems to split but in arrangement **(2)** it doesn't. Bohr concluded that whether or not the photon seems to split depends on how we set up the observational apparatus. What we are prepared to observe affects what seems to happen.

Wheeler made Bohr's interpretation more striking by noting that one may position the photodetectors *after* the photon has left mirror **A**, which splits the beam. We might think that at this point either the photon has split or it has followed one of the two paths, through **B** or **C**.

According to Wheeler's analysis, whether we see interference or see photons coming on separate paths still depends on the position chosen for the photodetectors.

Does this mean that the photon has split or stayed single as a consequence of a choice made later? Wheeler says no. He concludes, "No phenomenon is a phenomenon until it is an observed phenomenon." In other words, one can't say anything about the photon before the observation, which, so to speak, brings the observed phenomenon into existence. Wheeler generalizes on this by saying, "The universe does not 'exist, out there.' . . . It is in some strange sense a participatory universe."

Introducing Consciousness

Now, this might seem to tell us something profound about consciousness. It might seem to suggest that consciousness somehow plays a crucial role in the phenomena of nature.

But this is not the case. First of all, what is an "observer" in QM? In every case the observer is a *physical* device. Here the observer is a photodetector, which might consist of a photographic plate, an electronic photocell, or even the retina of someone's eye. Wheeler's analysis doesn't mention whether or not a conscious human being ever becomes aware of what the photodetectors are doing. We don't think of a photodetector itself as conscious (even when it is a retina), and in analyzing the experiment the idea of consciousness plays no role. The strange phenomena predicted by Wheeler's theory tell us nothing about consciousness.

Still, some physicists have tried to introduce consciousness into their analysis of quantum mechanical experiments. For example, John von Neumann suggested that the time when a phenomenon becomes an observed phenomenon can be delayed until the experimental data is perceived by the "abstract ego" of the human observer. It almost seems as though von Neumann's analysis of quantum phenomena has led him to posit a nonphysical soul.

But von Neumann's line of thought requires him to postulate that detectors **E** and **F** in position **(2)** go into a kind of schizoid state in which **E** fires but not **F**, and **F** fires but not **E**. Furthermore, the brain of the human observer must go into a state in which it registers **E** firing but not **F**, and **F** firing but not **E**.

This is the unsatisfactory state of affairs that Erwin Schrṭdinger discussed in his "cat paradox," in which quantum phenomena give rise to a cat that is simultaneously dead and alive. Wheeler avoids this problem by cutting short his analysis at the photodetectors and not bringing consciousness into the picture.

What happens if we try to introduce a universal observer—the Supersoul as described in *Bhagavad-gītā*? One might think that since the Supersoul is all-seeing, He must know whether the photon splits at mirror **A** or follows the path to **B** or **C** without splitting. But if quantum mechanics is correct, what the Supersoul sees must conform to the observations allowed by the arrangement of the physical detectors. According to QM, a phenomenon is not a phenomenon until physical devices "observe" it. If we posit a nonphysical observer who can see things independently of the physical apparatus, we get into trouble with the quantum theory.

A Deeper Theory of Nature

So what can we say about quantum mechanics and consciousness? Even though QM has an excellent record of accurately predicting certain physical phenomena, it is a physical theory afflicted by serious conceptual difficulties. I would propose that QM is not a fully correct description of physical reality, and a better theory may eventually replace it. Wheeler declares that he is sticking with the standard quantum theory because it is "battle-tested." But classical mechanics is also battle-tested, and in the late nineteenth century many expert physicists thought it was approaching perfection. Then, in the twentieth century, physics was revolutionized, first by relativity theory and then by quantum mechanics.

A great deal of evidence points to the existence of phenomena contrary to what quantum mechanics predicts. For example, many experiments show that the will of a human observer can influence physical events without the aid of physical actions initiated by the human body. A group of researchers headed by Robert Jahn of Princeton University has performed many experiments of this kind. The findings of this group contradict the predictions of the standard quantum theory, and I can attest from my own analysis that they deserve to be taken seriously.

The Jahn experiments involve small effects observable only by careful statistical analysis. Other reported phenomena, however, strongly violate the known laws of physics. For example, Ian Stevenson has accumulated and carefully analyzed a large body of data suggesting that a child will sometimes accurately remember events that took place in the life of a particular deceased person. These data are consistent with the idea of reincarnation, and by the known laws of physics they are unexplainable. Like the Princeton results, they also directly involve human consciousness.

I suggest we look forward to the unfolding of a deeper theory of nature, one that goes beyond QM, just as QM goes beyond classical physics. Consciousness and phenomena directly involving consciousness should play an integral role in this genuinely new physics. Only with such a theory shall we truly be able to understand in what sense we live in a "participatory universe."

EVOLUTION

14

Primordial Alphabet Soup

"Thirty-eight years ago what is arguably the greatest mystery ever puzzled over by scientists—the origin of life—seemed virtually solved by a single simple experiment." This is how the February 1991 issue of *Scientific American* begins a review of theories of the origin of life.[1]

The simple experiment, carried out by a University of Chicago graduate student named Stanley Miller, involved placing a mixture of methane, ammonia, hydrogen, and water in a sealed flask and zapping it with electrical sparks. The result was a tarry goo containing amino acids, the building blocks of the proteins found in living organisms.

To Miller it seemed but a few inevitable evolutionary steps from this primordial soup of water and biomolecules to the first living organisms. And from that day, college science students have been taught that science has explained life's origin. Indeed, many students are under the impression that life itself has been synthesized in a test tube. Unfortunately, as the article in *Scientific American* points out, scientists are far from understanding life's origins.

First of all, some scientists have argued that the conditions on the primordial earth would have been unsuitable for amino acids to form in. Miller's theory calls for a reducing atmosphere rich in hydrogen-based gases such as methane and ammonia. But the primordial atmosphere, some say, consisted mainly of nitrogen and carbon dioxide, so that the raw materials for amino acids and other small biological molecules would have been missing. In fact, scientists can only guess about what the earth was like billions of years ago, and the guesses they make can agree or disagree with Miller's theory.

Let's suppose, for the sake of argument, that amino acids would have formed on the primordial earth. And let's suppose they would have piled up with other simple biological molecules without being naturally destroyed or dispersed. We'd then run into another problem: Although the rules for chemical bonding may allow simple biological molecules to form, these same rules don't guarantee that the higher forms of organization found in living organisms will arise.

We can illustrate this by a simple example. We all know the story of the monkeys that randomly hit typewriter keys and by chance write Shakespeare's plays. Monkeys who strike keys completely at random are unlikely even to come up with English words, apart from short words like *is* or *at.* But we can improve on the monkeys' performance by introducing a simple rule.

Here's how the rule works. If a monkey has just typed *th,* we require that the next letter be fit for an English word including *th.* For example, the next letter might be *e,* forming the word *the,* or it might be *r,* since *thr* appears in *throw.* But the letter couldn't be *q* or *x,* since *thq* and *thx* don't come up in English words. By this rule, the monkey always randomly chooses a letter that in English could follow the last two letters he typed.

Another part of our rule is this: we instruct the monkey that the more often a letter appears in English after the two he has just typed, the more he should tend to choose it. For example, *e* follows *th* more often than *r* does, so after *th* the monkey is more likely to choose *e* than *r.* (We also let the monkey choose spaces, commas, and periods along with the twenty-six letters of the alphabet.)

You can think of this rule as an imitation of chemical bonding. An *e* or *r* can bond to *th,* but *q* or *z* can't. Allowing the monkey to type sequences of letters by this rule is like letting molecules form in a primordial soup by the rules of chemical bonding. I compiled a table of allowed three-letter combinations (letter-triples) by running an essay of mine, on Vedic astronomy, through a computer. Then I programmed the computer to generate sequences of letters

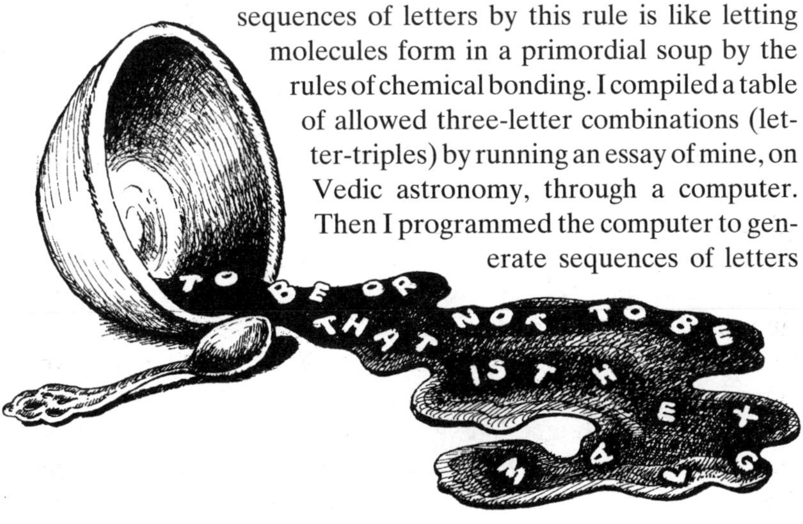

according to the resulting rule. I call these sequences of letters "sentences," even though they're generally not punctuated properly. Here's an example:

"To the local thers an ut once scorpith ese, ar and astar. The ma, wers a godern the sky srittailis othicein volumn of the onsmilky way, thears"

Evolutionists, this seems promising. The computer-monkey is coming up with many English words, and some even seem to convey a faint glimmer of meaning. One can imagine that in just a few evolutionary steps the computer will begin to express profound thoughts—with impeccable English grammar.

But unfortunately if we read a few pages of this stuff we find no signs of emerging complex order. We find short English words, often relating to astronomy, since the letter-bonding rule comes from such words. But there are no signs of the more complex order needed for the grammatical expression of thoughts. In the bonding rule, the information for these complex patterns is simply not there.

Biological chemistry puts before us a similar problem. By the rules of chemical bonding, atoms of hydrogen, oxygen, carbon, and nitrogen will tend to form amino acids and similar compounds under appropriate conditions. But these rules are not enough to bring together the highly complex structures found in even the simplest living cells.

Of course, our rule for generating letter sequences doesn't take into account Darwinian evolution by mutation and natural selection. Many scientists regard this process as essential for the development of complex order. So it's not surprising, one might say, that our simple rule cannot produce such order.

But the simple forming of molecules by chemical bonding in a primordial soup also doesn't involve Darwinian evolution. Darwinian evolution calls for a self-reproducing system of molecules. Indeed, one of the main tasks of origin-of-life theories is to explain how the first self-reproducing system arose.

In living organisms, self-reproduction is a dauntingly complex process involving proteins, deoxyribonucleic-acid (DNA) and ribonucleic acid (RNA). If Darwinian evolution can't take place until such a complex system is operating, scientists are at a loss to explain how that complex system has come about.

The only hope has been to suppose that the first self-reproducing system was much simpler than the simplest of today's living cells. If somehow a single molecule could reproduce itself under suitable conditions, then perhaps it could evolve, develop liaisons with other molecules, and eventually give rise to the kind of organisms that exist today.

One of the most popular scenarios for a self-reproducing molecule has been the so-called "RNA-world." The idea is that an RNA molecule might be able to catalyze its own replication and so be able to evolve in a Darwinian manner. It has been shown that RNA molecules can act as enzymes that act on other RNA molecules. And Manfred Eigen of the Max Planck Institute has shown that RNA molecules reproducing under the influence of *modern* cellular enzymes can undergo a process of Darwinian evolution.

But the RNA-world models have problems. One is that RNA would seem unlikely to form on the prebiotic primordial earth. Another is that RNA cannot readily make new copies of itself in the laboratory without a great deal of help from scientists. (For one thing, RNA replication calls for pure conditions that can be provided in a laboratory but would not be expected in nature.)

Still, let's suppose that a self-reproducing molecule (which might or might not be RNA) did arise on the primordial earth. What might we expect it to evolve into? To gain some insight into this, I introduced evolution into the computer-monkey model.

Darwinian evolution rests on the idea of survival of the fittest, or natural selection. So I defined the fitness of a monkey-generated "sentence" by looking at how often the letter-triples of that sentence appear in English. If a sentence has many frequent triples (like *the* or *ing*), it has high fitness; if it has few, it has low fitness. So if we replace infrequent or nonexistent triples (like *inz*) with common ones (like *ing*), we increase the sentence's fitness. Essentially, the closer a sentence gets to a real English sentence, the more fit it is.

I used survival of the fittest to simulate how evolution might take place in a population of twenty monkey-generated sentences. For a sentence to "give birth," I would simply add to the population a copy of the sentence that might differ by one letter. The copy would be the offspring, and the differing letter would correspond to a random mutation.

I divided time into generations. During each generation, the ten fittest sentences in the population would each give birth to ten offspring. At the same time, I cruelly killed off the ten sentences of least fitness, so that the fit sentences multiplied at the expense of the less fit ones. This was survival of the fittest.

I began with a population of twenty copies of the sentence "godern the sky srittailis othicein volumn of the onsmilky way," generated by the letter-bonding rule. Here is how the fittest sentence in the population changed at intervals of 200 generations:

> godern the sky srittailis othicein volumn of the onsmilky way,
> zodur, the sky mriquat isuothyzet, volum, of the oesmilky way,
> zodur. the sky wriqua. isuothyzed, volums of the oesmilky way.
> zodur. the sky wriqua. invothyzed. volums of the oesmilky way.
> zodur. the lky wriqua, unvothyzed. volums of theboesmilky way.
> zodur. the lky wriqua, anvothyzed. volums of theboesmilky way.

We see that the sentence is indeed evolving. But unfortunately it's not evolving into anything meaningful. This process of evolution is simply not able to generate the complex patterns of actual English speech.

My point is this: Assuming that self-replicating molecules could exist on a primordial earth, where can we expect their evolution to go? Nowhere meaningful. Such molecules may indeed evolve and grow molecularly more fit, but there is no reason to think they will evolve into living cells.

Molecular fitness will have something to do with how strongly a molecule's bonds hold it together and how well the molecule can catalyze its own replication. This kind of fitness may increase through Darwinian evolution. But there's no reason to think that anything will ever emerge from this, other than modified self-replicating molecules of the same type. There's no reason to suppose that the self-reproducing molecules will ever give rise to something completely different, such as an elaborate system of reproductive machinery based on DNA, RNA, enzymes, and the famous genetic code.

My purpose in giving these examples from sequences of letters is not to claim they *prove* anything about the origin of life. Rather, I'm simply illustrating some of the obstacles that theories of life's origin face. We can talk about these obstacles in purely chemical terms. Such discussions are necessarily technical.

So, again, here are the two obstacles we have discussed: (1) Natural rules for bonding between atoms may give rise to simple biological molecules under special circumstances (as in Miller's experiment), but they can't give rise to the complex structures needed for organisms to grow and reproduce. (2) If some hypothetical molecules were able to jump start their own replication, they might evolve by Darwinian natural selection and random variation. But no one has given any solid reason to suppose they would evolve into anything more than better self-replicating molecules. And, of course, it has not been shown that prebiotic molecular self-replication could happen.

In the thirty-eight years since Miller's famous experiment, scientists have come up with many complicated theories about how life might have originated, but they have failed to overcome these and other fundamental obstacles. Miller himself tends to disapprove of the futile speculations of the theorists. He argues that what the origin-of-life field needs is good experiments that actually demonstrate how life got started. But such experiments are not easy to devise. "I come up with a dozen ideas a day," Miller says, pausing to reflect, "and I usually discard the whole dozen."[2]

REFERENCES

1. Horgan, J., 1991, "In the Beginning . . . ," *Scientific American*, February, p. 117.
2. Horgan, p. 125.

15

Was There an Eve?

In a 1987 article in the prestigious journal *Nature,* three biochemists published a study of mitochondrial DNAs from 147 people living on five continents. The biochemists stated, "All these mitochondrial DNAs stem from one woman who is postulated to have lived about 200,000 years ago, probably in Africa."[1]

The story became a sensation. The woman was called the African Eve, and *Newsweek* put her on its cover. There she was—the single ancestor of all living human beings.

Eve was one in a population of primitive human beings. But all human lineages not deriving from her have perished. For students of human evolution, one important implication of this finding was that Asian populations of *Homo erectus,* including the famous Peking ape men, must not have been among our ancestors. Those ape men couldn't have descended from Eve, it was thought, because they lived in Asia before 200,000 years ago.

Mitochondrial DNA (mtDNA) carries genetic instructions for the energy-making factories of human cells. Unlike other genetic material, it is transmitted to offspring only from the mother, with no contribution from the father. This means that the descent of mtDNA makes a simple branching tree that is easy to study.

Computer studies on the sample of 147 people (who represent the world population) show that the original ancestral trunk divided into two branches. Only Africans descended from one branch. The rest of the population, as well as some Africans, descended from the other. The inference was that the stem was African. In 1991 another analysis of exact mtDNA sequences from 189 people confirmed this and indicated that Eve was roughly our ten-thousandth great-grandmother.

The Fall of Eve

Unfortunately, however, Eve quickly fell down. In 1992 the geneticist Alan Templeton of Washington University stated in the journal *Science,* “The inference that the tree of humankind is rooted in Africa is not supported by the data.”[2] It seems that the African Eve theory evolved from errors in computer analysis.

The ancestral trees had been drawn from mtDNA sequences through what is called the principle of parsimony. The figure below gives a rough idea of how this was done. To create the figure, I used sequences of four letters to stand for the genetic information in mtDNA. In (1) I started with *abcd* as the original ancestor, and by making single changes, or mutations, I produced descendants *avcd* and *abud.* Then from *avcd* I got two more descendants, *avcn* and *rvcd,* again by single mutations.

Let’s suppose we are given the sequences *avcn, rvcd,* and *abud* and we are asked to deduce their ancestry. How would we go about this? The method used by the scientists studying mtDNA was to say that ancestors and descendants should be as similar as possible. One way to measure how similar they are is to count the number of mutations from ancestor to descendant in the tree of descent. A tree with few mutations shows high similarity, so it is a good candidate for the real ancestral tree. Such a tree is said to be parsimonious.

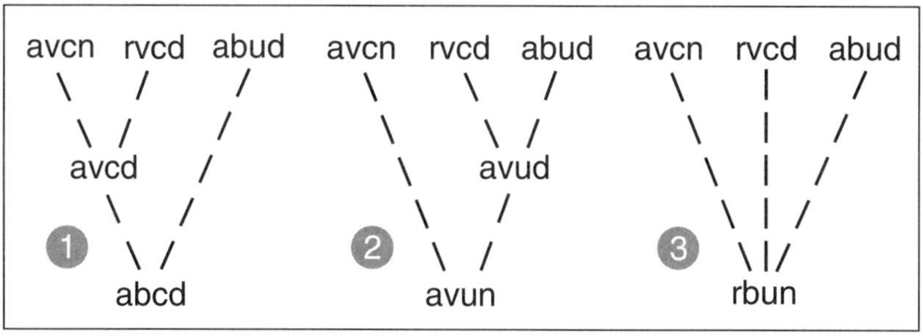

Examples of Evolutionary Trees. Tree 1 represents the evolution of a gene sequence. Each change from one letter to another represents a mutation. Trees 2 and 3 show other possible evolutionary histories yielding the same results. (The bottom row is the gene sequences before evolution; the top is after.) Such are the ambiguities involved in figuring out evolutionary histories from existing gene sequences. (See text).

For example, tree (1) has four mutations, and tree (3) has eight. Scientists would argue that (1) is therefore more likely to resemble the real ancestral tree. This seems promising, since in this case tree (1) is in fact the real tree. But tree (2) requires five mutations, and so it is nearly as parsimonious. Yet (2) shows a completely different pattern of ancestors.

The problem with the parsimonious tree method is that in a complex case there are literally millions of trees that are equally parsimonious. Searching through them all on a main-frame computer can take months. According to Templeton, the original findings on African Eve came from computer runs that missed important trees. When further runs were made, a tree with African roots turned out no more likely than one with European or Asian roots.

The parsimonious tree method rests on the idea that similar organisms should share close common ancestors, and less similar organisms more distant ones. This idea is the central motivating concept behind the theory of evolution. Since the span of recorded human history is too short to show evolutionary changes that mean very much, evolutionists are forced to reconstruct the history of living species by comparing likenesses and differences in living and fossil organisms.

For example, man and ape are said to share a close common ancestor because man and ape are very similar. In the late nineteenth century there was a famous debate between the anatomists Thomas Huxley and Richard Owen over whether or not human beings were cousins of apes. Owen maintained that they weren't, because a feature of the human brain, the hippocampus major, was not found in the brains of apes. But Huxley won the debate by showing that apes really do have a hippocampus major. Before triumphantly presenting his evidence for this to the British Association of Science, Huxley had written to his wife, "By next Friday evening they will all be convinced that they are monkeys."[3]

Why Man and Ape Are Similar

Of course, man and ape really are similar. So if they don't descend from a close common ancestor, how can one account for this? Biblical creationists propose that God created man and ape separately by divine decree. To many scientists this story seems unsatisfactory. The geneticist Francisco Ayala indicated why in a discussion of the close likenesses between human beings and chimpanzees. He remarked, "These creationists are implying God is a cheat, making things look identical when they are not. I consider that to be blasphemous."[4] In other words, why would God fake a record of apparent historical change?

To illustrate the idea behind Ayala's comment, consider the legs of mammals. In all known land mammals the leg bones are homologous, or similar in form. Thus all mammals have a recognizable thigh bone, shin bone, and so on. Now imagine that genetic engineering becomes highly perfected. A genetic engineer might want to create an animal with legs suitable for a particular environment. But would he do this by simply modifying the shapes of the standard mammalian leg bones to make another typical mammalian leg? Why not create a whole new set of bones suitable for the task at hand? And if human engineers might do this, why not God? The answer that God's will is inscrutable doesn't sit well with many scientists.

It is certainly not possible to second guess the will of God. But the Vedic literature offers an account of the origin of species that explains the patterns of similarity among living organisms. According to the *Śrīmad-Bhāgavatam,* living beings have descended, with modification, from an original created being. All species, therefore, are linked by a family tree of ancestors and descendants. Forms sharing similar features inherit those features from ancestral forms that had them. So the theory given in the *Bhāgavatam* accounts for the likenesses and differences between species in a way comparable to that of the theory of evolution.

But these two theories are not the same. The neo-Darwinian theory of evolution says that species descended from primitive one-celled organisms and gradually developed into forms more and more complex. In contrast, the *Bhāgavatam* says that Brahmā, the original created being, is superhuman. Brahmā generated beings called *prajāpatis,* who are inferior to him. These in turn produced generations of lesser beings, culminating in plants, animals, and human beings as we know them. From the *prajāpatis* on down, these successive generations generally came into being by sexual reproduction.

The theory of evolution says that species have emerged by mutation and natural selection, with no intelligent guidance. But the *Bhāgavatam* maintains that the entire process of generating species is planned in detail by God.

Intelligent Designer

This point brings us back to the question why species should be linked by patterns of homology.

Several points can be made. The first is that a genetic engineer designing one special-purpose mammal might find it convenient to introduce one special design. But if he wanted to create an entire ecosystem of interacting organisms, he might want to do it with a general scheme in which he could produce different types of organisms by modifying standard plans. So a standard mammalian plan could be used as the starting point for producing various mammals, and similar plans could be used for birds, fish, and so on. It would be most efficient to organize these plans into a parsimonious tree to make short the design work needed.

This idea can overcome one of the drawbacks of the theory of evolution. Many living organisms have complex structures that evolutionists have a hard time accounting for by mutations and natural selection. Observed intermediate forms linking organisms that have these structures to those that don't are notoriously lacking. Evolutionists have often found it hard to imagine convincing possibilities for what these intermediate forms might be. But the structures are easy to account for if we posit an intelligent designer.

To illustrate this point, consider the problem of writing computer programs. A programmer will often write a new program by taking an old one and modifying it. After doing this for a while, he winds up producing a family tree of programs. But the changes required to go from one program to the next are often extensive. They're not the kind you'd be likely to get by randomly zapping the first program with mutations and waiting to get a new program that operates in the required way.

The point could be made, however, that a finite human engineer may need efficient design methods but God is unlimited and does not need them. Why then should He use them? We can't second guess

God, but a possible answer is waiting for us to consider in the *Bhāgavatam* (2.1.36). There Kṛṣṇa, the Supreme Personality of Godhead, is celebrated as the topmost artist:

> Varieties of birds are indications of His masterful artistic sense. Manu, the father of mankind, is the emblem of His standard intelligence, and humanity is His residence. The celestial species of human beings, like the Gandharvas, Vidyādharas, Cāraṇas, and Apsarās, all represent His musical rhythm, and the demoniac soldiers are representations of His wonderful prowess.

Orderly patterns of design are also natural in artistic works. Just as Bach dexterously combines and modifies different themes in his fugues, so the Supreme Artist may orchestrate the world of life in a way that shows order, parsimony, and luxuriant novelty of form. The patterns of parsimonious change follow naturally from the procreation of species. The novelty flows from Kṛṣṇa's creative intelligence and cannot be accounted for by neo-Darwinian theory.

Subtle Energies

This brings us to our last point. The life forms descending from Brahmā include many species unknown to us. The higher species, beginning with Brahmā himself, have bodies made mostly of subtle types of energy distinct from the energies studied in modern physics. Manu, the Gandharvas, and the Vidyādharas are examples of such beings.

We may speak of the energies studied by modern physics as gross matter. The bodies of ordinary human beings, animals, and plants are all made of this type of matter. If they have descended from beings with bodies made of subtle energy, then there must be a process of transformation whereby gross forms are generated from subtle. Such a process, the *Bhāgavatam* says, does in fact exist.

So the *Bhāgavatam's* explanation of the origin of species makes the following two predictions: (1) There should exist subtly embodied beings that include the precursors of grossly embodied organisms, and (2) there should be a process of generating gross form from subtle form. It would be interesting to see if there is any empirical evidence that might corroborate these predictions.

REFERENCES

1. Cann, R., Stoneking, M., and Wilson, A., 1987, "Mitochondial DNA and Human Evolution," *Nature,* Vol. 325, January 1.
2. Begley, S., 1992, "Eve Takes Another Fall," *Newsweek,* March 1..
3. Wendt, 1972, p. 71.
4. Davis, J., 1980, "Blow to Creation Myth," *Omni,* August.

16

The Seeds of Reason

In the mid-nineteenth century Charles Darwin corresponded regularly with Asa Gray, a Harvard professor of botany who was an evangelical Christian. Gray was dedicated to scientific empiricism, but in those days he opposed the idea of the evolutionary transformation of species. He held the traditional view that God had individually designed and created the bodily forms of living organisms.

For some time, Darwin tried to break down Gray's resistance. For example, in 1860 Darwin wrote to Gray:

> I see a bird which I want for food, take my gun and kill it. I do this designedly. An innocent and good man stands under a tree and is killed by a flash of lightning. Do you believe (and I really should like to hear) that God designedly killed this man? Many or most persons do believe this; I can't and don't. If you believe so, do you believe that when a swallow snaps up a gnat, that God designed that that particular swallow should snap up that particular gnat at that particular instant? I believe that man and the gnat are in the same predicament. If the death of neither man nor gnat are designed, I see no good reason to believe that their first birth or production should be necessarily designed.[1]

Gray was quickly persuaded by Darwin's thesis that species evolve, but in spite of many powerful arguments like this one, he stuck to the idea of divine design. He would argue that species might evolve by Darwin's process of natural selection but God must somehow guide the process. In fact, even Darwin himself was swayed by Gray's arguments. Once he reprinted one of Gray's reviews of his theory at his own expense, and across the top he printed the slogan "Natural Selection not Inconsistent with Natural Theology."

Guided Evolution Rejected

Darwin soon rejected Gray's method of harmonizing evolution with theology, and so did many mainstream Christian scientists. As David Livingstone put it in his history of the Christian response to Darwinism, "Christians were soon to abandon this version [of Asa Gray] in favor of a more holistic design located in the regularity of natural law."[2] In other words, instead of guiding nature organism by organism to bring forth specific designs, God designed the laws of physics in such a way that all organisms would emerge automatically by Darwinian evolution.

The reason for abandoning Gray's guided evolution is this: The laws of physics (in Darwin's time and now) do not allow for some nonphysical agent to manipulate the course of events. Therefore, if God were to guide the natural processes to come up with particular species one by one, He would violate the laws of physics.

Gray argued in favor of evolution by saying, "If the alternative be the immediate origination out of nothing, or out of the soil, of the human form with all its actual marks, there can be no doubt which side a scientific man will take."[3] The scientist will certainly prefer a process of evolution that follows the course of nature. But if occasional big violations of the laws of physics are to be rejected, why accept large numbers of small violations? Thus the scientist who accepts Gray's argument for evolution is likely to opt eventually for a fully naturalistic evolutionary process that does not violate the laws of physics at all.

For Christian theologians, this choice is not hard to justify. This was demonstrated by George Frederick Wright, a geologist, evangelical minister, and friend of Asa Gray. Wright rejected guided evolution, and he used the doctrines of Calvinism to argue that God is concerned only with the ultimate cause of creation—the laws of nature. Wright was able to satisfy physical scientists and Darwinian evolutionists by asserting that Darwinism was "the Calvinistic interpretation of nature."

Creative Seeds

Of course, the real laws of nature may differ from the laws of physics. In Chapter 3 I pointed out that the Vedic literature clearly supports this view. Since no scientist has ever shown that all natural phenomena obey known physical laws, students of science and religion might be wise to seek alternatives to using physics as the basis for understanding God's role in nature. I would therefore like to describe in more detail the Vedic version of the creation of living species.

To do this, let me return to another topic mentioned in Chapter 3—Saint Augustine's idea of "seed principles." According to Augustine, at the moment of creation God planted in nature *rationes seminales,* or "rational seeds." In due course of time, these seeds produced the forms of living beings by a natural process of unfolding. The rational seeds cannot be directly perceived by human senses, but each seed contains the potential for manifesting a specific gross form. According to the Catholic philosopher Frederick Copleston, the idea of the rational seeds did not come from Christian scripture or tradition. Augustine got the idea from the pagan philosopher Plotinus, and ultimately it came from the Stoics.[4]

Some scientists say that Augustine's theory foreshadows the modern idea that the laws of physics unfold the development of species through Darwinian evolution. These scientists suggest that the physical laws can thereby be regarded as "seed principles" of creation. This is certainly not what Augustine had in mind, but Augustine's idea does turn out to be strikingly similar to the concept of divine creation presented in the Vedic literature.

According to the Vedic conception, Kṛṣṇa brings about creation by investing His potency in seed forms called *bījas.* This idea is illustrated by the following passage from a lecture on the *Śrīmad-Bhāgavatam* given by Śrīla Prabhupāda in 1972:

> Kṛṣṇa's energy is so powerful that He puts the potency in a seed. *Bījaṁ māṁ sarva-bhūtānām,* Kṛṣṇa says. *Bīja* means "seed." "For whatever is coming out, being manifested, I am the seed." This means, "It is manufactured under My supervision." Just find the seed of a banyan tree. It is a small grain, like a mustard seed. But you sow the seed, and a gigantic tree will come out. Unless the energetic tree is there within the seed, how does it come out?

Like Augustine's *rationes seminales,* the *bījas,* or creative seeds, are placed within matter at the initial moment of creation. This is described in the *Śrīmad-Bhāgavatam* (3.26.19), which says that the

Supreme Personality of Godhead (Mahā-Viṣṇu) impregnates the womb of material nature. Nature then delivers the sum total of cosmic intelligence. This cosmic intelligence includes specific information defining the karmic destiny of the conditioned souls.

Initially material nature is in a quiescent state, called *pradhāna.* At the moment of creation, Mahā-Viṣṇu injects into the *pradhāna* innumerable conditioned souls, along with seed information defining their karma. This information guides transformations of material nature which give rise to the bodily forms and situations of the conditioned souls.

Subtle Forms of Energy

A crucial difference between this model of creation and modern evolutionary theories is that the injected seed information involves specific details for individuals. Rather than compare this information to the laws of physics, we could better compare it to the software of a virtual-reality system. When virtual-reality software is inserted into a suitable computer, the computer generates illusory bodily forms, which the players in the virtual-reality game experience as real. The intelligent design of the software by the computer programmer corresponds to the intelligent design of the seed information by Mahā-Viṣṇu.

One might argue that a computer contains complex electronic circuits designed to run its software but in nature we find nothing but randomly moving atoms and subatomic particles. If "seed information" were injected into nature, how would it be able to generate the bodily forms of living organisms?

This question is not answered by Augustine's sketchy theory of the *rationes seminales.* The Vedic literature, however, gives an answer. Just as gross physical seeds are always produced and disseminated by living organisms, so the seed information injected by Mahā-Viṣṇu is always controlled and manipulated by living beings.

In the *Brahma-saṁhitā,* Chapter 5, texts 7–10, it is said that the impregnating glance of Mahā-Viṣṇu becomes manifest in the material world as a being named Śambhu. The conceiving potency of nature, known as Māyā, likewise appears from Ramā Devī, the eternal consort of Viṣṇu. From the union of Śambhu and Māyā, innumerable living beings are generated through sexual procreation. The bodies of these beings are made of spiritual and subtle forms of energy unknown to modern physics. The gross physical bodies of our experience are generated from subtle living forms by the interaction of gross and subtle forms of energy. Thus the basic rule is that life forms are generated from seeds by a process of reproduction, subtle forms giving rise to gross forms.

Asa Gray and George Frederick Wright felt that creation must be the work of God but it should not violate the course of nature. We can see that the Vedic account of creation satisfies these two requirements. It does so, however, by speaking about spiritual and subtle phenomena in nature that are completely outside the scope of modern physical science.

A Deeper View of Cause and Effect

The Vedic account also provides an answer to Darwin's questions about design in nature. The *Padma Purāṇa* explains that karmic reactions to activities exist in the form of seeds stored within the heart, or subtle mind, of an individual.[5] In due course of time, these seeds fructify in the form of specific physical events.

This is the Vedic explanation of why lightning strikes Darwin's "innocent and good man" standing beneath a tree. The lightning stroke is not delivered whimsically by a wrathful God; it comes naturally as a reaction to the man's past actions. But the natural system that brings about this reaction is designed by God for the explicit purpose of administering divine justice. Even the eating of gnats by swallows is part of the divine plan. Gnats and swallows also have souls, and the experiences they undergo in the course of nature are designed to bring about progressive evolution of their consciousness.

The karmic seeds culminating in the lightning stroke consist of subtle energy. They are transferred from body to body in the process of transmigration of the soul, and they manifest their effects through complex control systems operating within nature. According to Vedic literature, these control systems are directed by living beings known as demigods, and ultimately they are under the supervision of the Supreme Personality of Godhead.

Darwin's theory of evolution can be seen as an attempt to give an alternative to the idea of whimsical, sudden creation by divine fiat. The theory attempted to explain the origin of species rationally in terms of a natural process of cause and effect. According to the Vedic literature there is indeed a rational process of creation. But it involves concepts and categories of being that go far beyond the limits of present-day science.

REFERENCES

1. Darwin, Francis, ed., 1959, *The Life and Letters of Charles Darwin,* New York: Basic Books, p. 284.
2. Livingstone, David N., 1987, *Darwin's Forgotten Defenders,* Grand Rapids, Mich.: W. B. Eerdmans, p. 64.
3. Frye, Roland Mushat, ed., 1983, *Is God a Creationist?* New York: Scribners, p. 112.
4. Copleston, Frederick, 1963, *A History of Philosophy,* Vol. II, New York: Doubleday, p. 76.
5. Prabhupāda, A. C. Bhaktivedanta Swami, 1982, *The Nectar of Devotion,* Los Angeles: Bhaktivedanta Book Trust, p. 6.

COSMOLOGY AND ANCIENT CULTURE

17

Cross-Cultural Traces Of Vedic Civilization

The ancient Greek writer Aratos tells the following story about the constellation Virgo, or the virgin. Virgo, he says, may have belonged to the star race, the forefathers of the ancient stars. In primeval times, in the golden age, she lived among mankind as Justice personified and would exhort people to adhere to the truth. At this time people lived peacefully, without hypocrisy or quarrel. Later, in the age of silver, she hid herself in the mountains, but occasionally she came down to berate people for their evil ways. Finally the age of bronze came. People invented the sword, and "they tasted the meat of cows, the first who did it." At this point Virgo "flew away to the sphere"; that is, she departed for the celestial realm.[1]

The Vedic literature of India gives an elaborate description of the universe as a cosmos—a harmonious, ordered system created according to an intelligent plan as a habitation for living beings. The modern view of the universe is so different from the Vedic view that the latter is presently difficult to comprehend. In ancient times, however, cosmologies similar to the Vedic system were widespread among people all over the world. Educated people of today tend to immediately dismiss these systems of thought as mythology, pointing to their diversity and their strange ideas as proof that they are all simply products of the imagination.

If we do this, however, we may be overlooking important information that could shed light on the vast forgotten period that precedes the brief span of recorded human history. There is certainly much evidence of independent storytelling in the traditions of various cultures, but there are also many common themes. Some of these themes are found in highly developed form in the Vedic literature. Their presence in cultures throughout the world is consistent with the idea that in the distant past, Vedic culture exerted worldwide influence.

In this article we will give some examples of Vedic ideas concerning time and human longevity that appear repeatedly in different traditions. First we will examine some of these ideas, and then we will discuss some questions about what they imply and how they should be interpreted.

In the Vedic literature time is regarded as a manifestation of Kṛṣṇa, the Supreme Being. As such, time is a controlling force that regulates the lives of living beings in accordance with a cosmic plan. This plan involves repeating cycles of creation and destruction of varying durations. The smallest and most important of these repeating cycles consists of four *yugas,* or ages, called Satya, Tretā, Dvāpara, and Kali. In these successive ages mankind gradually descends from a high spiritual platform to a degraded state. Then, with the beginning of a new Satya-yuga, the original state of purity is restored, and the cycle begins again.

The story of Virgo illustrates that in the ancient Mediterranean world there was widespread belief in a similar succession of four ages, known there as the ages of gold, silver, bronze, and iron. In this system humanity also starts out in the first age in an advanced state of consciousness and gradually becomes degraded. Here also, the progressive developments in human society are not simply evolving by physical processes, but are superintended by a higher controlling intelligence.

It is noteworthy that Aratos' story specifies the eating of cows as a sinful act that cut mankind off from direct contact with celestial beings. This detail fits in nicely with the ancient Indian traditions of cow protection, but it is unexpected in the context of Greek or European culture.

One explanation for similarities between ideas found in different cultures is that people everywhere have essentially the same psychological makeup, and so they tend to come up independently with similar notions. However, details such as the point about cow-killing suggest that we are dealing here with common traditions rather than independent inventions.

Another example of similarities between cultures can be found among the natives of North America. The Sioux Indians say that their ancestors were visited by a celestial woman who gave them their system of religion. She pointed out to them that there are four ages, and that there is a sacred buffalo that loses one leg during each age. At present we are in the last age, an age of degradation, and the buffalo has one leg.[2]

This story is a close parallel to the account in the *Śrīmad-Bhāgavatam* of the encounter between Mahārāja Parīkṣit and the bull of Dharma. There, Dharma is said to lose one leg with each successive *yuga,* leaving it with one leg in the present Age of Kali.

According to the Vedic system, the lengths of the Satya, Tretā, Dvāpara, and Kali *yugas* are 4, 3, 2, and 1 times an interval of 432,000 years. Within these immense periods of time the human life span decreases from 100,000 years in the Satya-yuga to 10,000 years in the Tretā-yuga, 1,000 years in the Dvāpara-yuga, and finally 100 years in the Kali-yuga.

Of course, this idea is strongly at odds with the modern evolutionary view of the past. In the ancient Mediterranean world, however, it was widely believed that human history had extended over extremely long periods of time. For example, according to old historical records, Porphyry (c. 300 A.D.) said that Callisthenes, a companion of Alexander in the Persian war, dispatched to Aristotle Babylonian records of eclipses and that these records covered 31,000 years. Likewise, Iamblicus (fourth century) said on the authority of the ancient Greek astronomer Hipparchus that the Assyrians had made observations for 270,000 years and had kept records of the return of all seven planets to the same position.[3] Finally, the Babylonian historian Berosus assigned 432,000 years to the total span of the reigns of the Babylonian kings before the Flood.[4]

We do not wish to suggest that these statements are true (or that they are false). The point here is that people in the old Mediterranean civilization evidently had a much different view of the past than the dominant view today. And this view was broadly consistent with Vedic chronology.

Although the Bible is well known for advocating a very short time-span for human history, it is interesting to note that it contains information indicating that people at one time lived for about 1,000 years. In the Old Testament the following ages are listed for people living before the Biblical Flood: Adam, 930; Seth, 912; Enos, 905;

Kenan, 910; Mahaleel, 895; Jared, 962; Enoch, 365; Methuselah, 969; Lamech, 777; and Noah, 950. If we exclude Enoch (who was said to have been taken up to heaven in his own body), these persons lived an average of 912 years.[5]

After the Flood, however, the following ages were recorded: Shem, 600; Arphachshad, 438; Salah, 433; Eber, 464; Plelg, 239; Reu, 239; Serug, 230; Nahor, 148; Terah, 205; Abraham, 175; Isaac, 180; Job, 210; Jacob, 147; Levi, 137; Kohath, 133; Amaram, 137; Moses, 120; and Joshua, 110. These ages show a gradual decline to about 100 years, similar to what must have happened after the beginning of Kali-yuga, according to the Vedic system.

Here we should mention in passing that the Biblical Flood is traditionally said to have taken place in the second or third millennium B.C., and the traditional date in India for the beginning of Kali-yuga is February 18, 3102 B.C. This very date is cited as the time of the Flood in various Persian, Islamic, and European writings from the sixth to the fourteenth centuries A.D.[6] How did the middle-eastern Flood come to be associated with the start of Kali-yuga? The only comment we can make is that this story shows how little we really know about the past.

In support of the Biblical story of very long human life-spans in ancient times, the Roman historian Flavius Josephus cited many historical works that were available in his time:

> Now when Noah had lived 350 years after the Flood, and all that time happily, he died, having the number of 950 years, but let no one, upon comparing the lives of the ancients with our lives . . . make the shortness of our lives at present an argument that neither did they attain so long a duration of life. . . . Now I have for witnesses to what I have said all those that have written Antiquities, both among the Greeks and barbarians, for even Manetho, who wrote the Egyptian history, and Berosus, who collected the Chaldean monuments, and Mochus, and Hestiaeus, and beside these, Hiernonymus the Egyptian, and those who composed the Phoenician history, agree with what I here say: Hesiod also, and Hecataeus, Hellanicaus, and Acuzilaus, and besides Ephorus and Nicolaus relate that the ancients lived a thousand years: but as to these matters, let everyone look upon them as he sees fit.[7]

Unfortunately, practically none of the works referred to by Josephus are still existing, and this again shows how little we know of the past. But in existing Norse sagas it is said that people in ancient times lived for many centuries. In addition, the Norse sagas describe a progression of ages, including an age of peace, an age when different social orders were introduced, an age of increasing violence, and a degraded "knife-age and axe-age with cloven shields."[8] The latter is followed by a period of annihilation, called Ragnarok, after which the world is restored to goodness.

The Norse Ragnarok involves the destruction of the earth and the abodes of the Norse demigods (called Asgard), and thus it corresponds in Vedic chronology to the annihilation of the three worlds that follows 1,000 *yuga* cycles, or one day of Brahmā. It is said that during Ragnarok the world is destroyed with flames by a being named Surt, who lives beneath the lower world (appropriately called Hel) and was involved in the world's creation. By comparison, the *Śrīmad-Bhāgavatam* (3.11.30) states that at the end of Brahmā's day, "the devastation takes place due to the fire emanating from the mouth of Saṅkarṣaṇa." Saṅkarṣaṇa is a plenary expansion of Kṛṣṇa who is "seated at the bottom of the universe" (*Śrīmad-Bhāgavatam* 3.8.3), beneath the lower planetary systems.

There are many similarities between the Norse and Vedic cosmologies, but there are also great differences. One key difference is that in the *Śrīmad-Bhāgavatam,* all beings and phenomena within the universe are clearly understood as part of the divine plan of Kṛṣṇa, the Supreme Personality of Godhead. In contrast, in the Norse mythology God is conspicuously absent, and the origin and purpose of the major players in the cosmic drama are very obscure. Surt, in particular, is a "fire giant" whose origins and motives are unclear even to experts in the Norse literature.[9]

One might ask, If Vedic themes appear in different societies, how can one conclude that they derive from an ancient Vedic civilization? Perhaps they were created in many places independently, or perhaps they descend from an unknown culture that is also ancestral to what we call Vedic culture. Thus parallels between the accounts of Surt and Saṅkarṣaṇa may be coincidental, or perhaps the Vedic account derives from a story similar to that of Surt.

Our answer to this question is that available empirical evidence will not be sufficient to *prove* the hypothesis of descent from an ancient Vedic culture, for all empirical evidence is imperfect and subject to various interpretations. But we can decide whether or not the evidence is consistent with this hypothesis.

If there was an ancient Vedic world civilization, we would expect to find traces of it in many cultures around the world. We do seem to find such traces, and many agree with Vedic accounts in specific details (such as the location of Surt's abode or the sacred buffalo's loss of one leg per world age). Since this civilization began to lose its influence thousands of years ago, at the beginning of Kali-yuga, we would expect many of these traces to be fragmentary and overlain by many later additions, and this we also see. Thus the available evidence seems to be consistent with the hypothesis of a Vedic origin.

REFERENCES

1. Sachau, E. C., trans., 1964, *Alberuni's India*, Delhi: S. Chand & Co., pp. 383–84.
2. Brown, J. E., ed., 1971, *The Sacred Pipe*, Baltimore: Penguin Books, p. 9.
3. Neugebauer, D., 1975, *History of Ancient Mathematical Astronomy*, Berlin: Springer-Verlag, pp. 608–9.
4. North, J. D., 1977, "Chronology & the Age of the World," in *Cosmology, History, & Theology*, eds. Wolfgang Yourgrau and A. D. Breck, New York: Plenum Press, p. 315.
5. Patten, D. W. and Patten, P. A., August 1979, "A Comprehensive Theory on Aging, Gigantism & Longevity," *Catastrophism & Ancient History,* Vol. 2, Part 1, p. 24.
6. North, J. D., pp. 316–17.
7. Patten, D. W., p. 29.
8. Rydberg, V., 1889, *Teutonic Mythology*, R. B. Anderson, trans., London: Swan Sonnenschein & Co., pp. 88, 94.
9. Rydberg, pp. 448–49.

18

Astronomy And the Antiquity of Vedic Civilization

Traditional Chinese stories tell of a monkey named Sun who goes through remarkable adventures. In one story, two "harpooners of death" capture him, claiming he has reached the limit of his destiny on earth and is due to be taken to the underworld. The story's translator tells us that according to the Chinese, the constellation Nan Teou, the Southern Dipper, decides everyone's death, and the harpooners of death carry out the decision.[1]

In the last chapter I compared Vedic ideas about time with similar ideas found in cultures around the world. We saw that many cultures share highly specific Vedic thoughts about how long ancient people lived and what happened in ancient human societies. This suggests that an ancient cultural tradition existed worldwide, hinted at today in many cultures through fragmentary and poorly understood memories but spoken of in detail in the Vedic writings.

In this chapter we turn from time to space. And we find that ancient traditions about the layout of the universe bear similar traces of a common cultural background.

Vedic literature divides the visible heavens into regions, which transmigrating souls are said to reach according to their karma. We can think of the constellations of stars as a road map for the soul's travel after death. First I shall describe this map. Then I shall give some evidence that people in old cultures all over the world had a similar cosmic map, often agreeing with the Vedic map in many minute details.

To describe this map I need to introduce some basic ideas from astronomy. In both Indian and Western astronomy, the lines of latitude and longitude on the earth are projected onto the sky and set into a daily spin about the polar axis, so that to an observer on earth they seem to rotate once a day with the stars. This gives us a celestial coordinate system in which each star has a latitude, called its declination, and a longitude, called its right ascension.

We can think of the stars as points on a huge imaginary sphere, called the celestial sphere, surrounding the earth. Just as the earth has a northern and southern hemisphere separated by the equator, so does the celestial sphere.

Each year, against the background of stars, the sun completes a circuit called the ecliptic, a great circle tilted 23° degrees from the celestial equator. Around the ecliptic in a broad band stretch the twelve constellations of the zodiac and twenty-eight constellations called *nakṣatras,* or lunar mansions.

Books of Vedic astronomy list the *nakṣatras* and important stars. And more recent astronomers have identified the modern names of the constellations and stars to which these Vedic luminaries are thought to correspond. (The map on page 170 marks these correspondences, giving the ancient Sanskrit names and the modern locations.)

According to the *Viṣṇu Purāṇa,* north of the star Agastya and south of the three *nakṣatras* Mūla, Pūrvaṣādhā, and Uttarāṣādhā lies the road to the region of the Pitṛs, Pitṛloka.[2] This is said in Vedic literature to be the headquarters of Yamarāja, the demigod who punishes sinful human beings. The *Śrīmad-Bhāgavatam* (5.26.5) says that this region, along with the hellish planets, lies in the south of the universe, beneath Bhū-maṇḍala, the earthly planetary system.

The *nakṣatras* mentioned here match parts of the southern constellations Scorpio and Sagittarius, and Agastya is thought to be the star Canopus, which lies in the southern hemisphere. From the description in the *Viṣṇu Purāṇa,* therefore, we can locate Pitṛloka in terms of familiar celestial landmarks.

The Milky Way is seen in the sky as a great band of light, densely packed with stars, running roughly north and south, cutting the celestial equator at an angle of about 62 degrees. A very bright region of the Milky Way intersects the ecliptic in the constellation Sagittarius. This is close to the *nakṣatras* Mūla and Pūrvāṣādhā, which form the beginning of the path of the Pitṛs.

Just as Pitṛloka is south of the ecliptic, the higher planets are to its north. So the mystics who follow the path to these planets, the path of

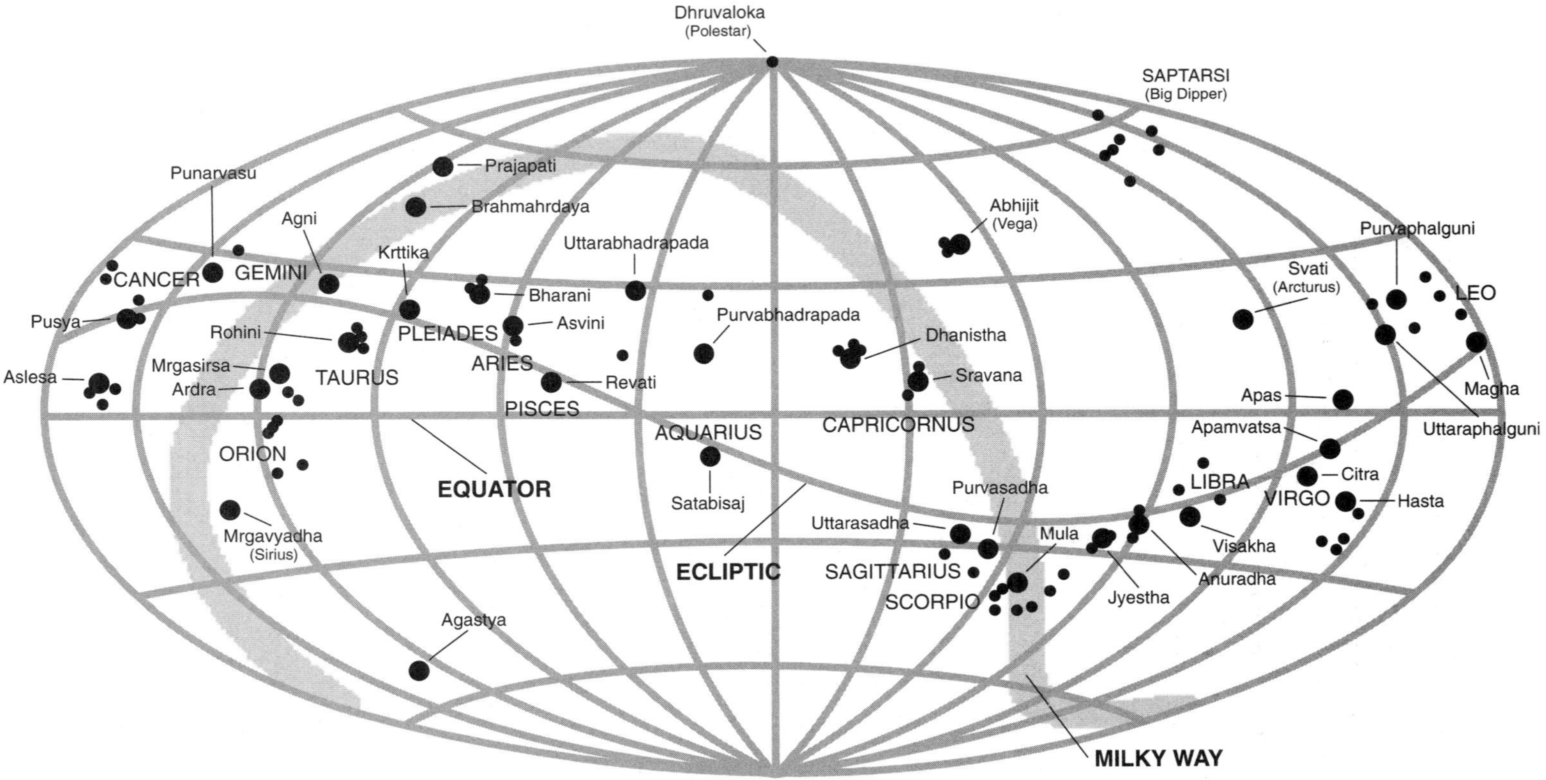

The location of Vedic star constellations on the celestial sphere.

the demigods, also begin at Mūla and Pūrvāṣādhā, but they travel northward. Their journey is described in the *Śrīmad-Bhāgavatam* (2.2.24–25) and in the *Viṣṇu Purāṇa.*

Moving along the ecliptic, the mystics travel up to Revatī. (This leg of their journey is called Vaiṣvānara.) From Revatī they move through the *nakṣatras* Aśvinī, Bhāraṇī, and Kṛttikā and travel on to the planet of the fire-god, Agni. There they are purified of all contaminations.

From Agni the mystics keep going north, through Brahmahṛdaya and Prajāpati, following the Milky Way, and as they reach the latitudes of the seven *ṛṣis* they enter Viṣṇupāda, the path of Viṣṇu. This is the path they follow until they at last reach the polestar, Dhruvaloka, a spiritual planet within the material universe.

In more familiar terms, Aśvinī, Bhāraṇī, and Kṛttikā match parts of the constellations Aries and Taurus. The seven *ṛṣis* (*saptarṣi*) correspond to the constellation Ursa Major, commonly known as the Big Dipper.

Opposite the point where the Milky Way meets the ecliptic in the southern hemisphere, it intersects the ecliptic in the north, at the boundary of Taurus and Gemini. It is here that we find the star Agni.

Once we locate the paths of the Pitṛs and the demigods on the celestial sphere, we can ask whether other cultural traditions offer similar accounts of the soul's celestial travels. It turns out that many do. Here are some examples:

1. We return to the story of the Chinese monkey, Sun, mentioned in the beginning of this chapter. The Chinese Southern Dipper consists of six stars in Sagittarius. It is interesting to note that this constellation shares stars with two of the *nakṣatras* marking the beginning of the path of the Pitṛs. So the start of the route to Yamarāja corresponds in this Chinese tradition to the place in the heavens where the fate of the dead is decided. The Chinese tradition also has messengers of death similar to the Vedic Yamadūtas.

2. The German scholar Franz Boll has analyzed ancient Greek traditions regarding Hades, the River Styx, and the ferryman of the underworld. We tend to think of Hades as lying beneath our feet, within the earth. Boll, however, cites texts placing this region in the

heavens around the southern crossroads of the Milky Way and the ecliptic.[3]

3. Boll points out a close relationship between Greek and Babylonian traditions. According to his analysis, the Babylonian god Dikud, the judge of Hades, may correspond to the star Theta Ophiuchi. This star lies close to the location mentioned in the Vedic writings as the beginning of the path of the Pitṛs. Boll cites a text referring to this star as "the beginning of the road of the lower heavenly vault."[4]

4. In North America the Pawnee and Cherokee say that the souls of the dead are received by a star at the northern end of the Milky Way. There the path divides. "He [God] directs the warriors on the dim and difficult path, and women and those who die of old age upon the brighter and easier path. The souls journey southwards; at the end of the celestial path they are received by the Spirit Star."[5]

The anthropologist S. Hagar thinks the Spirit Star is Antares. Antares (Jyeṣṭhā) lies, again, near the beginning of the path of the Pitṛs.

5. The Roman writer Macrobius, in his *Commentary on the Dream of Scipio,* says that souls of the dead ascend by way of Capricorn and, to be reborn, descend again through the gate of Cancer. Here Macrobius appears to have shifted everything by one sign of the zodiac; Capricorn is next to Sagittarius, and Cancer is next to Gemini. In fact, Macrobius says in his *Commentary* that Capricorn and Cancer lie where the zodiac crosses the Milky Way.[6]

6. In Honduras and Nicaragua the Sumo say that their "Mother Scorpion," who receives the souls of the dead, dwells at the end of the Milky Way. "And from her, represented as a mother with many breasts, at which children take suck, come the souls of the newborn."[7]

Here the "Mother Scorpion" is reminiscent of the constellation Scorpius. We note that the tail of the constellation Scorpius corresponds to the *nakṣatra* Mūla.

7. In general, Polynesians have traditionally believed in reincarnation and have held that the Milky Way is the pathway of transmi-

grating souls. The Mangaians of the Austral Islands in Polynesia believe that souls can enter heaven only on evenings of solstices (north islanders at one solstice and south islanders at the other).[8]

The important point here is that the solstices occur when the sun is near the intersection of the Milky Way and the ecliptic.

These astronomical examples, and our earlier examples about time, indicate that old cultures around the world shared a view of the cosmos similar in many ways to the Vedic one.

The details that appear again and again in these stories suggest the existence of a common cultural tradition. Yet the stories differ, and we have no clear historical records of their origin. This suggests that their common cultural source dates from the remote past. So the existence of these stories is consistent with the Vedic accounts of an ancient world civilization with a spiritual view of the origin and purpose of the universe.

REFERENCES

1. Ngen, Wou Tch'eng, 1957, *Si Yeou ki, ou le Voyage en Occident,* L. Avenol, trans. Paris, Vol. 1, p. iii.; Schlegel, G., 1875, *L'Uranigraphie Chinoise*, Leiden, pp. 172ff.
2. Wilson, H. H., 1865, *The Vishnu Purāṇa,* Vol. 2, London: Trubner & Co., pp. 263–268.
3. Boll, F., 1903, *Sphaera: Neue Griechische Texte und Untersuchungen zur Geschichte der Sternbilder*, Leipzig, pp. 246–51.
4. Boll.
5. Hagar, S., 1906, "Cherokee Star-Lore," in *Festschrift Boas,* p. 363; Alexander, H. B., 1916, *North American Mythology,* Mythology of All Races series, Vol. 10, p. 117.
6. Macrobius, 1952, *Commentary on the Dream of Scipio,* Stahl, W. H., trans., New York. Records of Civilization, Sources and Studies, vol. 48.
7. Alexander, H. B., 1920, *Latin American Mythology,* Mythology of All Races series, Vol. 11, p. 185.
8. Gill, W. W., 1876, *Myths and Songs from the South Pacific*, London, pp. 156ff, 185ff.

19

The Universe of the Vedas

The *Śrīmad-Bhāgavatam* presents an earth-centered conception of the cosmos. At first glance the cosmology seems foreign, but a closer look reveals that not only does the cosmology of the *Bhāgavatam* describe the world of our experience, but it also presents a much larger and more complete cosmological picture.[1] I'll explain.

The *Śrīmad-Bhāgavatam's* mode of presentation is very different from the familiar modern approach. Although the *Bhāgavatam's* "Earth" (disk-shaped Bhū-maṇḍala) may look unrealistic, careful study shows that the *Bhāgavatam* uses Bhū-maṇḍala to represent at least four reasonable and consistent models: (1) a polar-projection map of the Earth globe, (2) a map of the solar system, (3) a topographical map of south-central Asia, and (4) a map of the celestial realm of the demigods.

Śrī Caitanya Mahāprabhu remarked, "In every verse of *Śrīmad-Bhāgavatam* and in every syllable, there are various meanings." (*Caitanya-caritāmṛta, Madhya* 24.318) This appears to be true, in particular, of the cosmological section of the *Bhāgavatam,* and it is interesting to see how we can bring out and clarify some of the meanings with reference to modern astronomy.

When one structure is used to represent several things in a composite map, there are bound to be contradictions. But these do not cause a problem if we understand the underlying intent. We can draw a parallel with medieval paintings portraying several parts of a story in one composition. For example, Masaccio's painting "The Tribute Money" (Figure 1) shows Saint Peter in three parts of a Biblical story. We see him taking a coin from a fish, speaking to Jesus, and paying a tax collector. From a literal standpoint it is contradictory to have Saint Peter doing three things at once, yet each phase of the Biblical story makes sense in its own context.

Figure 1

Figure 2

A similar painting from India (Figure 2) shows three parts of a story about Kṛṣṇa. Such paintings contain apparent contradictions, such as images of one character in different places, but a person who understands the story line will not be disturbed by this. The same is true of the *Bhāgavatam,* which uses one model to represent different features of the cosmos.

The Bhāgavatam Picture at First Glance

The Fifth Canto of the *Śrīmad-Bhāgavatam* tells of innumerable universes. Each one is contained in a spherical shell surrounded by layers of elemental matter that mark the boundary between mundane space and the unlimited spiritual world.

The region within the shell (Figure 3) is called the Brahmāṇḍa, or "Brahma egg." It contains an earth disk or plane—called Bhū-maṇḍala—that divides it into an upper, heavenly half and a subterranean half, filled with water. Bhū-maṇḍala is divided into a series of geographic features, traditionally called *dvīpas,* or "islands," *varṣas,* or "regions," and oceans.

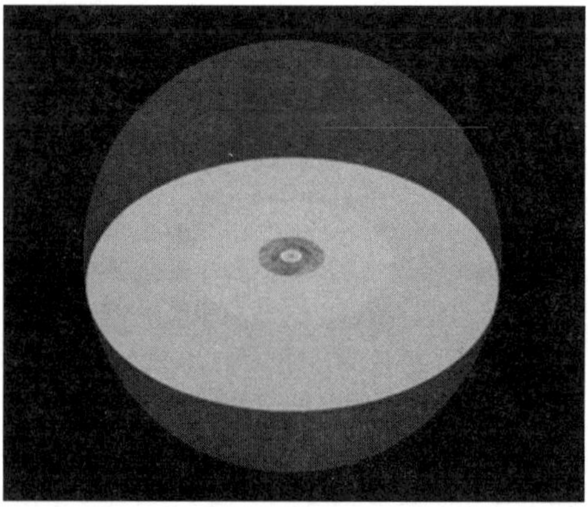

Figure 3

In the center of Bhū-maṇḍala (Figure 4) is the circular "island" of Jambūdvīpa, with nine *varṣa* subdivisions. These include Bhārata-varṣa, which can be understood in one sense as India and in another as the total area inhabited by human beings. In the center of Jambūdvīpa stands the cone-shaped Meru Mountain (Figure 5), which represents the world axis and is surmounted by the city of Brahmā, the universal creator. To any modern, educated person, this sounds like science fiction. But is it? Let's consider the four ways of seeing the *Bhāgavatam's* descriptions of the Bhū-maṇḍala.

Model 1: Bhū-maṇḍala as a
Polar Projection of the Earth Globe

We begin by discussing the interpretation of Bhū-maṇḍala as a planisphere, or a polar-projection map of the Earth globe. This is the first model given by the *Bhāgavatam.* A stereographic projection is an ancient method of mapping points on the surface of a sphere to points on a plane. We can use this method to map a modern Earth

Figure 4

globe onto a plane, and the resulting flat projection is called a planisphere (Figure 6). We can likewise view Bhū-maṇḍala as a stereographic projection of a globe (Figure 7).

In India such globes exist. In the example shown here (Figure 8), the land area between the equator and the mountain arc is Bhārata-varṣa, corresponding to greater India. India is well represented, but apart from a few references to neighboring places, this globe does not give a realistic map of the Earth. Its purpose was astronomical, rather than geographical.

Although the *Bhāgavatam* doesn't explicitly describe the Earth as a globe, it does so indirectly. For example, it points out that night prevails diametrically opposite to a point where it is day. Likewise, the sun sets at a point opposite where it rises. Therefore, the *Bhāgavatam* does not present the naive view that the Earth is flat.

We can compare Bhū-maṇḍala with an astronomical instrument called an astrolabe, popular in the Middle Ages. On the astrolabe, an off-centered circle represents the orbit of the sun—the ecliptic. The Earth is represented in stereographic projection on a flat plate, called the mater. The ecliptic circle and important stars are represented on

Indupati Dāsa

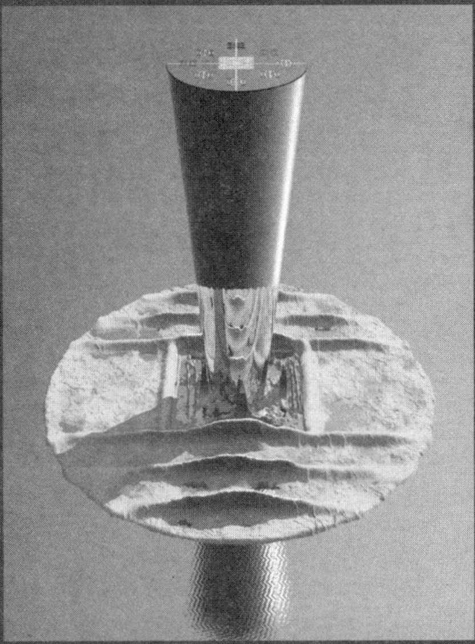

Figure 5—Jambūdvīpa: The *Śrīmad-Bhāgavatam* describes that the universe lies within a series of spherical shells which is divided in two by an earth plane called Bhū-maṇḍala. A series of *dvīpas*, or "islands," and oceans make up Bhū-maṇḍala. In the center of Bhū-maṇḍala is the circular "island" of Jambū-dvīpa (inset), whose most prominent feature is the cone-shaped Mount Meru. The main illustration here shows a closer view of Jambūdvīpa and the base of Mount Meru.

Indupati Dasa

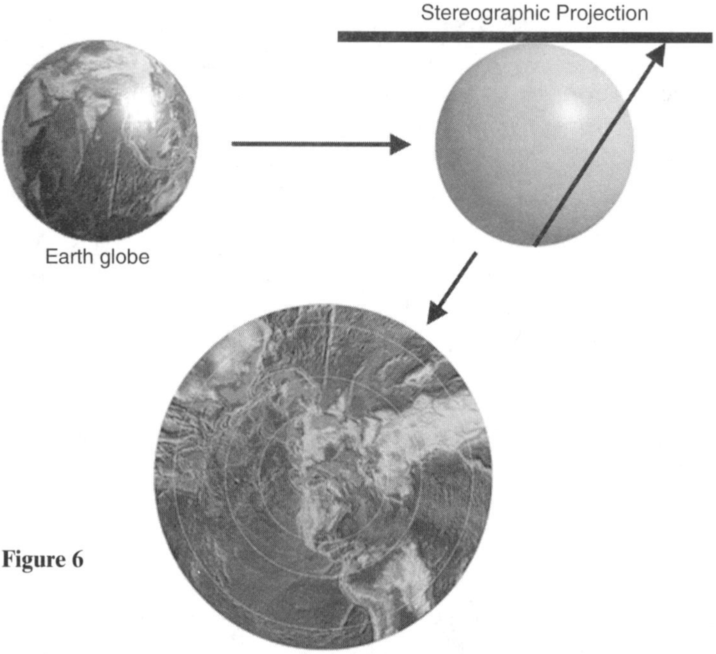
Stereographic Projection
Earth globe

Figure 6

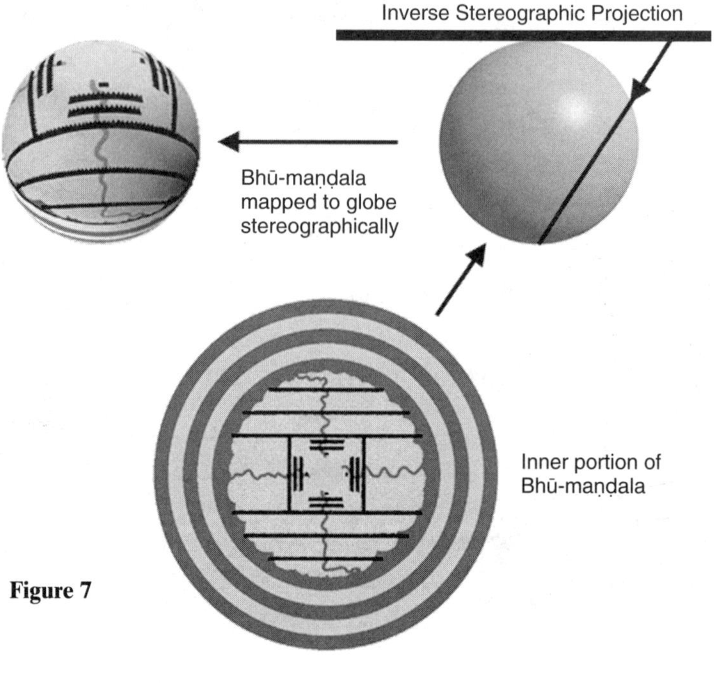
Inverse Stereographic Projection
Bhū-maṇḍala mapped to globe stereographically
Inner portion of Bhū-maṇḍala

Figure 7

another plate, called the rete. Different planetary orbits could likewise be represented by different plates, and these would be seen projected onto the Earth plate when one looks down on the instrument. The *Bhāgavatam* similarly presents the orbits of the sun, the moon, planets, and important stars on a series of planes parallel to Bhū-maṇḍala. Seeing Bhū-maṇḍala as a polar projection is one example of how it doesn't represent a flat Earth.

Model 2: Bhū-maṇḍala As a Map of the Solar System

Here's another way to look at Bhū-maṇḍala that also shows that it's not a flat-Earth model. Descriptions of Bhū-maṇḍala have features that identify it as a model of the solar system. In the previous section I interpreted Bhū-maṇḍala as a planisphere map. But now, we'll take it as a literal plane. When we do this, it looks at first like we're back to the naive flat Earth, with the bowl of the sky above and the underworld below.

The scholars Giorgio de Santillana and Hertha von Dechend carried out an intensive study of myths and traditions and concluded

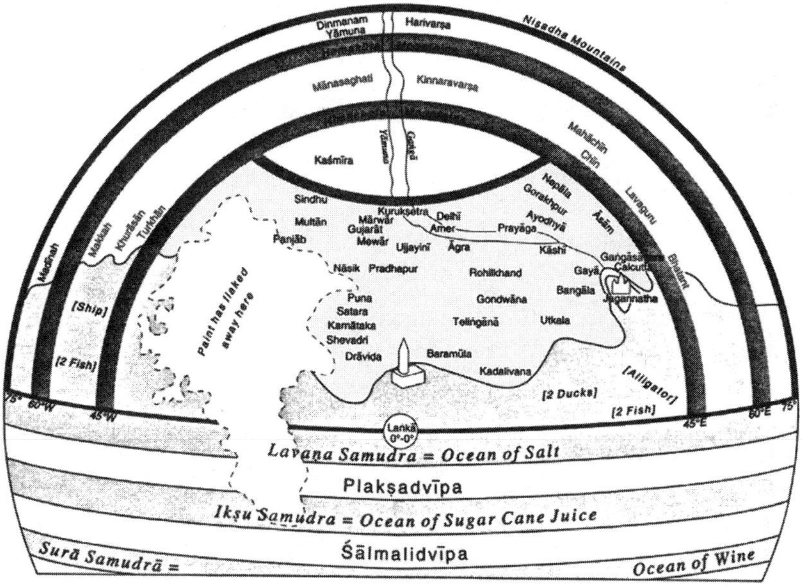

Figure 8

Figure 9

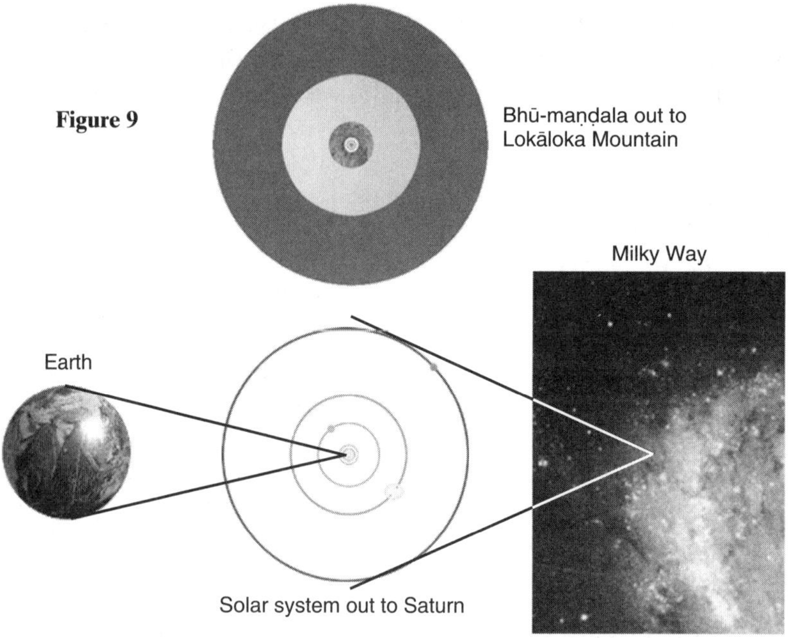

that the so-called flat Earth of ancient times originally represented the plane of the ecliptic (the orbit of the sun) and not the Earth on which we stand. Later on, according to de Santillana and von Dechend, the original cosmic understanding of the earth was apparently lost, and the Earth beneath our feet was taken literally as a flat plate. In India, the earth of the *Purāṇas* has often been taken as literally flat. But the details given in the *Bhāgavatam* show that its cosmology is much more sophisticated.

Not only does the *Bhāgavatam* use the ecliptic model, but it turns out that the disk of Bhū-maṇḍala corresponds in some detail to the solar system (Figure 9). The solar system is nearly flat. The sun, the moon, and the five traditionally known planets—Mercury through Saturn—all orbit nearly in the ecliptic plane. Thus Bhū-maṇḍala does refer to something flat, but it's not the Earth.

One striking feature of the *Bhāgavatam's* descriptions has to do with size. If we compare Bhū-maṇḍala with the Earth, the solar system out to Saturn, and the Milky Way galaxy, Bhū-maṇḍala matches the solar system closely, while radically differing in size from Earth and the galaxy.

Furthermore, the structures of Bhū-maṇḍala correspond with the planetary orbits of the solar system (Figure 10).

If we compare the rings of Bhū-maṇḍala with the geocentric orbits of Mercury, Venus (Figure 11), Mars, Jupiter, and Saturn, we find several close alignments that give weight to the hypothesis that Bhū-maṇḍala was deliberately designed as a map of the solar system. (For a discussion of geocentric orbits of planets, see pages 195–201.)

Until recent times, astronomers generally underestimated the distance from the earth to the sun. In particular, Claudius Ptolemy, the greatest astronomer of classical antiquity, seriously underestimated the Earth-sun distance and the size of the solar system. It is remarkable, therefore, that the dimensions of Bhū-maṇḍala in the *Bhāgavatam* are consistent with modern data on the size of the sun's orbit and the solar system as a whole. (See pages 190–205.)

Model 3: Jambūdvīpa as a Topographical Map of South-Central Asia

Jambūdvīpa, the central hub of Bhū-maṇḍala, can be understood as a local topographical map of part of south-central Asia. This is the third of the four interpretations of Bhū-maṇḍala. In the planisphere interpretation, Jambūdvīpa represents the northern hemisphere of

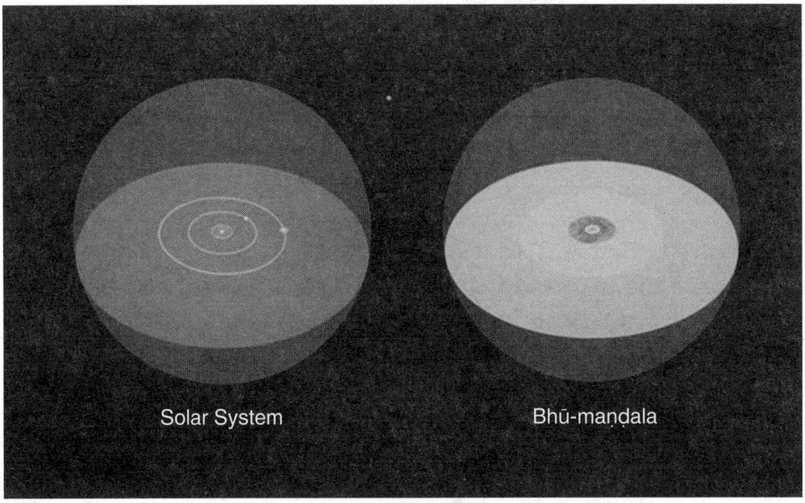

Figure 10

the Earth globe. But the detailed geographic features of Jambūdvīpa do not match the geography of the northern hemisphere. They do, however, match part of the Earth.

Six horizontal and two vertical mountain chains divide Jambūdvīpa into nine regions, or *varṣas* (Figure 12). The southernmost region is called Bhārata-varṣa. Careful study shows that this map corresponds to India plus adjoining areas of south-central Asia. The first step in making this identification is to observe that the *Bhāgavatam* assigns many rivers in India to Bhārata-varṣa. Thus Bhārata-varṣa represents India. The same can be said of many mountains in Bhārata-varṣa. In particular, the *Bhāgavatam* places the Himalayas to the north of Bhārata-varṣa in Jambūdvīpa.

A detailed study of Purāṇic accounts allows the other mountain ranges of Jambūdvīpa to be identified with mountain ranges in the region north of India. Although this region includes some of the most desolate and mountainous country in the world, it was nonetheless important in ancient times. For example, the famous Silk Road passes through this region. The Pamir mountains can be identified with

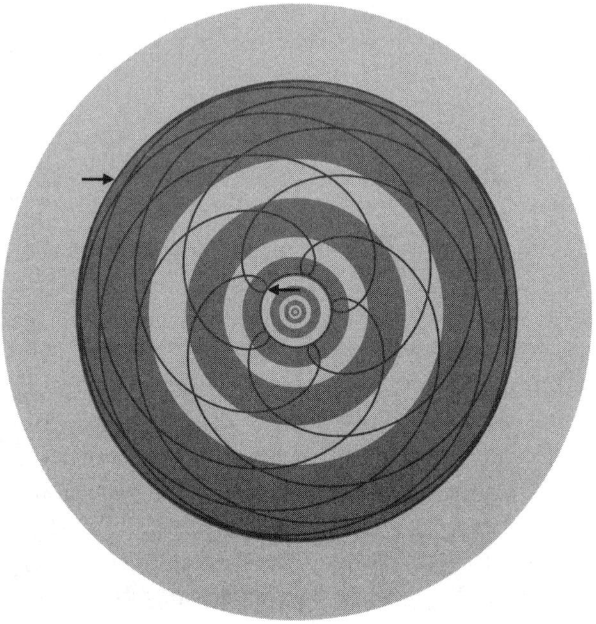

Figure 11— The two arrows indicate that the boundaries of the geocentric orbit of Venus align with the circular features of Bhū-maṇḍala.

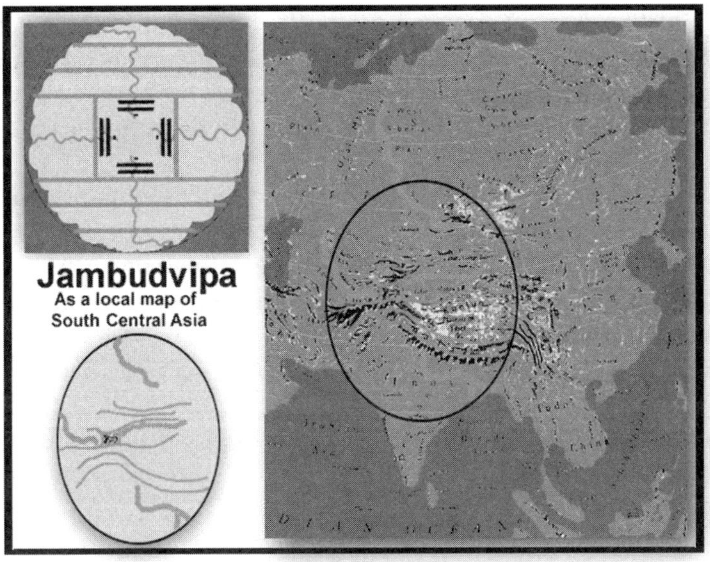

Figure 12

Mount Meru and Ilavṛta-varṣa, the square region in the center of Jambūdvīpa. (Note that Mount Meru does not represent the polar axis in this interpretation.) Other *Purāṇas* give more geographical details that support this interpretation.

Model 4: Bhū-maṇḍala as a Map of the Celestial Realm of the Devas

We can also understand Bhū-maṇḍala as a map of the celestial realm of the demigods, or *devas*. One curious feature of Jambūdvīpa is that the *Bhāgavatam* describes all of the *varṣas* other than Bhārata-varṣa as heavenly realms, where the inhabitants live for ten thousand years without suffering. This has led some scholars to suppose that Indians used to imagine foreign lands as celestial paradises. But the *Bhāgavatam* does refer to barbaric peoples outside India, such as Huns, Greeks, Turks, and Mongolians, who were hardly thought to live in paradise. One way around this is to suppose that Bhārata-varṣa includes the entire Earth globe, while the other eight *varṣas* refer to celestial realms outside the Earth. This is a common understanding in India.

But the simplest explanation for the heavenly features of Jambūdvīpa is that Bhū-maṇḍala was also intended to represent the realm of the *devas*. Like the other interpretations we have considered, this one is based on a group of mutually consistent points in the cosmology of the *Bhāgavatam.*

First of all, consider the very large sizes of mountains and land areas in Jambūdvīpa. For example, India is said to be 72,000 miles (9,000 *yojanas*) from north to south, or nearly three times the circumference of the Earth. Likewise, the Himalayas are said to be 80,000 miles high.

People in India in ancient times used to go in pilgrimage on foot from one end of India to the other, so they knew how large India is. Why does the *Bhāgavatam* give such unrealistic distances? The answer is that Jambūdvīpa doubles as a model of the heavenly realm, in which everything is on a superhuman scale. The *Bhāgavatam* portrays the demigods and other divine beings that inhabit this realm to be correspondingly large. Figure 13 shows Lord Śiva in comparison with Europe, according to dimensions given in one text of the *Bhāgavatam.*

Why would the *Bhāgavatam* describe Jambūdvīpa as both part of the earth and part of the celestial realm? Because there's a connection between the two. To understand, let's consider the idea of parallel worlds. By *siddhis,* or mystic perfections, one can take shortcuts across space. This is illustrated by a story from the *Bhāgavatam* in which the mystic yogini Citralekhā abducts Aniruddha from his bed in Dvārakā and transports him mystically to a distant city (Figure 14).

Besides moving from one place to another in ordinary space, the mystic *siddhis* enable one to travel in the all-pervading ether or to enter another continuum. The classical example of a parallel continuum is Kṛṣṇa's transcendental realm of Vṛndāvana, said to be unlimitedly expansive and to exist in parallel to the finite, earthly Vṛndāvana in India.

The Sanskrit literature abounds with stories of parallel worlds. For example, the *Mahābhārata* tells the story of how the Nāga princess Ulūpī abducted Arjuna while he was bathing in the Ganges River (Figure 15). Ulūpī pulled Arjuna down not to the riverbed, as we would expect, but into the kingdom of the Nāgas (celestial snake-like beings), which exists in another dimension.

Painting by Yadupriyā Devī Dāsī

Figure 13

Painting by Yadupriyā Devī Dāsī

Figure 14

Mystical travel explains how the worlds of the *devas* are connected with our world. In particular, it explains how Jambūdvīpa, as a celestial realm of *devas,* is connected with Jambūdvīpa as the Earth or part of the Earth. Thus the double model of Jambūdvīpa makes sense in terms of the Purāṇic understanding of the *siddhis.*

Concluding Observations: The Vertical Dimension in Bhāgavata Cosmology

For centuries the cosmology of the *Bhāgavatam* has seemed incomprehensible to most observers, encouraging many people either to summarily reject it or to accept it literally with unquestioning faith. If we take it literally, the cosmology of the *Bhāgavatam* not only differs from modern astronomy, but, more importantly, it also suffers from internal contradictions and violations of common sense. These very contradictions, however, point the way to a different understanding of *Bhāgavata* cosmology in which it emerges as a deep and scientifically sophisticated system of thought. The contradictions show that they are caused by overlapping self-consistent interpretations that use the same textual elements to expound different ideas.

Drawing by Bhārata Dāsa

Figure 15

Each of the four interpretations I've presented deserves to be taken seriously because each is supported by many points in the text that are consistent with one another while agreeing with modern astronomy. I've applied the context-sensitive or multiple-aspect approach, in which the same subject has different meanings in different contexts. This approach allows for the greatest amount of information to be stored in a picture or text, reducing the work required by the artist or writer. At the same time, it means that the work cannot be taken literally as a one-to-one model of reality, and it requires the viewer or reader to understand the different relevant contexts. This can be difficult when knowledge of context is lost over long periods of time.

In the *Bhāvagatam,* the context-sensitive approach was rendered particularly appropriate by the conviction that reality, in the ultimate issue, is *avāk-manasam,* or beyond the reach of the mundane mind or words. This implies that a literal, one-to-one model of reality is unattainable, and so one may as well pack as much meaning as possible into a necessarily incomplete description of the universe. The cosmology of the *Bhāgavata Purāṇa* is a sophisticated system of thought, with multiple layers of meaning, both physical and metaphysical. It combines practical understanding of astronomy with spiritual conceptions to produce a meaningful picture of the universe and reality.

REFERENCE

1. Thompson, Richard L., 2000, *Mysteries of the Sacred Universe,* Alachua, FL, Govardhan Hill Publishing.

20

Advanced Astronomy in The Śrīmad-Bhāgavatam

Today we take for granted that the earth is a sphere, but the early Greeks tended to think it was flat. For example, in the fifth century B.C. the philosopher Thales thought of the earth as a disk floating on water like a log.[1] About a century later, Anaxagoras taught that it is flat like a lid and stays suspended in air.[2] A few decades later, the famous atomist Democritus argued that the earth is shaped like a tambourine and is tilted downwards toward the south.[3] Although some say that Pythagoras, in the sixth century B.C., was the first to view the earth as a sphere, this idea did not catch on quickly among the Greeks, and the first attempt to measure the earth's diameter is generally attributed to Eratosthenes in the second century B.C.

Scholars widely believe that prior to the philosophical and scientific achievements of the Greeks, people in ancient civilized societies regarded the earth as a flat disk. So to find that the *Bhāgavata Purāṇa* of India appears to describe a flat earth comes as no surprise. The *Bhāgavata Purāṇa,* or *Śrīmad-Bhāgavatam,* is dated by scholars to A.D. 500–1000, although it is acknowledged to contain much older material and its traditional date is the beginning of the third millennium B.C.

In the *Bhāgavatam,* Bhū-maṇḍala—the "earth mandala"—is a disk 500 million *yojanas* in diameter. The *yojana* is a unit of distance about 8 miles long, and so the diameter of Bhū-maṇḍala is about 4 billion miles.[4] Bhū-maṇḍala is marked by circular features designated as islands and oceans. These features are listed in Table 1, along with their dimensions, as given in the *Bhāgavatam.*

There are seven islands, called *dvīpas,* ranging from Jambūdvīpa to Puṣkaradvīpa. Jambūdvīpa, the innermost, is a disk, and the other

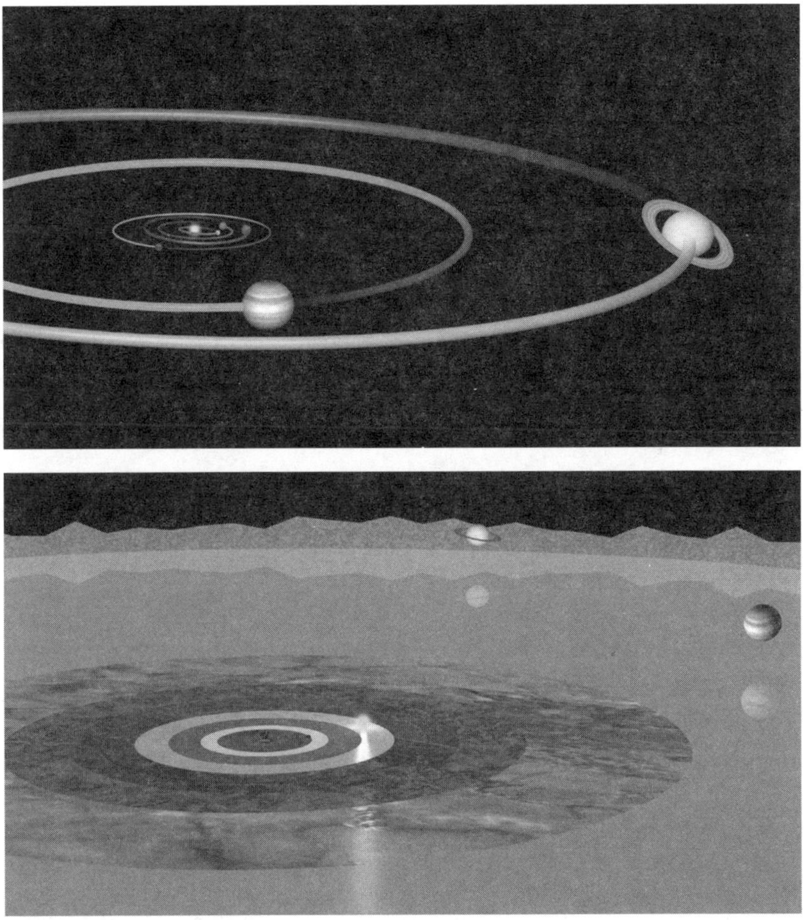

Figure 1—Above: The modern heliocentric solar system. Below: Bhū-maṇḍala, the "earth mandala" of the *Śrīmad-Bhāgavatam.* Although Bhū-maṇḍala appears at first glance to represent a flat earth, it is actually an accurate map of the solar system.

six are successively larger rings. The islands alternate with ring-shaped oceans, beginning with Lavaṇoda, the Salt Water Ocean surrounding Jambūdvīpa, and ending with Svādudaka, the Sweet Water Ocean. Beyond Svādudaka is another ring, called Kāñcanībhūmi, or the Golden Land, and then yet another, called Ādarśatalopamā, the Mirrorlike Land.[5]

N	Inner Radius	Outer Radius	Width	Feature
1	0	50	50	Jambūdvīpa
2	50	150	100	Lavaṇoda
3	150	350	200	Plakṣadvīpa
4	350	550	200	Ikṣura
5	550	950	400	Śalmalīdvīpa
6	950	1,350	400	Suroda
7	1,350	2,150	800	Kuśadvīpa
8	2,150	2,950	800	Ghṛtoda
9	2,950	4,550	1,600	Krauñcadvīpa
10	4,550	6,150	1,600	Kṣīroda
11	6,150	9,350	3,200	Śakadvīpa
12	9,350	12,550	3,200	Dadhyoda
13	12,550	15,750	3,200	Inner Puṣkaradvīpa
14	15,750	18,950	3,200	Outer Puṣkaradvīpa
15	18,950	25,350	6,400	Svādudaka
16	25,350	41,100	15,750	Kāñcanībhūmi
17	41,100	125,000	83,900	Ādarśatalopamā
18	125,000	250,000	125,000	Aloka-varṣa

Table 1—The radii in thousands of *yojanas* of the islands and oceans of Bhū-maṇḍala, as given in the *Bhāgavata Purāṇa.*

There are also three circular mountains we should note. The first is Mount Meru, situated in the center of Bhū-maṇḍala and shaped like an inverted cone, with a radius ranging from 8,000 *yojanas* at the bottom to 16,000 *yojanas* at the top. The other two mountains can be thought of as very thin rings or circles. The first, called Mānasottara, has a radius of 15,750 thousand *yojanas* and divides the island of Puṣkaradvīpa into two rings of equal thickness. (In Table 1 these are referred to as inner and outer Puṣkaradvīpa.) The second mountain, called Lokāloka, has a radius of 125,000 thousand *yojanas* and separates the inner, illuminated region of Bhū-maṇḍala (ending with the Mirrorlike Land) from the outer region of darkness, Aloka-varṣa.

At first glance, Bhū-maṇḍala appears to be a highly artificial portrayal of the earth as an enormous flat disk, with continents and oceans that do not tally with geographical experience. But careful consideration shows that Bhū-maṇḍala does not really represent the earth at all. To see why, we have to consider the motion of the sun.

In the *Bhāgavatam* the sun is said to travel on a chariot (Figure 2). The wheel of this chariot is made of parts of the year, such as months and seasons. So it might be argued that the chariot is meant to be taken metaphorically, rather than literally. But here we are concerned more with the chariot's dimensions than with its composition. The chariot has an axle that rests at one end on Mount Meru, in the center of Jambūdvīpa. On the other end, the axle connects to a wheel that "continuously rotates on Mānasottara Mountain like the wheel of an oil-pressing machine."[6] The wheel rolls on top of Mount Mānasottara, which is like a circular race track.

The sun rides on a platform joined to the axle at an elevation of 100,000 thousand *yojanas* from the surface of Bhū-maṇḍala. Since the

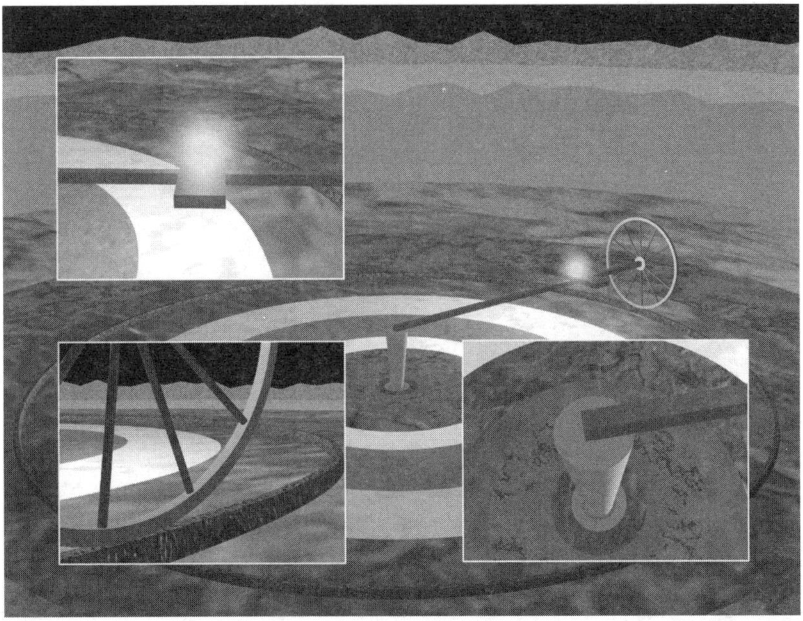

Figure 2—The chariot of the sun. The chariot's axle runs from Mount Meru to a wheel riding on Mānosattara Mountain. The sun rides on a platform on this axle. The wheel and Mount Meru have been greatly expanded here; if drawn to scale, they would be too small to see, and the sun would lie close to the plane of Bhū-maṇḍala.

axle extends from Mount Meru to Mount Mānasottara, its length must be 15,750 thousand *yojanas,* or 157.5 times as long as the height of the sun above Bhū-maṇḍala. Since the sun's platform is somewhere on the axle between Meru (in the center) and the wheel (running on the circular track of Mānasottara), it follows that to an observer at the center the sun always seems very close to the surface of Bhū-maṇḍala.

To see this, imagine building a scale model of the sun's chariot on a level field, with 1 foot representing 100,000 thousand *yojanas.* In this model, the sun is a ball riding 1 foot above the field on an axle 157.5 feet long. One end of the axle pivots around Mount Meru, which is about 1 foot high (or a little less), and the other end goes through a wheel about 1 foot in diameter which follows a circular track. If the sun is a good part of the way out from the center (say, 50 feet or more), it will seem close to the field from the point of view of an observer lying down with his eye close to the base of Mount Meru. The same is true if the model is scaled up to actual size.

Suppose that Bhū-maṇḍala represents our local horizon extended out into a huge flat disk—the so-called flat earth. Then an observer standing in Jambūdvīpa, near the center, must see the sun continuously skim around the horizon in a big circle, without either rising into the sky or setting. This is actually what one can see at the north or south pole at certain times in the year, but it is not what one sees in India. The conclusion, therefore, is that Bhū-maṇḍala does not represent an extension of our local horizon. Since the sun is always close to Bhū-maṇḍala, and since the sun rises, goes high into the sky, and then sets, it follows that the disk of Bhū-maṇḍala is tilted at a steep angle to an observer standing in India.

In brief, Bhū-maṇḍala is where the sun goes. It extends high into the sky overhead and also far beneath the observer's feet. Furthermore, it must be regarded as invisible, for if it were opaque it would block our view of a good part of the sky.

Bhū-maṇḍala is not the "flat earth," but what is it? One possibility is the solar system. In modern astronomy, each planet orbits the sun in a plane. The planes of these orbits lie at small angles to one another, and thus all the orbits are close to one plane. Astronomers call the plane of the earth's orbit the ecliptic, and this is also the plane of the sun's orbit, from the point of view of an observer stationed on the earth. To an observer on the earth, the solar system is a more-or-less flat arrangement of planetary orbits that stay close to the path of the sun.

Bhū-maṇḍala is far too big to be the earth, but in size it turns out quite a reasonable match for the solar system. Bhū-maṇḍala has a radius of 250 million *yojanas,* and at the traditional figure of 8 miles per *yojana* this comes to 2 billion miles. For comparison, the orbit of Uranus has a radius of about 1.8 billion miles.

If we move in from the outer edge of Bhū-maṇḍala we meet the Lokāloka mountain, with a radius of 125 million *yojanas,* or about 1 billion miles. From Uranus the next planet inward is Saturn, with an orbital radius of about 0.9 billion miles. Thus we find a rough agreement between certain planetary orbits and some circular features of Bhū-maṇḍala.

Of course, Bhū-maṇḍala is earth centered. Its innermost island, Jambūdvīpa, contains Bhārata-varṣa, which Śrīla Prabhupāda has repeatedly identified as the planet earth.[7] In contrast, the orbits of the planets are centered on the sun. How, then, can they be compared to earth-centered features of Bhū-maṇḍala?

The solution is to express the orbits of the planets in geocentric (earth-centered) form. Although the calculations of modern astronomy treat these orbits as heliocentric (sun-centered), the orbits can be expressed in relation to any desired center of observation,

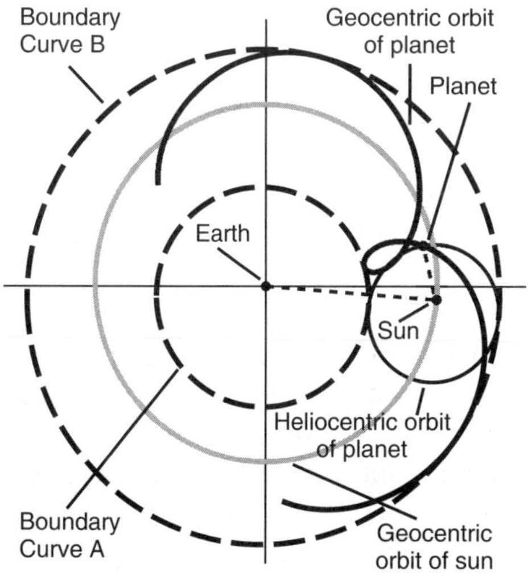

Figure 3—The geocentric orbit of a planet. From the viewpoint of a person standing on the earth, the sun moves around the earth and a planet (Mercury, in this example) orbits around the sun. The combination of the sun's motion around the earth, and the planet's motion around the sun forms the apparent orbit of the planet around the earth. This is called the planet's geocentric orbit. It lies between two curves: the inner boundary curve (A) and the outer boundary curve (B).

including the earth. In fact, since we live on the earth, it is reasonable for us to look at planetary orbits from a geocentric point of view.

The geocentric orbit of a planet is a product of two heliocentric motions, the motion of the earth around the sun and the motion of the planet around the sun. To draw it, we shift to the earth as center, and show the planet orbiting the sun, which in turn orbits the earth. This is shown in Figure 3 for the planet Mercury. The looping curve of the planet's geocentric orbit lies between two boundary curves, in the figure marked A and B. If we continue plotting the orbit for a long enough time, the orbital paths completely fill the donut-shaped area between these two curves.

If we superimpose the orbits of Mercury, Venus, Mars, Jupiter, and Saturn on a map of Bhū-maṇḍala, we find that the boundary curves of each planet's orbit tend to line up with circular features of Bhū-maṇḍala. Thus the inner boundary of Mercury's orbit swings in and nearly grazes feature 10 in Table 1, and its outer boundary swings out and nearly grazes feature 13. We can sum this up by saying that Mercury's boundary curves are tangent to features 10 and 13. The boundary curves of the orbit of Venus are likewise tangent to features 8 and 14 as shown in Figure 4, and those of the orbit of Mars are tangent to features 9 and 15. Figure 5 shows the alignments between features of Bhū-maṇḍala and the boundary curves of Mercury, Venus, and Mars. The inner boundary of Jupiter's orbit is tangent to feature 16, and the outer boundary of Saturn's orbit is tangent to feature 17. These alignments are shown graphically in Figure 6. If we include Uranus, we find that its outer boundary lines up with feature 18, the outer edge of Bhū-maṇḍala. The orbital alignments make use of over half the circular features of Bhū-maṇḍala. Each of the features from 8 to 18, with the exception of 11 and 12, aligns with one orbital boundary curve. But it turns out that features 11 and 12 also fit into the orbital picture. Unlike the planetary orbits, the geocentric orbit of the sun is nearly circular, since it is simply the earth's heliocentric orbit as seen from the earth. The sun's orbit lies almost exactly halfway between the circular features 11 and 12, and this is shown in Figure 5.

To compare geocentric orbits measured in miles with Bhū-maṇḍala features measured in *yojanas,* we have to know how many miles there are in a *yojana.* I began by using 8 miles per *yojana,* in accordance with

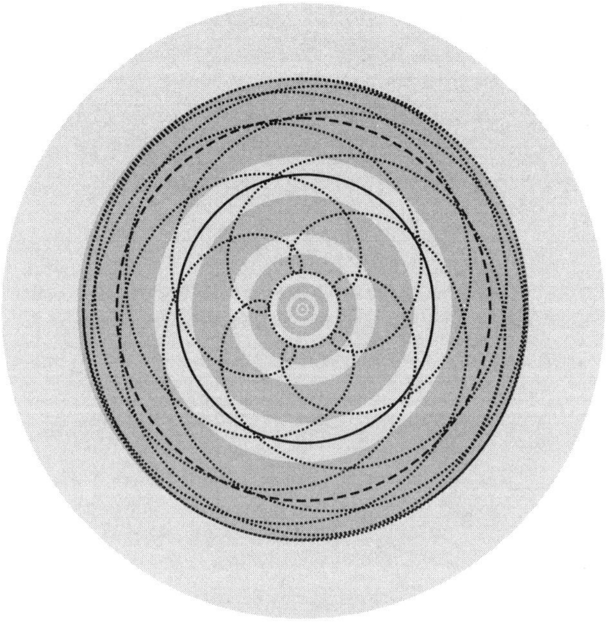

Figure 4—Plot of the geocentric orbit of Venus (dotted line) and its boundary curves and the geocentric orbit of the sun (solid ring), superimposed on Bhū-maṇḍala. The ring of dashes indicates Mānasottara Mountain.

Figure 5—Plot of the inner and outer boundary curves of Mercury (dot-dashed line), Venus (dotted line), and Mars (dot-dot-dashed line), superimposed on Bhū-maṇḍala. The geocentric orbit of the sun (solid ring) is also shown. The ring of dashes indicates Mānasottara Mountain.

Figure 6—Plot of the geocentric orbits of Jupiter (looping dotted line) and Saturn (looping solid line) and their boundary curves, superimposed on Bhū-maṇḍala. The geocentric orbit of the sun (innermost black ring) is shown to indicate the scale. The outer black ring indicates Lokāloka Mountain.

Prabhupāda's statement "One *yojana* equals approximately eight miles."[8] But there is a simple way to refine this estimate. We have seen that the boundary curves of the planets tend to line up with the circular features of Bhū-maṇḍala. The trick, then, is to find the number of miles per *yojana* at which the curves and features line up the best.

A boundary curve can touch a circular feature at either its apogee (point furthest from the earth) or its perigee (point closest to the earth). This gives us 4 points (apogee and perigee of curves A and B) that I call turning points. This is illustrated in Figure 7.

I use turning points to define a measure of "goodness of fit"[9] that tells us how good an alignment of features and orbits is. Figure 8 is a plot of goodness of fit against the length of the *yojana,* for lengths ranging from 5 to 10 miles. The curve has a pronounced peak at 8.575 miles per *yojana.* This value—reasonably close to the traditional figure of 8 miles—gives the best fit between features of Bhū-maṇḍala and planetary orbits.

To compute the geocentric orbits of the planets, I used a modern ephemeris program.[10] Such calculations must be done for a particular date. I used the traditional date for the beginning of Kali-yuga: February 18, 3102 B.C. But it turns out that the results are nearly the same for a wide range of dates. So the orbital calculations do not tell us when the *Bhāgavatam* was written, but they are consistent with the traditional date of about 3100 B.C.

Table 2 lists the correlations between planetary boundary curves and features of Bhū-maṇḍala, using 8.575 miles per *yojana.* The error percentages tell how far the radius of each feature differs from the radius of its corresponding turning point, and they show that there is a close agreement between planetary orbits and various features of

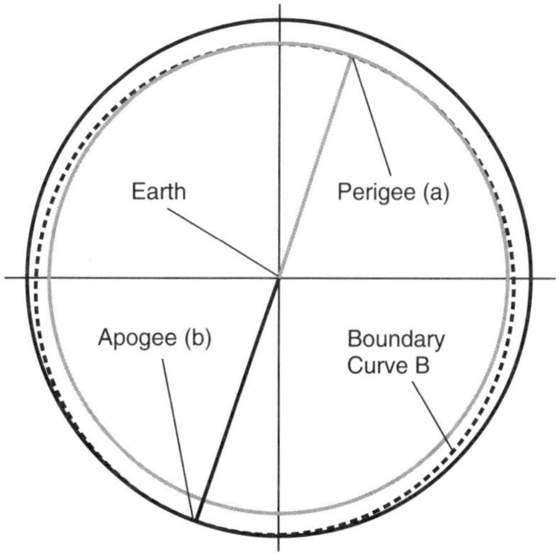

Figure 7—The perigee and apogee of a boundary curve. A boundary curve of a planet's geocentric orbit has a point (a) of closest approach to the earth (its perigee), and a point (b) of greatest distance from the earth (its apogee). At each of these points, the boundary curve is tangent to a circle centered on the earth.

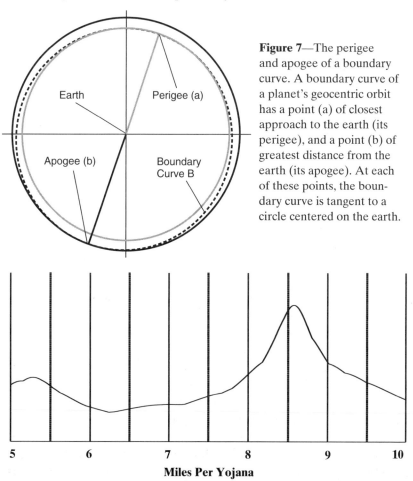

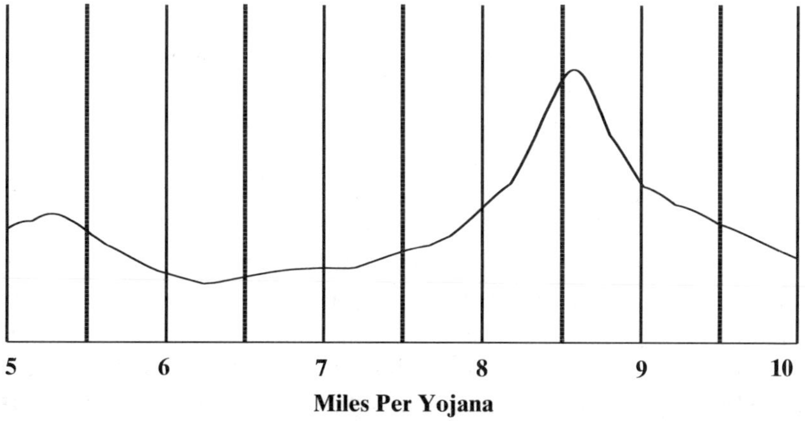

Figure 8—Plot of "goodness of fit" as a function of miles per *yojana* in the range 5 to 10. The peak is at 8.575 miles per *yojana.*

Bhū-maṇḍala.[11] Besides the planets Mercury, Venus, Mars, Jupiter, and Saturn, I have included the sun, the planet Uranus, and Ceres, the principal asteroid. These are interesting because they are also part of the total pattern, but the case for this pattern can and should be made without them.

The sun's mean orbital radius falls within 1% of the center of Dadhyoda (the Yogurt Ocean), which is bounded by features 11 and 12 in Table 1. This puts the sun about halfway between Mounts Meru and Mānasottara along the axle of its chariot.

N	Planet	Turning Point	Turning Point Radius	Feature Radius	Error %
1	Mercury	A perigee	5,976.0	6,150	2.9
2	Mercury	B apogee	15,701.1	15,750	0.3
3	Venus	A perigee	2,851.0	2,950	3.5
4	Venus	B apogee	18,813.0	18,950	0.7
5	Mars	A perigee	4,090.0	4,550	11.2
6	Mars	B perigee	25,736.5	25,350	-1.5
7	Jupiter	A perigee	43.422.8	41,100	-5.3
8	Saturn	B apogee	121,599.6	125,000	2.8
9	Sun	mean	10840.4	10,950	1.0
10	Ceres	B apogee	42,683.2	41,100	-3.7
11	Uranus	B apogee	229,811.0	250,000	8.9

Table 2—Correlation between radii of features of Bhū-maṇḍala and orbital turning points. The feature radii are from Table 1 and are in thousands of *yojanas*. Error percentage is the error in the feature radius relative to the corresponding orbital turning point. The orbital turning points are calculated for the beginning of Kali-yuga, using a modern ephemeris program. They are expressed in thousands of *yojanas* using 8.575 miles per *yojana*.

Although Uranus is not mentioned in the *Bhāgavatam*, its orbit lies near the outer boundary of Bhū-maṇḍala, in the region of darkness called Aloka-varṣa. It is noteworthy that the inner boundary of Aloka-varṣa is the circular Lokāloka Mountain, said to serve as the outer boundary for all luminaries.[12] This is consistent with the fact that the five planets visible to the naked eye are Mercury through Saturn (Saturn's orbit lies just within the boundary of Lokāloka Mountain).

As already mentioned, and as shown in Figure 8, the correlation between Bhū-maṇḍala and the planetary orbits is best at 8.575 miles per *yojana.* This length for the *yojana* was calculated entirely on the basis of the *Bhāgavatam* and the planetary orbits. Yet it is confirmed by a completely different line of investigation. As I explain in the next chapter, the *yojana* has close ties to the dimensions of the earth globe and to units of measurement used in ancient Western civilizations. My investigations of this led independently to a length of 8.59 miles for one standard of the *yojana,* a figure that agrees well with the length of 8.575 miles obtained from the orbital study. This agreement underscores the point that Bhū-maṇḍala does not represent the planet earth, since the 8.59 mile figure reflects accurate knowledge of the size and shape of the earth globe (including its slight polar flattening).

We should note that the *Bhāgavatam* lists heights of the planets

Planet	**Height (*Bhāgavatam*)**	**Height (*Modern*)**	**Mean Distance**
Sun	100	100	10,840
Venus	600	555	10,840
Mercury	800	572	10,840
Mars	1,000	690	14,480
Jupiter	1,200	1,733	56,381
Saturn	1,400	5,205	103,474

Table 3—Heights of the planets above Bhū-maṇḍala in thousands of *yojanas,* as given in the *Bhāgavata Purāṇa* and as calculated using modern astronomy. The modern heights denote the maximum distances the planets move perpendicular to the plane of the solar system, the plane I have suggested that Bhū-maṇḍala represents. For comparison, the mean distances of the planets from the earth are listed.[13] (The mean distance is the halfway point between the minimum and maximum distance of the planet from the earth, as computed using modern astronomy.)

above Bhū-maṇḍala. These heights are sometimes interpreted as the distances in a straight line from the planets to the earth globe, but they are far too small for this. Table 3 compares the heights listed in the *Bhāgavatam* with the mean distances of the planets from the earth, which are many times larger. The arguments presented here suggest that the planetary heights actually represent distances perpendicular to the plane of Bhū-maṇḍala. Since Bhū-maṇḍala represents the plane of the solar system, the heights listed in the *Bhāgavatam* should be compared to the furthest distances the planets move perpendicular to the ecliptic plane. (Since the sun in the ecliptic plane lies 100 thousand *yojanas* from Bhū-maṇḍala, the figures should be offset by that amount.) Table 3 makes this comparison and this is also indicat-

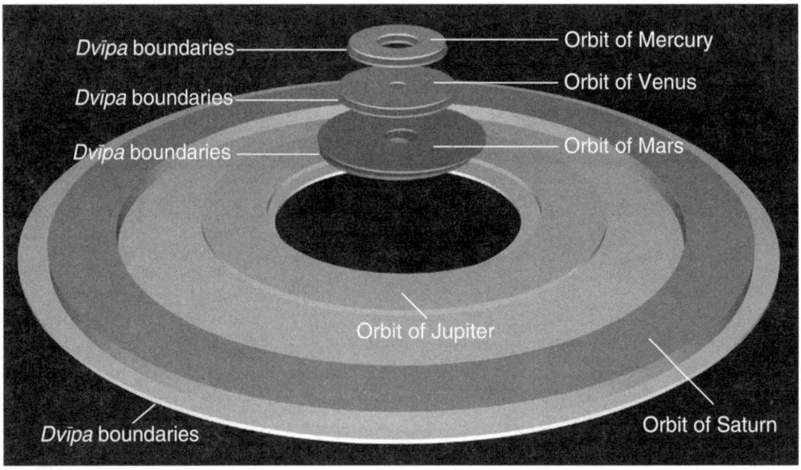

Figure 9—Exploded view of the solar system in three dimensions. Each pair of rings represents the three-dimensional form of a planetary orbit from modern astronomy, compared with a corresponding feature from the *Bhāgavatam.* In each pair of rings, the inner and outer diameters of the top ring represent the boundary curves of the planet's geocentric orbit in the plane of Bhū-maṇḍala, and its thickness represents the planet's maximum height perpendicular to Bhū-maṇḍala (from column 3 of Table 3). For comparison, the inner and outer diameters of the bottom ring represent the circular features of Bhū-maṇḍala that align with the planetary orbit, and the thickness represents the planet's height above Bhū-maṇḍala (from column 2 of Table 3). In nature, all of the rings are superimposed in the same space, but we have drawn them separately for easy visibility.

ed in Figure 9. We see that for the sun, Venus, Mercury, Mars, and Jupiter, the height listed in the *Bhāgavatam* roughly agrees with the modern height. For Saturn the modern height is about 4 times too large, but it is still much closer to the *Bhāgavatam* height than the mean distance, which is about 74 times too large.

I suggest that the heights listed in the *Bhāgavatam* give a simple estimate of the maximum movement of the planets away from the ecliptic plane. This supports the interpretation of Bhū-maṇḍala as a simple but realistic map of the planetary orbits in the solar system. The flatness of the solar system is also indicated by the small magnitude of the *Bhāgavatam* heights in comparison with the large radial distances listed in Tables 1, 2, and 3.

In conclusion, the circular features of Bhū-maṇḍala from 8 through 18 correlate strikingly with the orbits of the planets from Mercury through Uranus (with the sun standing in for the earth because of the geocentric perspective). It would seem that Bhū-maṇḍala can be interpreted as a realistic map of the solar system, showing how the planets move relative to the earth. Statistical studies (not documented here) support this conclusion by bearing out that when you choose sets of concentric circles at random, they do not tend to match planetary orbits closely and systematically like the features of Bhū-maṇḍala.

The small percentages of error in Table 2 imply that the author of the *Bhāgavatam* was able to take advantage of advanced astronomy. Since he made use of a unit of distance (the *yojana*) defined accurately in terms of the dimensions of the earth, he must also have had access to advanced geographical knowledge. Such knowledge of astronomy and geography was not developed in recent times until the late eighteenth and early nineteenth centuries. It was not available to the most advanced of the ancient Greek astronomers, Claudius Ptolemy, in the second century A.D., and it was certainly unknown to the pre-Socratic Greek philosophers of the fifth century B.C.

It would appear that advanced astronomical knowledge was developed by some earlier civilization and then lost until recent times. The so-called flat earth of classical antiquity may represent a later misunderstanding of a realistic astronomical concept that dates back to an earlier time and is still preserved within the text of the *Śrīmad-Bhāgavatam*.

REFERENCES

1. Kirk, G. S. and Raven, J. E., 1963, *The Presocratic Philosophers,* Cambridge: Cambridge Univ. Press., p. 87.
2. Kirk and Raven, 1963, p. 391.
3. Kirk and Raven, 1963, p. 412.
4. British readers, please note: The billions in this article are American; the British billion has three zeros less.
5. The translation of *Śrīmad-Bhāgavatam* 5.20.35 says that beyond the ocean of sweet water is a tract of land as wide as the distance from Mount Meru to Mānasottara Mountain (15,750 thousand *yojanas*), and beyond it is a land of gold with a mirrorlike surface. But examination of the Sanskrit text shows that the first tract of land is made of gold, and beyond it is a land with a mirrorlike surface. We have listed this as Ādarśa-talopamā, based on the text.
6. Bhaktivedanta Swami Prabhupāda, A. C., 1975, *Śrīmad-Bhāgavatam,* Fifth Canto - Part Two, Los Angeles: Bhaktivedanta Book Trust, text 5.21.13.
7. In several places Śrīla Prabhupāda has written that the planet earth was named Bhārata-varṣa after Mahārāja Bhārata, the son of Ṛṣabhadeva.
8. Bhaktivedanta Swami Prabhupāda, A. C., 1975, *Śrīmad-Bhāgavatam,* Fifth Canto - Part Two, Los Angeles: Bhaktivedanta Book Trust, Chapter 16, Chapter Summary, p. 89.
9. "Goodness of fit" can be defined as follows: For each planetary orbit, we can find the shortest distance from a turning point to a circular feature of Bhū-maṇḍala. The reciprocal of the root mean square of these distances for Mercury through Saturn is the measure of goodness of fit. This measure becomes large when the average distance from turning points to Bhū-maṇḍala features becomes small.
10. All orbital calculations were performed using the ephemeris programs of Duffett-Smith, Peter, 1985, *Astronomy with Your Personal Computer,* Cambridge: Cambridge University Press.
11. The 11.2% error of Mars stands out as larger than the others, since Mars partially crosses over feature 9, the outer boundary

of Krauñcadvīpa. The *Bhāgavatam* may refer to this indirectly, since it states in verse 5.20.19 that Mount Krauñca in Krauñcadvīpa was attacked by Kārtikeya, who is the regent of Mars.

12. Bhaktivedanta Swami Prabhupāda, A. C., 1975, *Śrīmad-Bhāgavatam,* Fifth Canto - Part Two, Los Angeles: Bhaktivedanta Book Trust, text 5.20.37.
13. The mean distances of the sun, Venus, and Mercury are the same because Venus and Mercury are inner planets that orbit the sun as the sun orbits the earth (when seen from a geocentric point of view).

21

Exact Science in The Śrīmad-Bhāgavatam

An encyclopedia article states that in early times length was defined by the breadth of the palm or hand, and the length from the elbow to the tip of the middle finger (the cubit). The article goes on to say, "Such standards were both changeable and perishable, and only within modern times have definite unchanging standards of measurement been adopted." (*Microsoft Encarta*)

The Middle Ages certainly saw many conflicting and poorly defined standards of weights and measures. But exact standards of measurement are not solely a modern invention.

Consider this example. In tenth-century England, King Athelstan decreed that the king's girth, in which the king's peace is in force, should extend from the royal residence for a distance of 3 miles, 3 furlongs, 9 acres, 9 feet, 9 palms, and 9 barleycorns. This sounds quaint. But it defines a circle with a diameter of 36,500 feet—almost exactly 1⁄10 of a degree of latitude in southern England.

Measuring with Latitude

To define a unit of length exactly, it is natural to use latitude as a standard, because latitude derives from the size of the earth, a constant that can be measured astronomically. So if a fire or invasion destroys the standard measuring rod stored in some government building, astronomical readings can be used to restore the lost standard. Of course, it seems unlikely that accurate astronomical measurements were being made in England in the days of King Athelstan. But if we look into the history of weights and measures, we find that distances were gauged in terms of latitude in ancient times, and medieval societies inherited many exact standards of measurement. These included volumes defined as length cubed and weights defined by filling such a volume with water.

Figure 1—The ancient Vedic unit of measure called the *yojana* appears to be based on the size of a degree of latitude and thus the size of the earth.

The Greek astronomer Eratosthenes is usually credited with being the first to measure the size of the earth by observing latitudes (see Figure 2). He is said to have noted that the sun, when directly overhead at Syene at the Tropic of Cancer, casts a shadow of 7.2 degrees at Alexandria. Knowing the distance between Syene and Alexandria, he could compute the length of a degree of latitude and estimate the circumference of the earth.

But there is reason to believe that the size of the earth was known long before Eratosthenes. The Italian scholar Livio Stecchini has given extensive evidence that the ancient Egyptians laid out their country using latitude and longitude. He argues that they had accurate knowledge of the dimensions of the earth and that such knowledge was inherent in the design of the great pyramid at Giza. Since the great pyramid dates to about 2500 B.C., this implies that the earth was measured scientifically at least that long ago.

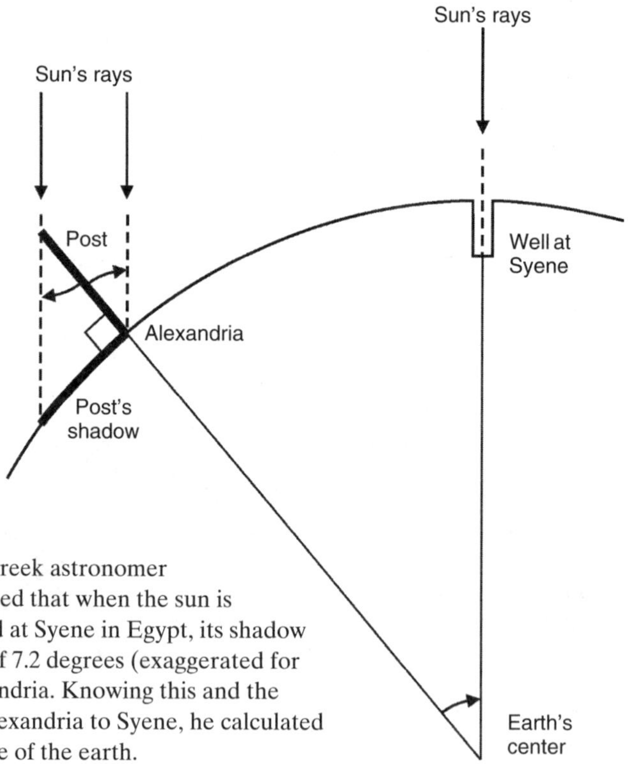

Figure 2—The Greek astronomer Eratosthenes noted that when the sun is directly overhead at Syene in Egypt, its shadow marks an angle of 7.2 degrees (exaggerated for clarity) at Alexandria. Knowing this and the distance from Alexandria to Syene, he calculated the circumference of the earth.

Defining the Yojana

Turning to India, we find a unit of distance—called the *yojana*—that at first glance seems as ill defined as the medieval English furlong or foot. The *yojana* is defined to be either 16,000 or 32,000 *hastas,* where a *hasta,* or cubit, is 24 *angulas,* or fingers. That there were at least two sizes for the *yojana* is upheld by the writings of classical Indian astronomers. The fifth-century astronomer Āryabhata used a *yojana* of about 8 miles, and the astronomy text *Sūrya-siddhānta* a *yojana* of roughly 5 miles.

The first hint of the ancient history of the *yojana* comes from Strabo, who describes the experiences of Megasthenes, a Greek ambassador to India in the period following Alexander the Great. Strabo cites Megasthenes as saying that along the royal road to the Indian capital of Palibothra (thought to be modern Patna), pillars were set up every 10 *stadia* (see Figure 3). The British scholar Alexander Cunningham argues that the pillars marked an interval of one *krośa.* Since there are traditionally 4 *krośas* per *yojana,* this implies 40 *stadia* per *yojana*. Stecchini gives 400 cubits per *stadium,* and this implies 16,000 cubits per *yojana.*

Since the smaller of the two definitions for the *yojana* assigns it 16,000 *hastas,* we can tentatively identify the *hasta,* or Indian cubit, with the Greek cubit. This unit is well known, and it enables us to

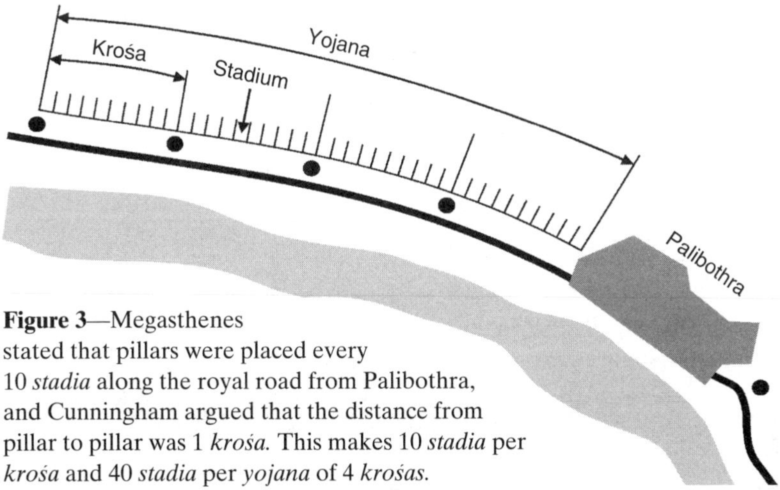

Figure 3—Megasthenes stated that pillars were placed every 10 *stadia* along the royal road from Palibothra, and Cunningham argued that the distance from pillar to pillar was 1 *krośa.* This makes 10 *stadia* per *krośa* and 40 *stadia* per *yojana* of 4 *krośas.*

compute the length of the *yojana.* The Greek cubit is 462.42 millimeters. This gives us a small *yojana* of about 4.6 miles, in rough agreement with texts such as the *Sūrya-siddhānta.*

Stecchini points out that the *stadium* was defined as 1/600 of a degree of latitude. This would mean that there are 15 small *yojanas* per degree. Likewise, there are 60 *krośas* per degree, or 1 *krośa* per minute.

Here we must make a technical observation about latitudes. Consider the earth to be a sphere, rotating on a line through the north and south poles called the polar axis. The latitude of a person facing north at some point in the northern hemisphere is the angle from his horizon up to the polar axis (see Figure 4). That angle is 0 degrees at the equator and grows to 90 degrees at the North Pole. The length of a degree of latitude is the distance a person would have to travel north for his latitude to increase by 1 degree. On a perfect sphere, this distance would be the same at all latitudes. But the earth is slightly flat at the poles and bulges at the equator. This makes for a degree of latitude slightly smaller at the equator than further north (see Figure 5).

Figure 4—To measure latitude in the northern hemisphere, imagine that you are standing on level ground, facing north. Sight along a protractor to the North Star, as shown. The angle L from the horizon to the North Star is your latitude.

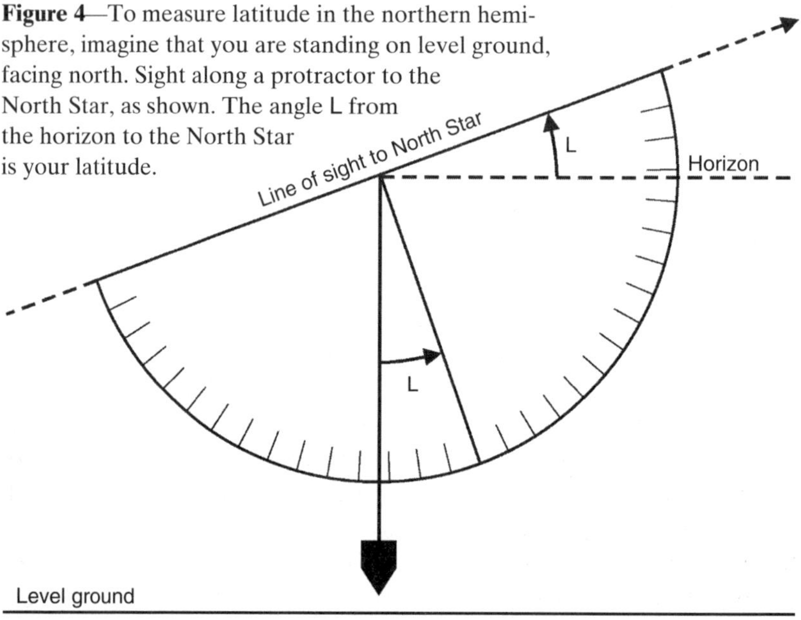

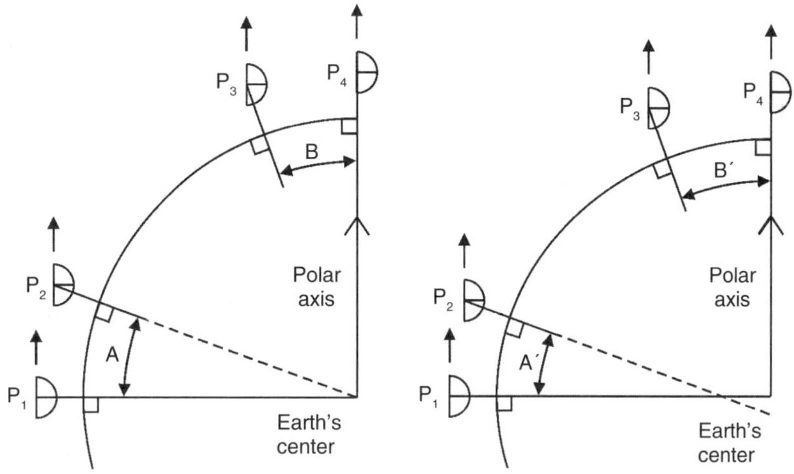

Figure 5—The length of a degree of latitude is the distance over which an observer's latitude changes by 1 degree. Latitude is measured by sighting the North Star along protractors (P_1 through P_4) in the same way as in Figure 4. The lengths A and B are each 20 degrees of latitude. Since A and B are measured on a perfect sphere, they are equal. But if the sphere is flattened like the earth, the distance A shrinks slightly to A′, and the distance B expands to B′. Here the flattening of the earth is greatly exaggerated to show the effect.

Stecchini noted that the Greek *stadium* is 1⁄600 of a degree of latitude at Mycenae in Greece, and he argued that it was deliberately defined this way in ancient times. I propose that to define the *yojana* in India the degree of latitude at the equator was used. This means that the *hasta* should be 460.7 millimeters instead of 462.4 millimeters (and the *yojana* would still be about 4.6 miles). I shall point out below why this fine distinction is important.

At first glance, the *yojana* of 32,000 *hastas* should be twice as long as this, or about 9.2 miles. But there is reason to think that these two *yojanas* use different standards for the *hasta* (see Figures 6 and 7).

Hiuen Thsang, a Buddhist pilgrim who visited India in the seventh century, wrote of *yojanas* in terms of a Chinese unit of measure called the *li.* He reported that a *yojana* consisted of 40 *li* according to Indian tradition but the measure in customary use equaled 30 *li* and the measure given in sacred texts was only 16. The *li* has taken on many values during China's history. But using values for the Thang dynasty, when Hiuen Thsang lived, we can compute that the *yojana* of 16 *li* matches the small *yojana* of 4.6 miles.

Could the *yojana* of 30 *li* match the larger *yojana* of 32,000 *hastas*? If it does, then the larger *yojana* has to use a slightly smaller *hasta,* 30⁄32 as long as the *hasta* in the shorter *yojana.* Multiplying our *hasta* of 460.7 millimeters by 30⁄32, we get a smaller *hasta* of 431.9 millimeters. The larger *yojana* of 32,000 *hastas* then comes to 8.59 miles. At the equator, that is ⅛ of a degree of latitude.

In an investigation reported in the previous chapter, I found that the geocentric orbits of the planets Mercury, Venus, Mars, Jupiter, and Saturn align closely with the dimensions of *dvīpas* in Bhū-maṇḍala. Bhū-maṇḍala and *dvīpas* are features of cosmic geography defined in the Fifth Canto of the *Śrīmad-Bhāgavatam.* To align planetary orbits with *dvīpas* we need to be able to convert the *yojanas* used in the *Bhāgavatam* into the miles or kilometers of modern astronomy. I found that the alignment of orbits and *dvīpas* works well if we assume about 8⅛ miles per *yojana.*

To compare orbits with the structure of Bhū-maṇḍala, I used modern ephemeris programs for orbital calculations. I was most interested in the epoch of about 3000 B.C., the traditional time of Kṛṣṇa's manifest pastimes on earth, as described in the *Bhāgavatam.*

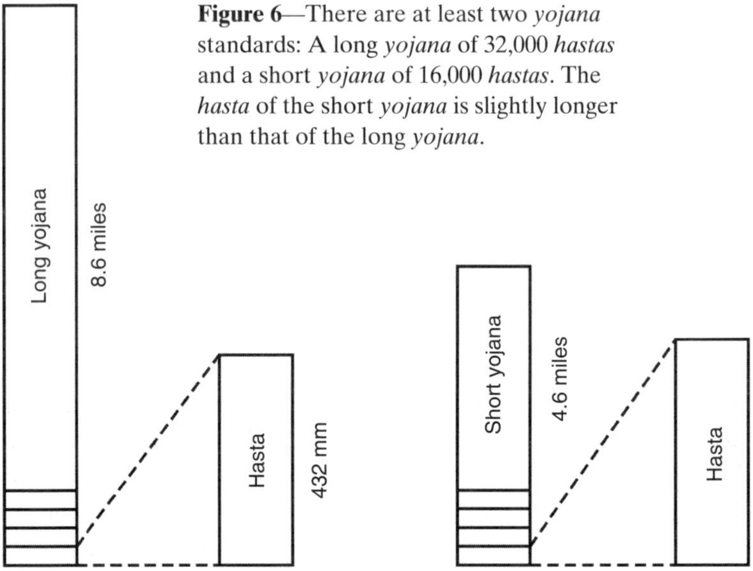

Figure 6—There are at least two *yojana* standards: A long *yojana* of 32,000 *hastas* and a short *yojana* of 16,000 *hastas*. The *hasta* of the short *yojana* is slightly longer than that of the long *yojana*.

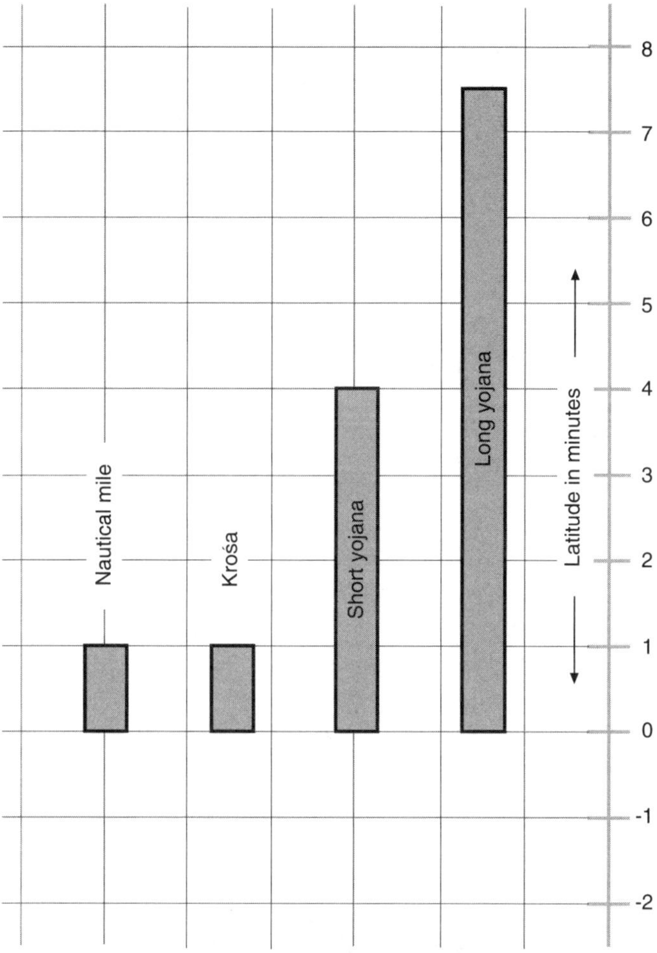

Figure 7—The *krośa* of the short *yojana* is 1 minute of latitude at the equator, and the modern nautical mile is defined in the same way. The short *yojana* is 4 minutes of latitude, and the long *yojana* is 7.5 minutes of latitude.

It turns out that at this epoch the planetary orbits align closely with *dvīpas* in Bhū-maṇḍala at a sharply defined value of 8.575 miles per *yojana.* This is very close to the figure of 8.59 miles based on the *hasta* of 432 millimeters. So the value of the *yojana* we get by historical research is confirmed by completely independent calculations having to do with planetary orbits and the astronomy of the *Bhāgavatam.*

Familiar Numbers

As explained above, we get the larger *yojana* of 32,000 *hastas* (and ⅛ of a degree of latitude) by using a *hasta* of 431.9 millimeters. This can be rounded off to 432, a familiar number in Vedic literature. (For example, 432,000 is the number of years in Kali-yuga, the current age.) It turns out that this familiar number may not be simply coincidental.

First of all, the meter itself derives from a measurement of latitude. The meter (one thousand millimeters) was originally defined in 1791 as 1 ten-millionth of the distance from the equator to the north pole through the meridian of Paris. That distance has been remeasured since then, but the change amounts to a tiny fraction of a percent.

So accepting for the larger *yojana* a *hasta* of 432 millimeters, we find that this *hasta* comes very close to 108 ten-billionths of the circumference of the earth through the poles (see Figure 8). (This is because $432 = 4 \times 108$ and there are 4 quadrants from equator to pole in the circumference.)

Another 108 comes up if we consider the mean diameter of the earth, 7917.5 miles, or 1,728.5 "small *yojanas*." This is close to 1728, or 16×108. (Recall the 1,728,000 years of Satya-yuga, the first in the cycle of the four ages.)

These observations suggest a simple experiment. Try setting the

Figure 8—The *hasta* of the long *yojana* is equal to 108 ten-billionths of the circumference of the earth, measured on a great circle through the poles. Here one polar great circle is shown.

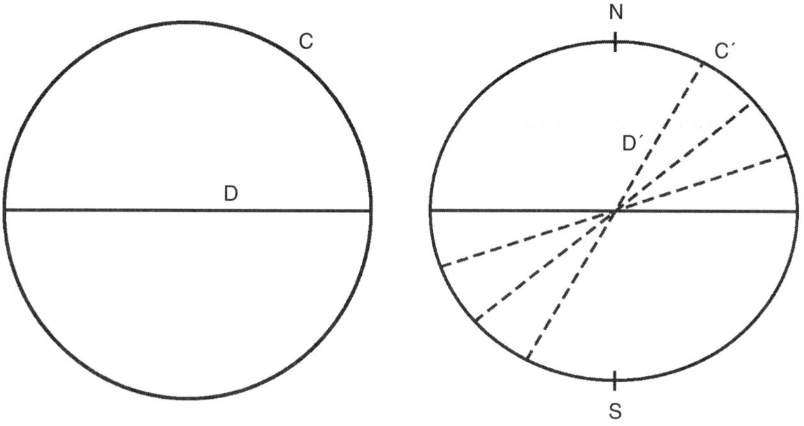

Figure 9—The ratio between the circumference C and the diameter D of a circle (shown on the left) is $\pi = 3.1415927$. Since the earth (shown on the right) is flattened at the poles, its diameter varies. The ratio between the circumference C′ through the poles and the mean diameter D′ is 3.13984, within 0.006% of the value calculated on the basis of the *yojana* (see the text). (The flattening of the earth is shown greatly exaggerated for clarity.)

mean diameter of the earth to exactly 1,728 small *yojanas* of 16,000 *hastas.* Suppose that $^{30}/_{32}$ of a *hasta* gives a smaller *hasta* exactly 108 ten-billionths of the circumference of the earth through the poles. If we multiply it all out, we find that the ratio between circumference and mean diameter comes to 3.13967.

This ratio expresses the degree of polar flattening of the earth (see Figure 9). (If the earth were a perfect sphere, the number would be π—the ratio of the circumference of a circle to its diameter.) As it turns out, 3.13967 is within 0.006% of the actual ratio, as calculated using modern data. That this calculation works out so well indicates strongly that we are dealing with design rather than coincidence.

In summary, simple arguments from the testimony of Megasthenes and Hiuen Thsang enable us to reconstruct two closely related *yojana* values. Both are precisely defined as fractions of a degree of latitude at the equator. Both relate to the earth by multiples of 108 (namely 432 and 1728), and this relationship gives us a very accurate estimate of the polar flattening of the earth. Also, the length of the larger *yojana* is confirmed independently by an investigation comparing modern astronomy with the cosmology of the *Bhāgavatam.*

The Great Pyramid

Let us return briefly to our replacement of the Greek cubit with a slightly smaller unit linked to a degree of latitude at the equator. All the calculations above would go through if we used the Greek cubit directly and did not make this substitution. But the errors would be larger. So I prefer to match the two *yojana* lengths to the degree of latitude at the equator rather than to Greece.

Curiously, we can find support for this in the design of the great pyramid of Egypt (see Figure 10). In 1925 an engineer named J. H. Cole made an accurate survey of the great pyramid using up-to-date instruments. He found that twice the perimeter is 1,842.91 meters. For comparison, a minute of latitude at the equator—or 1 *krośa* of the small *yojana*—is 1,842.93 meters. In other words, the perimeter of the great pyramid is almost exactly 1 *krośa.* Likewise, we find that the *hasta* of the small *yojana* goes almost exactly 500 times into each of the sides of the pyramid.

The Greek cubit and *stadium,* however, fit the pyramid less closely. (There is a 0.4% error.) So it would seem that the great pyramid was designed using units linked to the degree of latitude at the equator.

There is a further astronomical support for the length of the larger *yojana.* If we divide an up-to-date value for the distance from the earth to the sun by this length, the result is 10,821.6 thousand *yojanas.* This figure is close to 10,800, another multiple of the familiar 108. Elsewhere I have shown that this distance also fits naturally into the system of *dvīpas* in Bhū-maṇḍala, and I have given many examples of 108 in astronomy.

Wise Ancients

If the *yojana* was exactly defined as a fraction of the equatorial degree of latitude, then the people who defined it must have known that the earth is a globe. Indeed, they appear to have understood the dimensions of the earth's equatorial bulge.

Who were these people, and when did they live? The evidence considered here puts them at least as far back as the time of the great pyramid—a time when people supposedly believed that the earth is flat. Yet the correlation between planetary orbits and features of

Bhū-maṇḍala shows that the "earth *maṇḍala*" of the *Bhāgavatam* was far from being a naive flat earth. Its connection with planetary orbits shows that Bhū-maṇḍala represents the plane of the solar system, which (if we discount the slight inclinations of the planetary orbits) is actually flat.

The *Bhāgavatam* speaks of an ancient Vedic world civilization. Although the evidence we have looked at here does not prove that such a civilization existed, it does show that some people in the distant past attained an unexpectedly high level of scientific knowledge. Whether they lived in the East, the West, or both is hard to say. We do know that some evidence for this civilization is preserved in texts from India such as the *Śrīmad-Bhāgavatam,* and other evidence may be found in ancient ruins of the West. Perhaps there was an advanced civilization that was worldwide in its influence. It is worth our while to be on the alert for other evidence that may shed light on this hidden chapter in human history.

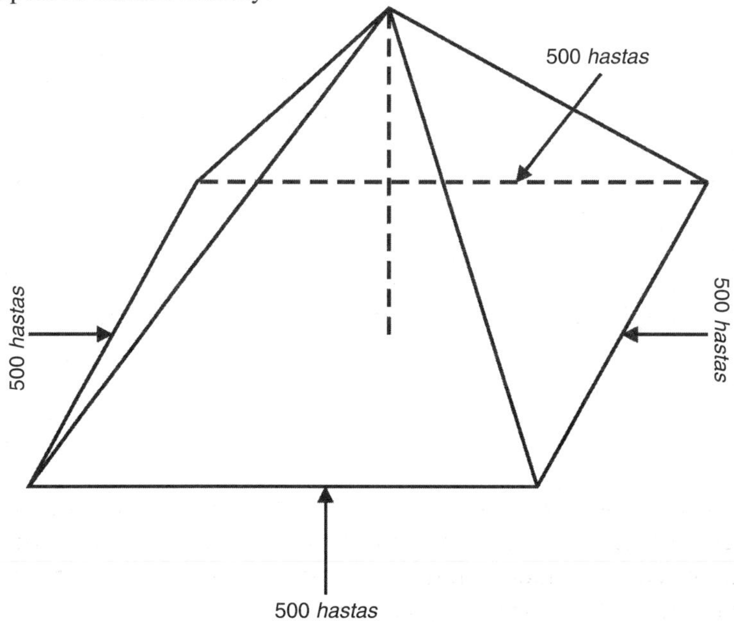

Figure 10—Based on accurate measurements made by J. H. Cole in 1925, we calculate that each side of the great pyramid of Egypt is almost exactly 500 *hastas* of the short *yojana.* The perimeter of the pyramid is almost exactly ½ *krośa* in length.

OTHER BOOKS BY
RICHARD L. THOMPSON
ON SCIENCE AND RELIGION

Maya: The World As Virtual Reality

This groundbreaking book shows how conscious beings could interact with a physically realistic virtual world. It shows how both paranormal phenomena and religious experiences can be reconciled in a natural way with the laws of physics, and it sheds light on paradoxes of time, on life beyond the body, and on cosmic and terrestrial evolution. In a sweeping synthesis, the ideas and data of modern science are used to illuminate the ancient theme of consciousness in a world of illusion.

Mysteries of the Sacred Universe

Traditional spiritual texts often seem wedded to outmoded cosmologies that show, at best, the scientific limitations of their authors. However, a closer examination of the *Bhāgavata Purāṇa,* one of the classical scriptures of Hinduism, reveals unexpected depths of knowledge in ancient cosmology. This cosmology is a sophisticated system, with multiple levels of meaning that encode at least four different astronomical, geographical, and spiritual world models. By viewing the text in the light of modern astronomy, Richard Thompson shows how ancient scientists expressed exact knowledge in apparently mythological terms. Comparison with the ancient traditions of Egypt and the Near East shows early cultural connections between India and these regions including a surprisingly advanced science. There is also a clear understanding of how the spiritual dimension was integrated into ancient Indian cosmology.

Mechanistic and Nonmechanistic Science

Attempts to explain consciousness, biological form, and inspiration with mechanistic models have met with difficulties, yet a nonmechanistic science of consciousness based on the *Bhagavad-gītā* can offer a valuable new paradigm.

For more information on these and other books, CDs, and videos by Richard L. Thompson, including how to order, visit Govardhan Hill Publishing at **www.sciencereligionbooks.com**, send e-mail to **info@sciencereligionbooks.com**, call 386-462-0466, or send a fax to 775-898-8310. Books and CDs are also available at Amazon.com.